The New Institutional Economics of Corruption

Corruption is a major barrier to sound development, affecting a wide range of economies across the world. Measuring and explaining corruption is no easy task; this book sets about it with real vigour.

Examining the institutional foundations of corrupt transactions, this book provides a new perspective towards the analysis of corrupt behaviour as well as the design of anti-corruption policies. It does so by identifying institutions that may facilitate corruption, such as particularistic trust, social norms that foster reciprocity, intermediaries, hierarchies and network-type organizations.

With an international troop of contributors, this book will impress academics with an interest in institutional economics, sociology and corruption. It will also prove to be a useful addition to policy-makers in the sphere of fighting corruption.

Johann Graf Lambsdorff is Chair in Economic Theory at the University of Passau, Germany. **Markus Taube** is Chair for East Asian Studies at the University of Duisberg, Germany. **Matthias Schramm** is Research Fellow for East Asian Studies at the University of Duisberg, Germany.

Routledge frontiers of political economy

The New Institutional Economics of Corruption

Edited by
Johann Graf Lambsdorff,
Markus Taube and
Matthias Schramm

 Routledge
Taylor & Francis Group

LONDON AND NEW YORK

First published 2005
by Routledge
2 Park Square, Milton Park, Abingdon, Oxon OX14 4RN

Simultaneously published in the USA and Canada
by Routledge
270 Madison Ave, New York, NY 10016

Routledge is an imprint of the Taylor & Francis Group

© 2005 Selection and editorial matter, Johann Graf Lambsdorff,
Markus Taube and Matthias Schramm; individual chapters, the
contributors

Typeset in Galliard by Wearset Ltd, Boldon, Tyne and Wear
Printed and bound in Great Britain by MPG Books Ltd, Bodmin

British Library Cataloguing in Publication Data
A catalogue record for this book is available from the British Library

Library of Congress Cataloging in Publication Data
A catalog record for this book has been requested

ISBN 0-415-33368-7

Contents

Figures

Tables

Contributors

Soji Apampa, Solutions Manager – Government, SAP Africa, Johannesburg, South Africa.

Christian Bjørnskov, Aarhus School of Business, Aarhus C, Denmark.

John Bray, Control Risks Group KK, Tokyo, Japan.

Peter Eigen, Chairman, Transparency International e.V., Berlin, Germany.

Peter Graeff, Department of Sociology, University of Bonn, Bonn, Germany.

Johann Graf Lambsdorff, Department of Economics, University of Passau, Passau, Germany.

Sonja Opper, Economics Department, University of Tübingen, Tübingen, Germany.

Martin Paldam, University of Aarhus, Aarhus C, Denmark.

Lambros Pechlivanos, Athens University of Economics and Business, DIEES, Athens, Greece.

Donatella della Porta, Department of Political and Social Sciences, European University Institute, Firenze, Italy.

Matthias Schramm, University of Göttingen, Institute of Agricultural Economics, Göttingen, Germany.

Hartmut Schweitzer, Seminar for Oriental Languages and Sociology, University of Bonn, Bonn, Germany.

Markus Taube, Department of Economics, Institute of East Asian Studies, Gerhard-Mercator-University Duisburg, Duisburg, Germany.

Sitki Utku Teksoz, University of Munich, Munich, Germany.

Eric M. Uslaner, Department of Government and Politics, University of Maryland, Maryland, USA.

Alberto Vannucci, University of Pisa, Pisa, Italy.

1 Corrupt contracting

Exploring the analytical capacity of New Institutional Economics and New Economic Sociology

Johann Graf Lambsdorff, Markus Taube and Matthias Schramm

Introduction

Corruption has emerged high on the agenda of multinational development agencies, private firms and policy-makers. This increased interest in the phenomenon of corruption has produced a multitude of policy prescriptions, reform initiatives and conferences. The world is not short of ideas on how to tackle corruption. While good intentions abound we currently know little about their likely success. Being short of empirical evidence and profound experience, there is not even a theory available that allows us to put the various approaches into comparative perspective. How should bureaucrats be punished? How should administrative procedures be reformed? How far should parliamentarians be accountable to the public? What piece of information should be made publicly available? Is transparency always helpful? Is it possible to reward honesty? Can corruption be effectively fought by focusing on technical and organizational issues? What should be the role assigned to civil society? How far can we expect bureaucrats to follow their narrow self-interest as opposed to ethical considerations? How many resources should we spend for improving the judiciary? How should we deal with whistleblowers?

While there are numerous questions that are crucial to anti-corruption, mostly a holistic approach is suggested. This is due to the fact that corruption in one sector breeds malfeasance in another. Anti-corruption therefore is similar to destroying the Gordian knot; piecemeal approaches appear futile. However convincing such a holistic approach may appear, it does not clearly provide direction to reform. It alerts the public that much has to be done, without suggesting preferences. We need more theoretical inspiration that is able to better direct our energies in the fight against corruption. A consistent economic theory may provide valuable insights, but the task is too complex to rely on a single theoretical tradition. If we want to generate sound policy advice, only an interdisciplinary approach is likely to be successful. This is what this book is about.

We must understand the link between norms, trusts and the precise mechanisms by which corrupt relationships are established. A theoretical approach that links the corrupt exchange of goods and services with the underlying social patterns, moral sentiments and the necessity to find trusted partners is provided by New Institutional Economics (NIE) and its closely linked sociological correlate, the New Economic Sociology (NES). This volume is interdisciplinary by embracing contributions from political scientists, sociologists and economists. But the methodological approaches are not as diverse as one would expect. All contributions meet in a working environment that is concerned with institutions, both formal and informal ones. We intend to identify those institutions that are employed or especially evolve in order to meet the coordination needs of corrupt exchange. This is a task where economics and sociology meet and their joint approaches may greatly enrich our understanding of the phenomenon of corruption.

Therefore, this volume embraces the puzzle of corrupt transactions from two directions. A sociologist's viewpoint investigates the role of norms, trust and social embeddedness in corrupt transactions. Adhering to a more sociologist tradition, individuals tend to regard these institutions as a given. They optimize their behaviour given these exogenous normative and moral constraints. A more economic line of thought is to regard institutions as being themselves the result of individual optimization. They are deliberately chosen due to their capacity in organizing everyday life – and they are equally chosen when they prove superior in organizing corrupt exchange.

Corruption: norms, institutions and society

The phenomenon of corruption in society

Corruption is a global phenomenon. News on corruption is not bound to come from developing countries and transforming countries but is also easily found in leading industrial countries of the world. But corruption crosses more than geographical boundaries; it also crosses all periods of history. One of the oldest Indian sources on corruption dates back more than 2,300 years (Klitgaard 1988: 23). In China, the penal code of the Qin Dynasty (221–207 BC) already included the phenomenon of corruption and placed heavy penalties on it.

In the end, corruption seems to be a phenomenon manifesting itself in all societies that pass a certain degree of complexity (Fleck and Kuzmics 1985) and dates back to the very first instances of organized human life (Klitgaard 1988: 77). The problem of corruption seems to be closely linked to the institutional conditions of humans living together: once a constitution permits the escape from the Hobbesian jungle, this step also establishes and codifies the power of Leviathan and enables its (parasitical and self-seeking) exploitation in societal interaction (Hobbes [1651] 1985: 202, 228). Such institutional power over (economic) resources and transactions seems inevitably to lead to corrupt behaviour. The power of formal institutions to put order to social life within a society poses one of the oldest dilemmas: the Leviathan's institutional power to protect transactions and (re-)distribute resources also means constituting a monopoly which enables this opportunistic exploitation of the institutional power (Greif, Milgrom and Weingast 1994: 745).

On the other hand, economists commonly wonder why levels of corruption are not even higher. With self-seeking being the presumed nature of human beings, opportunities for self-enrichment should always be followed; distrusting public decision-makers should be the natural consequence; trusting them appears to be a deplorably naïve attitude. Given that we sometimes have reason to wonder about astonishingly high levels of integrity, economists must confess that they are lacking a theoretical explanation. Also, in recent experiments researchers have found that rational self-seeking optimization is not universally followed and that an intrinsic motivation lowers an individual's corrupt zeal (Schulze and Frank 2003). This puts the role of norms into the spotlight. Corruption is always closely interrelated with norms, formal and informal rules and of course the particular legal culture of a specific society (Goudie and Stasavage 1998: 131). Analysing, explaining and fighting corruption must consider these special circumstances. The New Institutional Economics and the New Economic Sociology have devoted themselves to the analysis of these formal and informal institutional arrangements and the resulting constraints that shape the interaction of human actors in every day life. In this volume corruption is analysed, focusing on these institutional arrangements, their ability to provide an infrastructure to conduct corrupt transactions and also on their power to prevent corrupt relationships from being established.

Analysing corruption: between New Institutional Economics and New Economic Sociology

Approaching corruption from an institutional economic perspective, as well as from a sociological one, can enrich our understanding of the causes of corruption and the scope for reform. Instead of focusing on legal institutions and their potential to contain corruption, institutional economics, as well as economic sociology, can approach the topic from inside the corrupt relationship. Partners in a corrupt exchange face a challenging task in negotiating the terms of their agreement and in making sure that each side adheres to its promises. At the same time they are constantly tempted to betray each other. The case presented in Box 1.1 illustrates just one such incident, where a long-standing corrupt system suddenly breaks apart leaving one party enraged by the betrayal of his 'business partners'. Such betrayal can be a good thing because it assures that corruption is a troublesome business and convinces others to refrain from corruption.

Although economics and sociology are separate and distinct sciences they have recently been found trying to work on very similar phenomena. One of these is the formal and informal institution. Reaching from the constitutional codices and legal systems to the informal norms and arrangements, social scientists agree that institutions matter in social and economic life. One of the most important functions of institutions is to safeguard transactions against

Box 1.1

Thai sex king sees staid new world
by Seth Mydans

Bangkok: The sheer injustice. Nobody had worked harder to pay off the police with wine, women, wristwatches and sacks full of cash.

And now this.

'I'm like a mad snow dog now and I'll bite anyone,' said Chuwit Kamolvisit, the owner of six industrial-size massage parlors who is proud to be known as Thailand's sex tycoon.

'I used to buy whole trays of Rolex watches for police officers,' he said in one of his almost daily news conferences. 'I used to carry cash in black plastic bags for them. But they are still harassing me.'

In the dim netherworld of Thailand's black economy, it is hard to know just who is doing what to whom.

But somehow Chuwit seems to have lost his immunity, and the tell-all ruckus he is raising has the country transfixed.

All at once, after 10 years of bribes that he says added up to US$ 2.5m, Chuwit has been accused of involvement in the midnight bulldozing of a rival's entertainment plaza and of procuring underage girls to perform what is politely called massage.

That is not how it's supposed to work. If a corrupt society is to function smoothly, each party has to do its part. The protectors have to protect.

'I have donated items for their comfort, including tables and chairs, not to mention computers and refrigerators,' Chuwit told delighted local reporters.

Also car maintenance, home repair, boxing tickets, golf memberships, bowling and, of course, free pleasure at Victoria's Secret, Honolulu, Hi-Class, Emmanuelle, Copacabana, and Sea of Love.

None of this comes as a surprise to anybody.

Holding news conferences, waving arms, kneeling in prayers, sealing his mouth with masking tape, saying he had been kidnapped by police officers and then rolling on the ground to show reporters how it happened – Chuwit, it turns out, is a one-man entertainment venue all by himself.

Chuwit may not be naming names – not yet – but tossing around broad hints in what one paper said had become a sort of national quiz show.

[. . .]

International Herald Tribune, 31 July 2003, S. 1–5

opportunistic behaviour. Yet these safeguarding mechanisms can be used in two different ways: some can protect legal transactions and help to economize on transaction costs, while others are used to carry out transactions that run counter to the formalized canon of legal activities – corrupt transaction being one of them.

Most often, the boundaries between economics and sociology, and even more those between NIE and NES, are not clear cut (Velthuis 1999). Both tend to emphasize the role of norms, trust and reciprocity in economic transactions. Sociologists, though, rather tend to regard these institutions as being beyond individual human design and focus on the way they are socially constructed. In contrast, economists emphasize how individuals shape their institutional environment and how norms and trust may result from individual optimization. These differences will also be observed in this volume. Most economic writers ask how corrupt individuals shape their institutional environment so as to carry out a corrupt transaction securely. Sociologists, on the other hand, tend to investigate the normative preconditions that are favourable to the development of corruption.

Economics may explain the cost-utility calculus carried out by every single individual, while the New Economic Sociology can explain the social ties beyond the economic-rationale. Or, as Durkheim puts it in his sociological view of *The Division of Labor in Society*:

> [economic actors] are . . . solidly tied to one another and the links between them function not only in the brief moments when they engage in exchange or service, but extend considerably beyond.
>
> (Durkheim [1893] 1984: 21)

The NES points at the importance of informal and formal norms as a way to order social and economic life. The work of Granovetter discovers the importance of networks and relationships for social and economic action (Granovetter 1974). In re-discovering the importance of the social fabric for economic life, the discussion on the importance of networks, clans and families, social norms and values, as well as trust and reciprocity, has been revived (DiMaggio 1990; Granovetter 1985). But the 'embeddedness' of economic activities within social relationships and institutional arrangements poses a serious problem to neoclassical theory, as well as to some parts of neo-institutional theory: it is fundamentally incompatible with the model of economic man as a homo oeconomicus. If the social embeddedness of economic actors really does 'influence and simplify the way we think and act, what we observe, how we interpret what we observe, our standards of evaluation' (Brunsson and Olsen 1993: 21), then the free choice of individuals is limited by the institutions they face. This is what the New Economic Sociology lays emphasis on. Economic action is analysed within the social context it is situated in. Concerning the acting individuals, three analytical guidelines are created that distinguish NES from NIE (Granovetter 1992: 4):

1   the pursuit of economic goals is normally accompanied by that of non-economic ones such as sociability, approval, status and power;
2   economic action (like all action) is socially situated, and cannot be explained by individual motives alone; it is embedded in ongoing networks of personal relations rather than carried out by atomized actors;
3   economic institutions (like all institutions) do not arise automatically in some form made inevitable by external circumstances, but are socially constructed.

Economic and social exchange – legal and illegal – is thus facilitated by being embedded in a social structure, something that is beyond individual control and motivation (Granovetter 1985). Such social structures also play an important role for corrupt transactions (Rose-Ackerman 1999: 98; Cartier-Bresson 1997: 163). The analysis of corruption must in this perspective start with the analysis of institutional preconditions that help to facilitate corrupt transactions.

Building on the basic principles of neo-classical economics the New Institutional Economics is accepting the importance of all kinds of formal and informal constraints placed upon the individuals by the institutional setting. In addition to this, institutional arrangements are used to economize on transaction costs; that is, they are set up and used by the actors to minimize the costs of transacting with each other and to safeguard transactions against opportunistic behaviour. Thus, institutions are created as a direct consequence of the maximizing behaviour of economic actors. NIE is focused on how institutions evolve, how they are designed and how they emerge as a consequence and result of maximizing behaviour, and thus, lastly, on how they economize on transaction cost. Nevertheless, a large amount of informal institutions are not the result of human design. As Hayek points out, these informal institutions play an important role in human civilization:

> We flatter ourselves undeservedly if we represent human civilization as entirely the product of conscious reason or as the product of human design ... Many of the greatest things man has achieved are the result not of consciously directed thought, and still less the product of a deliberately coordinated effort of many individuals, but of a process in which the individual plays a part which he can never fully understand.
>
> (Hayek 1979: 149–50)

In this sense we must observe that economists sometimes consider institutions to be purposefully designed by humans, but that others regard them to be the outcome of evolution, competition and the market's capacity to select superior institutional arrangements. It becomes more troublesome, henceforth, to establish a universally accepted dividing line between economics and sociology.

A broader understanding of individuals as economic and social actors departs from a narrow notion of a human as a homo oeconomicus. It is hardly possible, of course, to mention all the modifications made to homo oeconomicus and the economic theory in economics, sociology and cognitive science. There are numerous developments in these sciences that contribute to our understanding of humans as economic and social actors, and only few of them are mentioned within this book. If there is one main trend of theorizing, it is the one pointed out by Smelser and Swedberg, who show that 'the sharp boundary between economics and sociology seems to be weakening' (Smelser and Swedberg 1994: 17). The New Institutional Economics are contributing to this development with their presumption of bounded rationality, which modifies the pure economic man to become more realistic. At the same time, in sociology and of course in the New Economic Sociology, the introduction of the Rational Choice approach leads to stronger 'economically' oriented modelling of human behaviour.

Both traditions of economic thought emphasize that corruption is deeply interwoven with the norms of society. Understanding the underlying principles of corrupt transactions and their embeddedness in the web of relationships also helps to develop new strategies for combating corruption. Thus, within this book two views are combined: on the one hand, a sociological view of how norms and institutions arise, how they vary in different social settings and how they embed a corrupt transaction into a broader framework; on the other, an economically oriented analysis on how they are purposefully designed by corrupt actors.

The NES approach to norms and society

The interplay between self-seeking behaviour and (behaviour constraining) norms has a profound impact on corruption and may give rise to questions like: can norms survive in a highly corrupt environment? With little reason to trust one another, is it likely that corruption will be fought? Is it possible to make technical improvements to a country's institutions and to improve the more informal aspects of trust and norms afterwards? The contributions collected in this volume are not affirmative to these questions. Generalized trust appears continuously to be a crucial factor for integrity and low levels of corruption. This emphasizes an issue that is easily overlooked when being 'too technical' in the fight against corruption. Improved administrative procedures may be helpful, more transparency and accountability in politics appear crucial, but anti-corruption must go deeper into understanding conflicts and a country's system of norms. The sociological studies presented in this volume emphasize the role of particularistic norms in striking corrupt deals. Corrupt actors must find an environment that is favourable to carrying out illegal transactions. Networks have to be available, ensuring that favours are reciprocated even where this contradicts with other virtues. Corruption flourishes where institutions allow trust to relate only to conspirators rather than to the whole of society.

Two sociologists, Hartmut Schweitzer and Peter Graeff, discuss the relationship between corruption and norms. Schweitzer argues that corruption is not necessarily a violation of norms. Rather, conflicts between universalistic norms and particularistic norms are crucial to the emergence and spread of corruption. Universalistic norms compete against particularistic norms, creating situations of normative ambiguity. Corruption may emerge when particularistic norms are more binding than universalistic norms, for example. The varying strengths of particularistic norms and universalistic norms can cause the spread of corruption within societies. Graeff provides a more micro viewpoint to the role of norms in singular corrupt transactions, asking which situational aspects assure the fulfilment of mutual promises. In the case of an anonymous exchange between corrupt partners this fulfilment may be supported by norms, such as rules of fairness in dividing the corrupt gains or of reciprocity in sticking to one's promises. He distinguishes these loosely binding norms from the strategic trust that can emerge in a more closely knit, long-term relationship between corrupt partners. Here, reciprocity can originate from the personal relationship between the actors. The prospect of dealing with each other again adds the opportunity to reinforce or punish non-performance by the corrupt partner. The transaction ceases to be anonymous and starts to be relation-specific.

Eric Uslaner provides further detail to a comparison of general trust and trust among conspirators. The first type has a moral dimension and is an expression of optimism. The second type has a strategic intention and relates only to particular people and situations where experience of trustworthiness has been gathered prior to interaction. Uslaner argues that corruption and generalized trust are polar opposites. Entrenched corruption arises only where societies function largely with particularistic forms of trust. A moral community fails in extending trust to all of its members. He shows that generalized trust is a crucial factor in anti-corruption. This suggests that increasing generalized trust might help in lowering corruption; but he shows that empirical results are ambiguous here. While generalized trust strongly impacts on corruption in simple regressions, he argues that these results are not robust to instrumental variables technique. Thus the causality may only run from generalized trust to corruption and not vice versa. The pessimistic viewpoint thus brought forward relates to those who intend to find approaches for increasing generalized trust. Without corruption having an impact, reformers lose an important instrument. The pessimism would not apply to anti-corruption crusaders, who can be grateful to Uslaner's findings: if methods can be sought to improve generalized trust the effect is likely to spill over to lower levels of corruption. On the other hand, decreasing particularistic trust may emerge as a successful approach to containing corruption.

This relationship is further corroborated by Christian Bjørnskov and Martin Paldam. While corruption is commonly investigated in cross-section analysis, the authors attempt to determine the causes of changing levels of corruption. They start with the difficult task of detecting trends in levels of corruption. The Transparency International Corruption Perceptions Index (TI CPI) they employ is not necessarily a valid time series because there are slight methodological changes in the methodology from year to year. These changes are due to a different composition of sources used every year and the fact that these sources, albeit highly correlated, tend to differ in their methodology. But the authors argue that with the help of a nonparametric approach the more erratic methodological changes would impact less on the results when compared to the rather smooth trends that persist in reality. They actually find negative trends between 1995 TI CPI and 2002 TI CPI for some countries while positive significant trends are identified for others. Using these trend data as the dependent variable, the authors test a variety of explanatory variables. They detect an insightful dynamic that largely corroborates Uslaner's contribution to this volume: changes in social capital, measured by generalized trust, are an important cause for changes in levels of corruption. The variation in generalized trust, along with levels of corruption and social capital, emerges as the only significant variable. This result alerts us that reform will be incomplete without considering the role of civil society. Reform must address the question of how we may start trusting our public decision-makers, and how we can continue trusting our fellow countrymen.

The NIE approach to corrupt transactions

Norms are often an exogenous entity that determines economic behaviour. But sometimes actors will seek to develop an environment where they can securely exchange their corrupt favours. As they seek methods for organizing their exchange, norms and trust may become part of their optimizing behaviour. This is commonly the economist's approach to institutions, suggesting that these are part of an individual's calculus, of a mechanism design. That corrupt actors have scope in designing the institutions of their exchange becomes apparent when observing that corrupt transactions usually do not take place in an anonymous marketplace. Reciprocity, loyalty and honesty in corrupt transactions can be increased by a variety of institutions. The contributions by Donatella della Porta and Alberto Vannucci, by Johann Graf Lambsdorff and Sitki Utku Teksoz, by Matthias Schramm and Markus Taube, by Lambros Pechlivanos, and by John Bray provide insights on this topic. They all share the arguments that corruption is vulnerable to opportunism. The focus is related to transaction costs. These are costs that occur as a consequence of exchanging services or goods for a return. They include costs associated with searching for partners, determining contract conditions, and enforcing the agreement. Identifying transaction costs of corruption agreements demonstrates that these differ from those of legal contracts. First, corruption does not allow for legal recourse.[1] Second, corruption must be hidden from the public. Third, because of the ever-present threat of mutual denunciation, partners of a corrupt agreement are 'locked-in' to each other even after an exchange has been finalized. As a consequence, there is consensus that opportunism is particularly difficult to avoid in case of corrupt contracts. Transaction costs are higher than in the case of legal contracts. These institutional difficulties motivate partners in a corrupt exchange to explore private solutions to make their agreement self-enforcing. Various forms of institutional solutions come into play and provide direction to reform.

Lambros Pechlivanos provides a formal modelling of our topic. He develops a principal–agent–client model where deals between the agent and the client are open to opportunism. He allows only one mechanism for enforcing the corrupt contracts: repeated exchange. This is taken as a starting point for the optimal incentives to be set by the principal. This approach allows for interesting insights that are partly in contrast to mainstream arguments. One reform proposal derived by Pechlivanos relates to a special type of audit or four-eye principle: the superior can sack the decision of his subordinate without communicating this decision to third parties. In this situation bribers face the uncertainty of whether the corrupt favour was sacked by the superior or whether it was deliberately withheld by an opportunistically acting agent. This insecurity makes it difficult for corrupt partners to enforce their illegal agreements. The results by Pechlivanos therefore question the universal use-fulness of transparency in containing corruption. But this is a caveat that anti-corruption activists can easily live with. Transparency is a principle that aims at providing the public with crucial information. If it instead helps to fuel information to those with a corrupt intention, transparency would be detrimen-tal to anti-corruption. Imagine that bureaucrats could simply post their corrupt offers in a daily newspaper – such a rare type of transparency would equally have to be dismissed. Some level of transparency can therefore help in containing corruption. This suggests avenues for future research: the limits of helpful transparency have to be determined with more accuracy. Another sug-gestion by Pechlivanos relates to the role of penalties. He argues that penalties can be informative to corrupt parties because they signal the willingness of a bribee to reciprocate. Less transparent forms of punishment may turn out to be superior. These results suggest that punishments should either be of a mild form that is not transparent to outside parties, or that they should include the firing of the corrupt bureaucrat, thus ending their corrupt exchange with clients.

How corrupt actors actively organize their institutional environment so as to carry out corrupt transactions is closely investigated by John Bray. He analyses some of the strategies used to 'sneak through' legal requirements, at the same time enforcing corrupt agreements. In this context he puts special emphasis on the role of middlemen in facilitating corrupt transactions. He posits that corrupt parties who lack trust in each other often employ middlemen. These can build bridges from one side to another by being trustworthy to both. Such intermedi-aries can help in identifying corrupt partners, where searching in the open is too risky. They may even provide a legal appearance to a corrupt deal, camouflaging a bribe as a commission. Middlemen can monitor how well public servants stick to their promises, providing reasons for public servants to invest in a reputation as an 'honest bribee'. Based on these requirements Bray derives a pattern of requirements that middlemen must fulfil in order to become attractive to multinational companies. But John Bray also demonstrates the risks that using middlemen can bring about to their clients: middlemen might be costly, cheat their clients, sign unenforceable contracts, and render their clients vulnerable to blackmail. Bray provides compelling case studies and survey results to provide a lively illustration of his arguments.

Middlemen are at best an imperfect solution to the problems faced by corrupt actors. Corrupt opportunities may be missed when enforcement problems remain unresolved. Another approach for enforcing corrupt agreements emerges for business partners who have already established an ongoing exchange with each other. Once a relationship of mutual trust, of repeated legal exchange or of hierarchical control has been established, this can be misused for striking a corrupt agreement. A corrupt transaction would be embedded into a broader context of exchange. A legal transaction may thus act as a 'guarantor' for the corrupt deal. For example, a repeated legal market exchange between business partners can serve as a basis for a corrupt deal because the threat to end the legal relationship effectively prevents opportunism regarding the corrupt deal. Also, a hierarchical relationship within a firm may help in arranging a corrupt exchange because it provides control mechanisms to sanction opportunism and to harass an offender. Johann Graf Lambsdorff and Sitki Utku Teksoz show that various types of market or hierarchical interactions can be exploited for striking a corrupt deal. Once trusted relationships have developed and legal threats established these can be misused for guaranteeing a corrupt side contract. This stresses that corruption usually does not take the form of market exchange but is restricted to well-acquainted business partners, whose relationship at some stage deteriorates into one that involves crime.

Donatella della Porta and Alberto Vannucci deepen the investigation of middlemen and hierarchy. They show that middlemen's tasks and their roles can exhibit remarkable differences. First, middlemen can be employed either by the private sector or by the public sector. Second, they may either operate by building trust to both sides in a corrupt transaction, or by having hierarchical instruments at their disposal that allow sanctioning malfeasance of either side. The latter types of middlemen are not just bridging corrupt parties but operate as a 'guarantor' – someone who makes sure that either side plays along with the rules of the game. An invaluable and vivid portrait of corruption in Italian politics by della Porta and Vannucci identifies political parties (as a public sector type) and the Mafia (as a private sector type) as two types of guarantors. A successful guarantor must be regarded as an unbiased arbitrator in case of conflict. If this is achieved, a guarantor can establish a sound reputation and his verdict will be sought by more clients. At the same time, a guarantor is well embedded into a hierarchy and a network. He does not operate by himself but is linked via a variety of legal channels to fellow members of his political party or the Mafia. This serves to ensure his own credibility and provides him with the instruments necessary for sanctioning a client in case of malfeasance.

This argument carries over to the functioning of networks in facilitating a corrupt transaction. This is investigated by Matthias Schramm and Markus Taube for the case of the Chinese *guanxi* networks. These networks have for centuries been used in order to protect transactions in an environment devoid of a reliable formal system of order. By binding investments in social capital they are able to transform risky business relationships into self-implementing contracts. Schramm and Taube argue that today these networks also constitute a formidable enforcement mechanism for corrupt transactions in Chinese society. Guanxi networks may transcend their normal functions and coordinate illegal, corrupt transactions by embedding these deals in trusted social relationships that contain opportunistic behaviour by any party. These networks therefore facilitate the sealing of corrupt contracts and are helpful in spreading information on corrupt opportunities.

Reform

In the perspective of NIE as well as NES, the contributions by Sonja Opper, Peter Eigen, and Soji Apampa may serve as a first illustration how effective anti-corruption policies may look like without yet being able to embrace the whole range of reform topics that emanate from our theoretical focus.

Courts commonly reject the enforcement of corrupt agreements. But this deficiency of corrupt agreements is not necessarily a disadvantage as compared to legal claims. In extreme cases of corruption, legal property rights may be just as vague and unenforceable as favours owed by a trusted person or the word of a friend. The enforcement of property rights requires impartial and efficient courts. If verdicts can be bought, legal claims lose their value. This is the starting point from which Sonja Opper focuses on deficiencies in a country's institutional environment, in particular in its legal, political and administrative system. Only if property rights have a sound legal basis is there a chance that business people will respect them more than the informal reciprocity (involving also corruption) they would rely on otherwise. Opper explains a variety of other mechanisms through which sound property rights limit corruption. She describes in detail the Chinese stock market and the insufficient incentives for monitoring. She explains in detail how these deficiencies are likely to contribute to leakage of funds and corruption. Strengthening property rights emerges as another important tool for anti-corruption.

Peter Eigen is currently the most prominent figurehead devoted to fighting corruption. He picks up the ideas of New Institutional Economics in a variety of instances. His plea for a responsible WTO rests on the idea that corruption impedes competition and that anti-corruption therefore falls into the core responsibility of this multinational organization. The transactional difficulties that arise for corrupt partners are responsible for allocative inefficiencies. Because the risk of being caught does not clearly increase with the value of a transaction, large one-off purchases create a more efficient base for a kickback. This biases the decisions made by corrupt politicians and bureaucrats in favour of capital-intensive, technologically sophisticated and custom-built products and technologies. In essence this often implies overpriced arms purchases. Economists tended to observe a prisoner's dilemma faced by private firms, with bribing being the dominant strategy. But the transactional difficulties of corrupt transactions imply that honesty may be a superior profit-maximizing strategy.

First, the secrecy necessary to carry out corrupt transactions increases the costs for contracting and negotiating; second, in exchange for paying a bribe firms obtain nothing else but the vague promise that a corrupt service will be reciprocated; third, if known to resist demands for bribes, firms may also be safe from blackmail; finally, a firm's employees often misuse the secrecy surrounding corrupt agreements to pocket parts of the bribes for themselves. Eigen provides evidence for different standards of ethics to persist in international markets. This evidence is well related to the survey responses described by Bray in this volume. This provides clear direction for the WTO to start levelling the playing field. In contracts where bribes are requested the law-abiding firms obtain a competitive disadvantage that cannot be accepted.

Soji Apampa provides another application, the establishment of a 'Convention On Business Integrity'. He portrays the dim outlook for Nigeria and the difficulties for starting with anti-corruption in an environment characterized by entrenched corruption. Business people in such an environment have little incentive to establish a reputation for integrity. Instead, they want to be regarded as people who reciprocate favours. Network ties are then open to being exploited for corrupt transactions. The resulting type of corruption is so deeply disorganized that they hardly attract legal business dealings. Apampa attempts to design a network that fosters integrity. While networks are commonly regarded as rather informal institutions, he attempts to introduce formal control mechanisms and transparent procedures. By establishing more formal procedures of membership, peer review and oversight systems he envisages a system that is able to provide business people with incentives for integrity. If functioning, for example, corrupt middlemen would quickly be expelled from the system. The success of the approach will clearly hinge on whether whistleblowers will be effectively encouraged, even if their behaviour would endanger the reputation of the group as a whole.

Outlook

A first wave of anti-corruption activities related to more draconic penalties and higher probabilities of detection of malfeasance. This approach had its merits, but it is uncertain whether it can be the guiding principle for the future. If the effects follow an economic law of decreasing marginal gains and increasing marginal costs, the likely outcome is that criminals are decreasingly deterred by increased penalties while the pursuit of absolute integrity becomes increasingly expensive. Law enforcement requires an honest judiciary, it is costly to carry out, administrative procedures may become more complex, and the intrinsic motivation of the bureaucracy may decline. These drawbacks of law enforcement may be felt increasingly in the future, and other guiding principles will be sought that inspire anti-corruption. We believe that New Institutional Economics (especially when in interplay with the New Economic Sociology) can provide us with a vivid starting point for future reform approaches. It can stimulate more innovative reform ideas in promising areas. The general approach suggested by New Institutional Economics for reform would be to encourage betrayal among corrupt parties, to destabilize corrupt agreements, to disallow contracts to be legally enforced, to hinder the operation of corrupt middlemen and to find clearer ways of regulating conflicts of interest.

Acknowledgements

The idea for this volume was born at the international conference 'Corrupt Transactions – Exploring the Analytical Capacity of New Institutional Economics', organized by the editors on 15 and 16 November 2002 in Göttingen. We are grateful to the German Research Foundation and SAP who provided financial support for this conference.

Note

1 Interestingly, Uslaner provides one counter-example in his contribution to this volume. An Italian court ruled that the non-deliverance of a promised (corrupt) favour would have been penalized. Clearly, this example is an exception rather than the rule.

References

Brunsson, N. and Olsen, J.P. (1993) *The Reforming Organization*, London.
Cartier-Bresson, J. (1997) 'The Economics of Corruption', in D. della Porta and Y. Mény (eds) *Democracy and Corruption in Europe*, London, pp. 148–65.
DiMaggio, P. (1990) 'Cultural Aspects of Economic Action and Organization', in R. Friedland and A.F. Robertson (eds) *Beyond the Marketplace*, New York, pp. 113–36.
Durkheim, É. ([1893] 1984) *The Division of Labor in Society*, New York.
Fleck, C. and Kuzmics, H. (1985) 'Einleitung', in C. Fleck and H. Kuzmics (eds) *Korruption – Zur Soziologie nicht immer abweichenden Verhaltens*, Königstein.
Goudie, A.W. and Stasavage, D. (1998) 'A Framework for the Analysis of Corruption', *Crime, Law & Social Change*, vol. 29, pp. 113–59.
Granovetter, M. (1974) *Getting a Job: A Study of Contacts and Careers*, Cambridge.
Granovetter, M. (1985) 'Eonomic Action and Social Structure: The Problem of Embeddedness', *American Sociological Review*, vol. 91, pp. 481–510.
Granovetter, M. (1992) 'Economic Institutions as Social Constructions: A Framework for Analysis', *Acta Sociologica*, vol. 35, pp. 3–11.
Greif, A., Milgrom, P. and Weingast, B.R. (1994) 'Coordination, Commitment, and Enforcement: The Case of the Merchant Guild', *Journal of Political Economy*, vol. 102, pp. 745–76.
Hayek, F.A. (1979) *The Counterrevolution of Science*, Indianapolis.
Hobbes, T. ([1651] 1985) *Leviathan*, London.
Klitgaard, R.E. (1988) *Controlling Corruption*, Berkeley.
Lambsdorff, J. Graf (2002) 'Making Corrupt Deals – Contracting in the Shadow of the Law', *Journal of Economic Behavior and Organization*, vol. 48, no. 3, pp. 1–21.
Rose-Ackerman, S. (1999) *Corruption and Government. Causes, Consequences and Reform*, Cambridge.
Schulze, G. and Frank, B. (2003) 'Deterrence Versus Intrinsic Motivation: Experimental

Evidence on the Determinants of Corruptibility', *Economics of Governance*, vol. 4, no. 2, pp. 143–60.

Smelser, N.J. and Swedberg, R. (1994) 'The Sociological Perspective on the Economy', in N.J. Smelser and R. Swedberg (eds) *The Handbook of Economic Sociology*, Princeton, pp. 166–80.

Swedberg, R. (1992) 'Major Traditions in Economic Sociology', *Annual Review of Sociology*, vol. 17, pp. 251–76.

Transparency International (1999) *Newsletter Berlin*, Transparency International, September.

Velthuis, O. (1999) 'The Changing Relationship Between Economic Sociology and Institutional Economics: From Talcott Parsons to Mark Granovetter', *American Journal of Economics and Sociology*, vol. 58, no. 4, pp. 629–49.

2 Corruption – its spread and decline

Hartmut Schweitzer

Introduction

This chapter presents an approach for explaining different stages of corruption by stressing the importance of norms and their influence on the individual cost–benefit calculation for determining a decision for corrupt exchanges. Corruption emerges when the different areas of applicability become mixed and particularistic norms are interpreted as valid instead of the actually valid universalistic norms. Several constellations that are not structurally identical are called corrupt, but all are based on differences in norms. Corruption is based on voluntary decisions; actions made under duress, or blackmail, do not fit into this category.

First, a classification of corruption is presented, followed by the draft of a theory of corruption. Then different kinds of corruption are distinguished. After that follows an explanation of why corrupt actions are socially differently valued. Next comes an outline of the general conditions for the changes of the spread of corruption. Finally it will be shown that this draft is applicable to all societies organized by the state.[1]

The theoretical foundation of this approach may be called an individualistic cost–benefit approach[2] modelling the actors as men rationally pursuing their self-interest, which is calculated in dependence on institutional and normative restrictions.

Towards a classification of corruption

There is a far-reaching agreement between social scientists that corruption covers the problem of the violation of norms, a point which is clarified by Acham (1981: 29) who generally says: 'Corruption is an action which deviates from the normative expectations of the whole society and is combined with personal gains to the detriment of the public.'

Similarly, Freisitzer's definition reads:

> From a sociological point of view corruption is a kind of deviant behaviour aiming at gaining special advantages for oneself and (or) others (mainly by the misuse of a suitable function). The relevant behaviour (acting, toler-

ation, refraining) contradicts formal and (or) informal regulations of
behaviour, and therefore violates the ethical-moral standards of that social
system (society, organization, group) within which it happens.[3]

(Freisitzer 1981: 152)

But both definitions are also applicable to fraud or embezzlement, thus showing
that they miss out the decisive ingredients of corruption: the social element of
exchange. And in general it must be doubted that definitions emphasizing the
normative discrepancy between individual actions and the expectations of the
state get to the core of the problem. A specific concrete corrupt behaviour very
often corresponds exactly with the expectations of the society, at least as it is
manifested in the individuals coming with the bribes in their hands into the
office. An action may be illegal but that does not mean it will be automatically
judged as illegitimate, even by those 'negatively' concerned. The action will be
accepted despite the fact that all know that it is illegal and thus violates fixed
norms (laws) of the state. But obviously it does not violate the norms of the
society (the public) and therefore does not lead to any reaction as long as the
society (or the involved parts of it) does not see its culturally transferred idea of
a 'justice of exchange' violated. Thus in many countries an illegal behaviour is
accepted, while in other countries with the same fixed norms it will provoke
fierce reactions.[4]

An analysis of corruption has to deal first with the differences between the
standards of behaviour resulting from the compliance with particularistic norms
on the one hand or universalistic norms on the other.[5] Particularistic norms are
related to primary or secondary groups; they are neither status-neutral nor per-
sonal-neutral and therefore vary greatly depending on the persons and/or the
social strata involved. Particularistic norms are rarely codified because they regulate our everyday social contacts, and almost everybody 'knows' how to behave
correctly in these situations. The reaction to unadjusted behaviour is usually
rather direct, thus making the actor violating the norm understand the connection between behaviour and response.

Universalistic norms are aimed at so-called tertiary groups, and at least in
Western societies they are status- and person-neutral and are usually codified.
They are designed and 'guarded' by external social authorities who generally
take these rules as known. That is why it says, at least in Germany: 'Ignorance
does not protect against penalty.' But the fact that protecting these rules
requires a considerable amount of public resources proves that the knowledge is
either not very widespread or that these rules are not very effective.

Particularistic and universalistic norms match only partially because of their
different areas and extent of validity. Thus there are problems arising at those
parts where both areas meet if the hierarchy of the values is vague or even controversial. In such conflicting cases Western societies usually give a clear priority
to universalistic norms.

Therefore the elites of societies in the transition from a patrimonial system[6]
to modern states with universalistic rules for regulating social processes have

often been blamed for being corrupt in many respects by the representatives of the *new moral* (Klaveren 1985; Hirschman 1988: 139). But the opposite also happens, as one can learn from Tocqueville (1988: 220–1) or di Lampedusa's *Il Gattopardo* (1961), where the representative of the new economic efficiency, Don Calògero, appears as morally disreputable to the Prince of Salina, the representative of the old, noble moral. And even certain kinds of social structures (e.g. the Sicilian Mafia, the Chinese Triads or the Japanese Yakuza) are called corrupt, and it is quite common to classify complete societies as corrupt ('a state of affairs as in Old Rome' or as in 'Old China'). Also, many countries of the so-called Third World (World Bank 1991: 128ff.), or of the bygone socialist system, are seen as extraordinarily corrupt (Voslensky 1984). Here the term 'corruption' is the symbol of decline or even of the fall of a state or a culture, and the word bears a significant connotation of rottenness or vileness.[7]

Thus on the one side personal exchange relations will be called corrupt, while on the other it will be structures. But where is the common denominator?

Drafting a theory of corruption

The core of corrupt actions is the obtaining of individual or group-specific advantages by unaccepted and/or unacceptable proceedings. However, this core is not only a universal fact but obviously, looked at from the interests of the individuals, a more 'natural' one than a decency which not only takes the interests of others into account *sine ira et studio* but most often has to give them priority over the very own interests. The universality of this disposition suggests not to concentrate exclusively on the specific conditions for the development of manifest corruption but to accept this behaviour, or at least the disposition for it, as quasi-natural. Rather, one should look out for those cultural constellations which afford to value negatively the pursuing of private aims, this presumably being a better way of understanding and thus minimizing corruption. The fixation of the interest on manifest corruption results most likely from normative dispositions and from a felt urgency of political problems, and this is most likely not the right basis for a scientific analysis.

The approach outlined here still has to undergo many tests with regard to its explanatory power and validity, and that is why for the time being much must remain plausible speculation.

Some axiomatic assumptions

To avoid the danger of using an empty formula, inherent in a cost–benefit approach, some axiomatic hypotheses on human behaviour will be introduced, thus making possible *a priori* decisions about the chances of realization of the current alternatives. According to our knowledge these axioms can be accepted as generally valid, although not valid for every single individual.[8]

One basic condition of social life is to win appreciation and love by caring for the members of the family. This behaviour can be seen as a kind of natural constant and it is taken into account in some way or another in all cultures. Similar caring will also be transferred to group members in a wider meaning. Most pronounced is care for offspring; that is, the care of the parents for the survival of children. Within hierarchically organized societies this care implies that the children will be helped to get a place as favourable as possible within the social fabric. Another form of this care is the respect children show to parents, which still has very great importance in Asia where children are obliged to look after the parents when they are old.

Guaranteeing the survival of relatives may require them to secure a lasting lead over the competitors.[9] This mechanism is also valid – although weaker – for relations with secondary groups, defined by symbols of identification: sporting clubs, students' associations, churches, political parties, etc. In highly differentiated societies the acquisition and/or provision of certain highly esteemed symbols is very often necessary for securing individual and social well-being: awarding an order of merit, a honorary professorship, or something similar.[10]

Particularistic norms have been guiding the behaviour of individuals and groups long before fixed or written norms came into existence. Therefore the importance of these norms can hardly be overestimated. Therefore if somebody is benefiting from his/her social position by gaining individual advantages this behaviour completely concurs with the highly binding particularistic norms. In this way a man cares for himself and 'his' people, or he collects the material and symbolic means which secure the vitally important appreciation of his social environment. This desire is so fundamental and so strong that it can be reduced, or even temporarily prevented, only by severe negative sanctions and by a deep-reaching symbolic re-evaluation, most often based in a religion[11] ('thou shalt love thy neighbour as thyself').[12] Such a re-evaluation profoundly changes the individual cost–benefit calculation; namely, for socially dependent people provision for the family can be secured only if one disregards the particularistic norms to a large extent. But there is no general separation of particularistic from universalistic norms because particularistic norms can also become incorporated into the system of the universalistic norms as, for example, a look at Confucian ethics proves or, in German law, where marriage partners cannot be forced to bear witness against each other.

For an intercultural analysis one also has to observe that the idea of what are particularistic and what are universalistic norms can and actually does differ strongly from society to society. Moreover (and this is more important in this context), within the same society the fields in which the validity of particularistic norms in relation to universalistic norms is accepted may vary considerably. Such changes of the areas of validity are inevitable consequences of social change. Looking back on the last hundred years such changes can be seen very clearly in our culture – for example, not only in the area of social welfare and care for the aged but also in the whole field of family laws. Many regulations which nowadays are regarded as universalistic norms as a matter of course would until recently have been judged as an undue intrusion of the state into the privacy and therefore would have been rejected as unacceptable – for example, the laws concerning violence in a marriage or laws concerning paternal rights over children.

Social differentiation and the development of norms

Inevitably, the organization of societies as states established social hierarchies and a social differentiation, together with unequal access to the social resources or even a complete cut off for some. This has been formally safeguarded by:

1   The codification of rules (and their forcing through and securing by threat with physical power).
2   The pushing back of particularistic norms and related actions in favour of those which aim at greater social units; that is, in favour of universalistic norms.

Now the logical basic conditions for the emergence of corruption are outlined. The various kinds of norms are vested with differing validity and are controlled by different institutions, of which roughly three authorities of sanctions can be identified:

* relatives (kinship) and friends;
* the public (the society);
* the state.

With regard to the strength of the binding nature of the norms one can refer to Dahrendorf's differentiation of Can-, Ought to- and Have to (Must)-expectations with the respective threats of sanctions (Dahrendorf 1967: 146ff.), a rank order which is said to indicate the importance which the societies ascribe to certain states of affairs. But it is more likely that this rank order reflects the difficulty societies attribute to the observance of the norms in relation to their importance.

During the development of the organization of the state hierarchies emerged generating unequal access to the resources. Moreover, at the same time different systems of norms came into existence: particularistic and universalistic norms in culturally specific variations. The system of universalistic norms is represented by the quoted 'norm authorities', which (must) demand and control their observance. Because of social neutrality each universalistic norm should be largely without internal contradictions, a demand which does not apply to particularistic norms.

That the values behind the realization and fixing of the universalistic norms (the laws) very often are not homogeneous – often even cannot be – elucidates the 'rule' prohibiting murder. It does not establish anything different from the *rule of a game*: 'If you are doing this or that then you have to expect these or those consequences', and inasmuch it does not formally differ from the rules of chess. The values behind the rule do not appear in the wording of the relevant law but have to be disclosed by interpretation and comparison. In the cases of the statutory requirements prohibiting murder these are ideas of the value of a human being, of social peace, of justice or revenge or retaliation, etc.

Because the materialization of norms in a certain law usually cannot be traced back definitely to one norm, or to a single principle only, it follows that despite their fixing laws need interpretations, resulting in the fact that even in a seemingly clear case different and even partly contradictory legal interpretations of that case can be expected.

In connection with discussing corruption it is necessary to point out the difference between what one might call fixed and fundamental universalistic norms, a difference which grows with increasing differentiation and complexity of the laws.[13] Moreover, when analysing the probability of the appearance of corrupt actions one also has to take into account the long duration of legal proceedings because men generally value a short-term advantage higher than an uncertain loss in the relatively distant future.

In his analysis of anomie, Merton (1968) distinguished culturally defined goals and the institutional means of achieving these goals. If a society places great emphasis on the goals but obstructs a particular social group from access to the legally accepted means by some kind of discrimination, it will push individuals of this group into adopting technically highly efficient means to the goal even if they are illegal. This is so because many individuals will prefer to strive illegally for the socially appreciated goals than to refrain from acting anyway.

Applying this idea to corruption implies that corrupt actions can also be interpreted as the result of a conflict of goals or of conflicting hierarchies of goals, meaning here a conflict between (1) the envisaged goals, and (2) the permissible means.

The individual decision to follow a norm or to neglect it can be considered to be the result of an assessment of the costs and benefits to expect. Thus an analyst of a specific case of corruption must reconstruct the individual's value hierarchies and explain the decision on the basis of this reconstruction. But at the same time the relevant organizational and institutional aspects of the social environment must always be kept under consideration.

Taking this approach as an analytical basis makes one expect that the probability of the appearance of corruption varies in dependence on the structure of social situations. It therefore seems reasonable to suppose that corrupt actions are more frequent (or at least are attempted more often) in situations where goals and means do not (or do not seem to) go together. Thus corruption can be expected to increase if

1   the situation is normatively ambiguous, meaning that it is not really clear which norm has to be applied in a concrete case;
2   great gains can be expected (or great losses can be avoided);
3   the number of (realistic) alternatives is (very) small;

4   the costs in relation to the gains are calculably lower, e.g. because the legal authorities work slowly, are incompetent, or can easily be influenced or even manipulated. Such situations are relatively frequent in everyday life and thus the appearance of corrupt actions is not surprising.

Different kinds of corruption

Based on the foregoing explanations one general definition and three classifications of corruption can be formulated:

General definition

Corruption is defined as the obtaining of individual advantages by exchange where the legitimation and/or the moral entitlement is at least doubtful or where the methods used are regarded as morally or legally not acceptable. Thus corruption is a manifestation of an unsolved competition between particularistic and universalistic norms, or of an unresolved conflict between different universalistic norms which are not compatible or even contradictory.

Thus one can distinguish two kinds of corruption which are constituted by the kind of conflict of the norms or the competition between the norms which they represent.

Classification 1: particularistic corruption (PC)

Actions which were derived from particularistic norms but must be subject to universalistic norms – for example, when particularistic and universalistic norms are not compatible with each other.

Classification 2: universalistic corruption (UC)

Actions which are based on specific universalistic norms but are assessed by a majority, the society or the judiciary system on the basis of different universalistic norms which are – more or less – incompatible with the first.

UC evolves if and when universalistic norms are subject to strong conflicts, and individuals or groups are – or think they are – in a position to (re)define the value hierarchy in specific situations. The ability for this independent definition is based on the fact that no social group is strong enough to give prominence to the validity of a deviating definition.

Classification 3: systemic corruption (SC)

Where structural constellations allow 'corrupt actions' to appear as (largely) normal and as being in conformity with the social system (or at least very influential parts of it) over a longer period of time – for example, the actions of the 'old' Mafia in Sicily. Such a constellation develops if a society does not succeed in solving the conflict between the normative systems in favour of the universalistic norms – for example, in Sicily the state almost never succeeded in pushing through its laws; thus the individuals were not hindered from pursuing their private interests to the disadvantage of the public or the state. With the Mafia, or the Yakuza in Japan, even organizations have been developed which are giving their support to particularistic norms and therefore basing their power on these norms. It must be clear that this does not mean that the actions are legal, it only says that legality is the guideline neither for the individual nor for the collective actors – and that only a few really care.

Wide versus narrow norms

To ascertain the existence of a difference between particularistic and universalistic norms is not sufficient for a comprehensive explanation. An additional condition is necessary: an exchange is designated corrupt if the norms called in by a third party[14] for the assessment of this exchange (most often universalistic norms) explicitly define a narrower space of action (i.e. allowing only a smaller number of alternatives for a decision) than the norms on which the actors rely – most often particularistic norms.

A different situation can be seen in Europe's history, for example, when the bourgeoisie established itself as the politically and socially leading power. Wide universalistic norms, which have been seen by the representatives of feudalism and absolutism as legitimated traditionally by their special social position, were no longer accepted by a private bourgeois moral which became increasingly puritanical, and on this basis the old system became to be judged as corrupt; in the course of time these norms became the universalistic norms of Western European societies.

One example for actions being legal, but valued increasingly from the society as illegitimate and corrupt, was the practice of the pursers of the Royal Navy (partly being exercised until the nineteenth century) to keep as commission a share of the paid-out wages of the sailors. This was a legal practice, but it had been restricted during the seventeenth century because greater parts of the public – and especially the sailors and their relatives – opposed it and called it corruption.

The ambiguity of the assessment

One phenomenon related to corruption puzzles many observers: the ambiguity of the assessment of seemingly clear corruption is very obvious and important. Norms are almost always supported by specific social groups, and therefore the dispute over actions being corrupt or not always includes a dispute over the validity of specific norms and the interests behind them, and it would be most astonishing if there were no ambiguity in the valuation. The assessment of an action is only secondarily a legal problem, being primarily a political one and therefore a question of power in determining the norm. The ambiguity can and will disappear only when the question of power has been answered, thus clearing which norms will be socially valid.

By that the difference between corruption and 'normal crimes' can be illustrated: 'normal corruption' is far from being an unambiguous criminal act, although some writers hold this position. That will rather be an exception. One of the distinguishing features of corruption is that it misses the normative unambiguousness of a crime and unambiguousness can be gained only by a longer 'tuning process' after an action, a process usually called scandal. Within the development of a public scandal the competition of the norms or their compatibility will be negotiated in the public (Neckel 1990: 5–7), and the result will be the assessment of an action as corruption or not. Here the general public has the opportunity to play the important role of giving or corroborating a norm.

This ambiguity is one reason for the popularity of charging political opponents with corruption because by means of that method one can easily scandalize a political opponent (Fleck and Kuzmics 1985: 16). But for several reasons even a scandal in a seemingly unambiguous affair of corruption can end without any result because a scandal also has the function to generate, or can be used to generate, a clear separation between the *in-group* and the *out-group*, between *us* and *them*. This is the more probable; the more the public identify themselves with the parties involved in a corruption scandal, the higher they value their membership in or their identification with one of the parties (Wagner and Philips 1993). The stronger the identification is, the more difficult it will be to come to a common assessment across the boundaries of the parties, because the corrupt individual belonging to one's own group will be held in higher esteem than the opponent and will be excused more easily. Here we encounter the typical mechanism of dissonance reduction in which incriminating arguments are principally devalued and relieving arguments are overvalued by the partisans.

Corruption within the bureaucracy

Time and again corruption has been identified above all at the borderline between the private and the public sector. Many publications convey the impression that corruption is mainly a problem of the morals of civil servants and the elimination of tempting opportunities, and this approach regularly gives room to manifold thoughts regarding the refinement of the control mechanisms for the civil servants.

This opinion is recurrently based on the assumption that parts of the state bureaucracy are (illegally) offering goods on a market which must not be offered there, e.g. licences, building permits, visas, residence permits, etc.). This idea is usually combined with more or less sophisticated considerations about the specific character of the market concerned. Regularly from this scheme all exchanges which refer to symbolic gratifications only are omitted, or there are daring attempts to define such symbols as commodities.

The real reason for this phenomenon is that here particularistic and universalistic norms clash more directly and more often than in any other social area, and thus the conflict between different value hierarchies becomes more obvious. But it is remarkable that the same behaviour in the private sectors of our economies is only rarely called corruption and is hardly ever punished.

Additionally, in the public area corruption, like crime, is judged as more serious than the same action in the private sector because it seems to affect and undermine the basis of the social order (Fleck and Kuzmics 1985: 15).

Corruption in the private sector

If relatively small changes in the professional position cause great differences in income the legitimacy of the universalistic norms which postulate pay according to performance and the field of responsibility will be questioned, and therefore the disadvantaged will consider the differences in remuneration to be unjustified and look for compensation.

The spread of rationalistic, universalistic norms, even to fields which originally were non-public (e.g. the private economy), with the adoption of many principles of the public administration, leads to an increasing mixture of particularistic and universalistic norms. This explains why corruption is increasingly found in these fields where nowadays competition of norms occurs, and the question is: what can be called private, what (company-) public?

Schuller (1985), for example, has argued that the enormous spread of corruption in the Roman Empire of the 3rd and 4th centuries AD had been caused exactly by the fact that the private and the public sectors were never clearly separated. This is valid even for actions which we used to ascribe clearly to the state sector. Therefore a great uncertainty in value validity prevailed, with the consequence that corruption seldom or never could be punished appropriately.

The emergence and the quantitative change of corruption

As mentioned above, corruption emerges on the one hand when particularistic norms are seen as more valid or individually more binding than the universalistic norms; on the other it emerges if at least two universalistic norms are incompatible, when the acting party defines a more favourable one as relevant while the public or the law enforcement insists on the validity of the other. This explains why there are no corrupt bushmen, as Fleck and Kuzmics (1985) have pointed out, because societies with a low complexity have not yet developed these two systems of norms and therefore there is not yet any noteworthy hierarchically or functionally differentiated (state or pre-state) authority of disposal of scarce goods. Moreover, because of the prevailing face-to-face relations the social control is still very strict and therefore the probability that offences against norms are detected, with negative sanctions immediately following, is very high.

These conditions change dramatically with the progressing differentiation of the societies. The selective power of disposal of scarce goods of some individuals increases, while at the same time the tightness of the social control decreases. If the validity of the particularistic norms remains unchanged corruption emerges because the real costs and the opportunity costs of a detection are decreasing while the benefit remains high.

For safeguarding the validity of the universalistic norms the control shifts from more or less informal social control to intentionally established formal institutions. Then the corruption decreases because the costs increase, while the benefit remains the same. At this point it becomes important to investigate how far universalistic norms can become parts of the particularistic norms, i.e. to what extent the formal law can gain validity for the system of norms of the individuals and to what extent rules prescribing social neutrality will be accepted by the society concerned.

This is a great problem in China, for example. There law has been understood traditionally as the negotiation of a social compromise and in this tradition the reference to fixed rules which postulate social neutrality is almost completely unknown. Generally speaking, up to now in most so-called developing countries the fixed laws have developed only very weak influences on private life and the individual habit of thinking.

If the socially accepted space of validity of particularistic norms changes in relation to the universalistic norms the individual risk assessment also changes. If the norm becomes wider the public assessment changes and the actual chance of detecting an act of corruption decreases – because people don't care so much – as well as the assessment of the threat and the seriousness of the sanctions.

It is evident that even under the 'most favourable' conditions not all men act corruptly. Therefore Lüdtke and Schweitzer (1993) supposed an individual disposition influencing the probability of corrupt collusions, and they found a clear – though not very strong – positive correlation between a positive Machiavellianism-value[15] and actions of proto-corruption. Machiavellianism is here understood as the disposition of an individual to act more or less without ideological constraints, being (relatively) insensitive to group pressure, not taking moral guidelines too seriously, and using the room to move for one's own advantage thus enabling the individual to value without constraints the pursuit of private interests higher than that of public interests when it comes to a decision. In a situation where there is a conflict between the validity of a universalistic and a particularistic norm an actor with a high Machiavellianism-value is much more likely to follow the particularistic norms, thus promoting his private interests, than is an actor with a low Machiavellianism-value. The negligence of universalistic norms and the pursuit of particularistic norms in favour of pushing through the private interests and Machiavellianism go together like twins.

In a society where persons with this Machiavellianistic disposition are advancing, and therefore are socially more successful, an increasing number of individuals with this disposition will emerge because it will be encouraged within the socialization process. The consequence is the growing pursuit of particularistic norms at the expense of universalistic norms, thus causing a stronger social emphasis on self-interest. With the numerical increase of individuals with a Machiavellianistic disposition the aggregated valuation of the scruples, of the risk, and the sanctions, as well as the assessment of the benefits of the conformity with the norms for the society, will undergo distinct changes – and that means nothing else than the fading away of the social binding force of universalistic norms.[16]

Corrupt actions

When and why do individuals finally act corruptly? As already mentioned from the point of view of a cost–benefit theory, corrupt actors resemble free-riders. The interests of many individuals meet in a common result (a collective good) so that everybody has an incentive to promote this outcome. The free-rider refrains from such a contribution because for him the whole result is worth less than his individual costs: he can participate in the outcome even if he refuses to donate while all the others contribute. From the special perspective of corruption this means the following calculation of ego: I have an incentive to gain additional resources in exchange to a good of which I have plenty. If I refrain from this exchange (a private gain) I will contribute to the continuation of the social order, but this contribution does not match the value of my particularistic gain because most probably most other men will act in conformity with the norms, thus supporting the order. For that reason I will perform the exchange, especially as I run only a low risk of detection and sanctions, even if both, together with the missed benefit, weigh heavily (Lüdtke and Schweitzer 1993: 469).

This calculation can be described roughly as follows: corrupt actions will be performed if the actors expect the particularistic gain to be considerably higher than the universalistic gain. This expectation comprises the anticipated probability of detection and sanctions (this probability is greater than zero), the costs of the sanctions of detection and the weight of 'scruple', understood as the interaction of disposition with the personality and the situational incentives as well as the estimation of their benefit from their conformity with the norms for the whole system. This calculation has to be made by both actors, and the result of both calculations must be very similar; at least their calculations have to point in the same direction. If the result of one actor's calculation is not in agreement with that of the other then there will be no corrupt exchange. If one of the actors is in a position to enforce a corrupt action without the consent of the other side, but only by threat, we cannot call this corruption; rather, it can be called intimidation or extortion.

Now some simple models can be sketched of the various normative situations in which corruption emerges; that is, the illustrations will be rather abstract. These will also show under which conditions variations in the extent of corruption are likely because of changes in the individual cost–benefit calculation.

Figure 2.1 shows the (ideal-type) 'picture' of an almost static society with constant distances between the particularistic norms (PaN) and the universalistic or collective norms (UN). The distances do not vary even if the norms themselves change over the course of time and either become more liberal (upwards) or more narrow (downwards). In such a situation men (actors) know very well

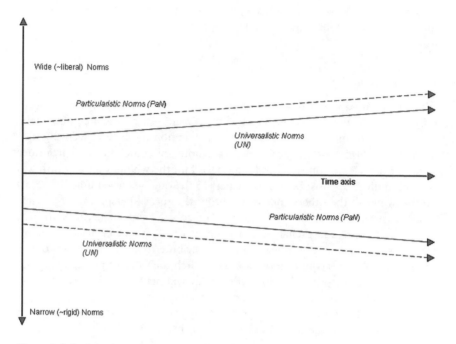

Figure 2.1 Static society where corruption is almost non-existent.

which action space the single norms grant to them; they obey the norms (relatively) exactly and therefore corruption, like other forms of deviant behaviour, very seldom happens.

As can be seen in Figure 2.2 the universalistic norms stay unchanged while the particularistic norms get more liberal. From a certain point on – when the distance between the PaN and the UN is large enough – corruption will emerge and continuously increase; this in turn will lead from another point onto countermeasures against corruption. Of course this sketch displays a very theoretical situation because in reality not only will the PaN change, the UN will also.[17]

Compared with the preceding ones, model 3 (as shown as in Figure 2.3) is much more realistic: a relatively wide UN is facing a narrower PaN. Preceding developments have already caused the development of corruption – at the left side, still outside the figure – and now the universalistic norms are getting more rigid while the particularistic norms are getting wider; that is, both kinds of norms change and one day the curve of the PaN will intersect the curve of the UN in the direction of relatively wider particularistic norms. The left part of the curve indicates the tendency for systemic corruption (which will be dealt with further down), while the right part indicates the trend to particularistic, individual corruption.

As already mentioned, these approaches are highly abstract. For more realism some additional and empirically testable marginal conditions will be introduced.

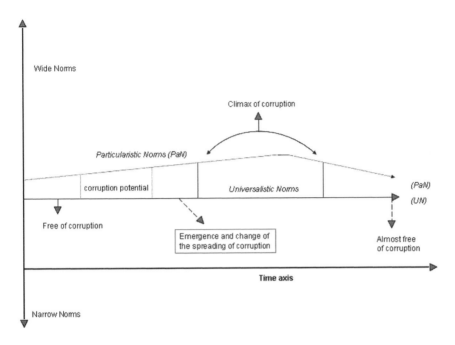

Figure 2.2 Changes of particularistic norms with unchanged universalistic norms.

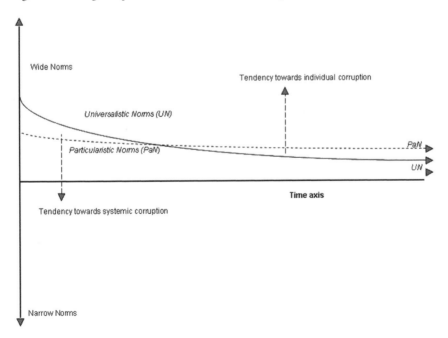

Figure 2.3 Changes in the trends towards corruption.

The degree of security of the life conditions of one or both of the exchange partners certainly influences the probability of the emergence of corrupt actions. (Hypothesis: the probability of corrupt actions increases the more the subsistence or even the survival of at least one of the two exchange partners is endangered.)

Corruption in the form of the negligence of professional duties becomes inevitable if the 'official' job does not render enough resources, either for making a living or for the adequate subsistence of the family, and no other opportunities for earning are available (Alatas 1985; Klitgaard 1988). In such a case the subjective binding force of the particularistic norms becomes so overwhelming that all threats of negative sanctions (punishment) will have no real influence. Another variable is constituted by the legitimacy which is given to the universalistic norms and by which the relation between the binding force and the sanctions will be modified. An additional factor influencing the size and spread of corruption is the culturally determined different acquaintance with written laws which, for example, is important when analysing corruption in China.

Systemic corruption, or the corrupt society

Now we are ready to deal with what may be called 'corrupt societies' or 'corrupt structures', already touched on above. Societies or structures can be called corrupt if they do not succeed, over a longer period (which is almost impossible to define exactly), to make the different norm systems sufficiently compatible within the society and/or between the society and the state. The effect of this state of affairs is that individuals or groups (organizations) can pursue their particular interests, even when doing harm to the public, without being hindered substantially by binding universalistic norms.[18] This situation can be identified, for example, within Japanese society and its relation to the Yakuza, within Sicilian and Italian society and its relation to the Mafia, and even in parts of Chinese societies (Hong Kong or Taiwan[19]) and the Triads, where these organizations have emerged during hundreds of years and usurped the rights of the state to their own advantage. But we can also have similar situations arising without such specific organizations if sections of a state's machinery act like the Mafia, the difference being that they will not be hindered by law enforcement agencies – for example in the Soviet Union, as Voslensky (1984) has described.

It is not only the difference between the particularistic and the universalistic that generates problems but also the coexistence of incompatible universalistic norms or norm systems, as one can see in the case of insider trade or the unresolved norm differences within societies dominated by groups relying on divergent interests or ideologies.

Figure 2.4 illustrates the emergence of systemic corruption by a particularistic norm gradually becoming less liberal than the universalistic norm. This is the situation mentioned above at the end of absolutism in Europe when the traditional norms of the nobility in many public affairs have been clearly more liberal

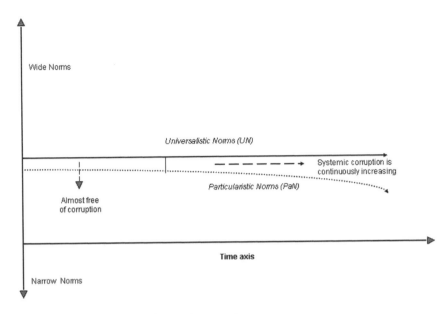

Figure 2.4 The emergence of systemic corruption.

than the norms of the rising bourgeoisie. But not only particularistic and universalistic norms can and do differ or develop differences but also two or more universalistic norms, which shows in Figure 2.5. Among other things this scheme can be applied to cases of the forbidden use of insider knowledge to a person's own advantage or to that of closely related persons.

There isn't a more impressive example for the clash of universalistic norms, which exclude one another almost completely and which must lead almost inevitably into corruption, than the case of forbidden use of insider knowledge. There is a law, an official universalistic norm: insider knowledge must not be used for the purpose of personal gain. All knowledge must be made accessible to the interested public, without preferring to any persons or groups. This norm is enforced by very severe sanctions, as it is obviously not very binding by itself and because offences are very hard to prove. In addition, an offence presents itself as a permanent and great temptation due to the enormous possible gains. This derives – at least in the capitalist social system – from another universalistic norm: earn as much money as possible. Capitalist societies (or at least very great parts of them) allot social appreciation to an individual almost exclusively according to wealth acquired, also allowing a lot of scope to acquire such wealth. In addition, we have the particularistic norm which partly concurs with the last universalistic norm.

Taking into account the enormous sums which are at stake in specific cases then, corruption (i.e. the breach of the prohibition of the use of insider knowledge) is not only most probable but more or less unavoidable in such a combination of norms. Here we have two universalistic norms with incongruous

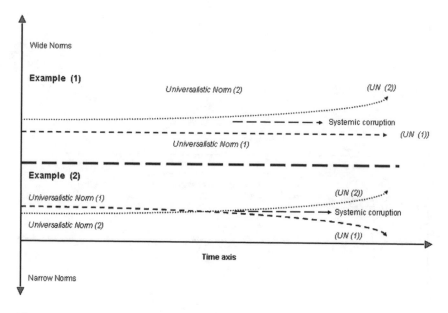

Figure 2.5 Development of discrepancies between different universalistic norms.

official and individual validities, difficult to put under one umbrella, and a particularistic norm inducing corrupt behaviour.

Such a situation cannot be eliminated by tightening up the laws because this would only raise the costs of the sanctions. Considering the chances for enormous profit the problem can be solved only by no longer exposing the actors to such a tempting difference of norms which can be borne only by the very honest. Thus a lasting solution to the problem of insider trade can only be found in a restructuring of the situations in which the people who have the opportunity to do this are acting.

In principle Figure 2.6 shows the same situation as Figure 2.5, but with the addition here of the particularistic norm, making the structural pressure which is exerted on the actors more obvious. The connection between the individual level of the actors and the social-structural level is illustrated in Figure 2.7, which shows in a quite abstract manner the influence of aggregated individual corrupt behaviour on the whole of society and the change of the social value system on the basis of Figures 2.1–2.6 and the text. The starting point is when unequal but reciprocal interests meet, the process going from (1) to (4), from left to right. If such encounters happen successfully quite often this will have repercussions on the socialization process of the individuals within a society (B), forming Machiavellianistic personalities at the least, which will also change the society's value system (C).

Some time ago Smelser ([1971] 1985) has already formulated the insight that societies under great developmental pressures are especially vulnerable to

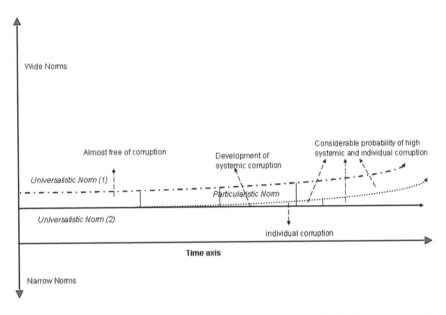

Figure 2.6 Overlapping and reinforcement of the development of individual and systemic corruption.

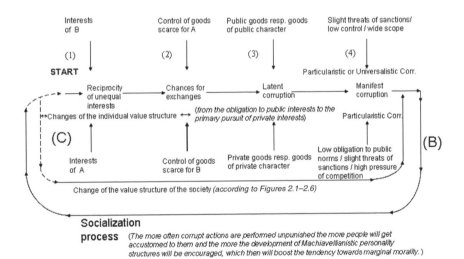

Figure 2.7 Emergence and change of the extent of corruption.

corruption, and in an essay of fundamental importance Olson (1963) has shown that economic growth is very likely to have destabilizing effects on the societies concerned by mixing up the norm systems, an insight which Durkheim has already described incisively in his classical study on suicide in 1897. Pinto-Duschinsky (1987: 42) summarized the prevailing opinion on the developmental policies of the 1950s and 1960s as follows: 'Corruption was seen as a transitory phenomenon, which was likely to decline as economic and social progress was achieved'. This opinion had been underpinned at that time by the experiences of US society, as well as by those of West European societies. This optimistic view, however, seems to have been disproved by the 'Watergate scandal', the party donation scandals in Germany, the scandal of Elf-Aquitaine in France and the *mani pulite* (clean hands) in Italy, to name but a few. In all modern European states one can prove cases of very severe corruption, with different kinds of actors coming from all social settings and nations.

From this we can derive four hypotheses on the changes of the extent of corruption.

Hypothesis 1

Corruption in a society will always be on a large scale if due to changes in the political, social or economic structures new and differing norms emerge which people perceive as expectations of behaviour. In this case corruption can be interpreted as the overstretching of the 'adaptive capacity' of the systems of norms of a society: the rearrangement and differentiation of the norms cannot keep pace with the speed and complexity of the social differentiation.

Hypothesis 2

If and when in the course of social development a new type of social structure is emerging, the old, previously accepted privileges – which together with their supporting values are inseparably connected to the old system – will become increasingly defamed as corrupt by the representatives of the new development and the new ethics.

This type of development can be clearly seen from the rise of the bourgeoisie in Europe. The bourgeois efficiency criteria succeeded slowly in the military sector also, by which the old virtues of chivalry with all their rituals had been undermined, even when these had survived only as a piece of pure ideology. So in the seventeenth century the Royal Navy had been forced by its secretary, Samuel Pepys – not by the military commanders – to restrict or even to stop the selling of officers' commissions.

Hypothesis 3

With the final success of the new structures a new system of norms becomes established as binding and a period of less corruption will start – because societies change continuously – in the course of time this will be followed by a new growth of corruption. Therefore, when looking at the changing extent of corruption within a society, we can speak of *life cycles of corruption.*[20]

The victory of the working ethics and thrift has led – more or less inevitably – to richness and wealth, thus undermining exactly those ethical norms out of which they have developed. The new, presumably hedonistic ethics will be denounced by representatives of the old morality as decline, as corruption of the manners, until new ethics develop again, only to be undermined in turn.

Hypothesis 4

The outlined course can be expected only if the new system really succeeds. If two systems exist side by side corruption will not decrease but increase – or at least stay on a high level because the universalistic norms do not rest on the same more or less coherent normative basis. This can be read as the present situation, not only in developing countries but also in many industrialized countries; all are under great pressure, this being induced by rapid technological developments, forced economic changes (globalization) and political challenges resulting from the fall of the Communist system in most parts of the world. This brings us back to Hypothesis 1.

Final remarks

In this chapter only some of the relevant questions regarding the connection between actors, norms, institutions and corruption have been touched upon. For example, the following have been omitted:

- an examination of the complex interdependence between the establishment of social relations, networking and corruption;
- a discussion of the influence of the mass media on the social perception of corruption;
- a discussion of the influence of face-to-face communication on the individual and on social perception and the valuation of corruption;
- an examination of the problem of how particularistic and universalistic norms work in dependence on different social environments.

The above considerations suggest that corruption is not an independent historical and social force that can destroy a society, an opinion that appears for example in the reasoning about the defeat of the Guo Mindang of Chiang Kai-Shek by the Communists of Mao Zedong. Above all the degree of corruption is an indicator as to what extent a society is capable of establishing a far-reaching compatibility or even a congruence of norms. In turn, inability to accomplish this indicates deep-reaching and perhaps irreconcilable differences within the society concerned. As a phenomenon corruption is not a primary cause of weakness; rather, it is a reliable indicator of weakness in a system. Yet corruption may intensify the social weakness which existed anyhow, thus leading into a self-reinforcing process of moral decline and social disintegration, known by sociologists as *anomie*.

If one accepts this view the question is unnecessary if there are positive social functions of corruption, a question to which many authors have devoted their arguments, very often in regard to developing countries. On the level of the whole society corruption has no positive function except as an indicator that something is seriously wrong.

Moreover, corruption reminds us clearly of the fragility of our civilizational achievements (e.g. the validity of the law) and shows us how close we always are to possible chaos without controlling institutions. Societies without corruption do not exist and never have existed. One can realize them only at an unbearably high price: the complete abolishment of individual freedom. Corruption therefore forces us also to consider the question as to what extent of control we are willing to accept; this question has been answered quite differently in the course of history and in different societies.

A considerable amount of individual and social self-responsibility and tolerance of ambiguity is necessary in order to learn to accept a certain amount of violation of norms to keep restrictions on individual freedom as small as possible. This will not be carried out in societies with very rigid systems of norms; they always try to avoid even minor violations of a norm by a complete set of rules secured by tight control. An individual interpretation of a norm will automatically be seen as a deviation from the binding interpretation of norms because this interpretation is seen as the prerogative of the people in power.[21] Any individual interpretation is therefore defined as a forbidden misinterpretation, and such occurrences should be minimized in scope and number. This is the cause for a frequent situation which seems to be paradoxical at the first glance: in dictatorial states the corruption blossoms without any penal consequences for the individuals on the high ranks while at the same time it is severely punished at the lower ranks.

Following the reasoning of Kirsch (1987) concerning alienation and transferring it to the case of corruption, an amount of corruption is – like alienation – the price for individual freedom. Corruption is one of the dark consequences of the development and success of the norms which have released us from narrow family and clan bonds and at the same time widened the scope for individual decisions. Thus possibilities have been created to destroy the sense of these norms which enable individual freedom.

If this approach is correct then corruption represents the regression into a pre-societal 'state of nature', because obeying universalistic norms instead of following the binding force of particularistic norms is an enormous cultural achievement and constitutes by that a line of civilization beneath which a society must not fall at any case.

Notes

1 However, the important problem of quantification and measurement has not yet been touched. At present there are only strongly subjective estimations available.

2 This sociological cost–benefit approach is akin to, but not identical with, the economic cost–benefit approach.

3 All translations from German to English are by the author.

4 Quite often one can turn over the arguments and say that the non-corrupt actions – according to modern Western standards – violate the fundamental normative expectations and standards of behaviour of the public.

5 The twin terms *universalistic/particularistic* are very common in sociology since they have been introduced by Parsons (Parsons and Shills 1951) as part of his 'pattern variables'. But the terms are applicable not only to the classification of norms but also to differentiate other matters – for example, public and private gains.

6 In which the separation of official and private affairs, and therefore also of official and private property, is the exception (Weber 1964: 768ff.).

7 Acham (1981: 59ff.) also mentions a corruption of morality and intellectuality which shall not be analysed here, because all corruption concerns morality. But the corruption of intellectuality often contains an interesting combination of circumstances, mainly because it usually does not centre round the exchange of the media power vs. money but acceptance (or flattery) vs. appreciation, which sometimes may result in a higher remuneration.

8 Here I lean extensively on the 'set of human bio-psychological selective principles' presented in Harris (1980: 62) and his following arguments: 'The more parsimonious we are about granting the existence of bio-psychological constants, the more powerful and elegant will be the ... theories ... Our object is to explain much by little' (p. 63), which can be read as another version of Ockham's razor: 'Pluralitas non est ponenda sine necessitate.'

9 This mechanism is the same all over the world, taking into consideration different concrete socio-cultural conditions.

10 This mechanism has been beautifully illustrated by the Austrian dramatist Schnitzler in Act 5 of *Professor Bernhardi* where he lets Professor Tugendvetter ask for the awarding of the title 'Hofrat' just in time for the birthday of the 'Gnädige Frau', his wife.

11 The Ten Commandments which – according to the Deuteronomy – Moses proclaimed to the people of Israel as God's command, can be read as the obligation to limit the validity of particularistic norms in favour of universalistic norms.

12 The third book of Moses, 19: 18; quoted from the King James version of the Bible, from the CD: Greatest Book Collection, World Library, Inc., Irvine, Calif., 1995–96.

13 A differentiation which de facto occurs parallel with the functional differentiation of the society.

14 This third party one might imagine as Adam Smith's 'impartial spectator' (see Smith, 1985).

15 Machiavellianism as measured with the modified Machiavellianism-scale of Henning and Six (see Zuma 1983, part D 08).

16 This social change can be linked with the concept of the *marginal moral* which originally had been designed by Briefs ([1957, 1963] 1980) for the analysis of the social consequences of capitalist competition.

17 As a historic example for this kind of change of norms one can take changes to the sexual morals in the 1960s and 1970s. In Germany, for example, the Particularistic Norms have changed much faster than the relevant laws, the Universalistic Norms. But it took years for the laws concerning procuration to be abolished, although most people had not taken them seriously for some time.

18 Regrettably, at present I am not yet able to offer a solution to the problem of where

the threshold is when 'sufficiently compatible' turns into 'not sufficiently compatible any more', if one thinks of both as conditions on a continuum running from 'fully compatible' to 'not at all compatible'.

19 At present it is not certain how powerful the influence of the Triads is in mainland China.

20 I am grateful to Markus Taube for suggesting this term during the workshop.

21 Therefore the slogan demanding zero tolerance seems to me incompatible with democratic norms.

References

Acham, K. (1981) 'Formen und Folgen der Korruption', in C. Brünner (ed.) *Korruption und Kontrolle*, Wien.

Alatas, S.H. (1985) *The Sociology of Corruption*, Singapore.

Briefs, G. ([1957] 1980) 'Grenzmoral in der pluralistischen Gesellschaft', in H.B. Streithofen and R. von Voss (eds) *Ausgewählte Schriften*, vol. 1, Berlin.

Briefs, G. ([1963] 1980) 'Zum Problem der Grenzmoral', in H.B. Streithofen and R. von Voss (eds) *Ausgewählte Schriften*, vol. 1, Berlin.

Coase, R.H. (1960) 'The Problem of Social Cost', *Journal of Law & Economics*, vol. 3, no. 1.

Cooter, R.D. (1989) 'The Coase Theorem', in J. Eatwell, M. Milgate and P. Newman (eds) *The New Palgrave: Allocation, The Invisible Hand*, vol. 1, London and New York, pp. 64–70.

Dahrendorf, R. (1967) 'Homo Sociologicus', *Pfade aus Utopia*, München.

di Lampedusa, G.T. (1961) *Der Leopard* (Italian original title: *Il Gattopardo*), Berlin, Darmstadt and Wien.

Durkheim, É. (1987) *Le Suicide*, Paris.

Fleck, C. and Kuzmics, H. (1985) 'Einleitung', in C. Fleck and H. Kuzmics (eds) *Korruption. Zur Soziologie nicht immer abweichenden Verhaltens*, Königstein, Ts.

Freisitzer, K. (1981) 'Gesellschaftliche Bedingungen der Korruption – Versuch einer verhaltenswissenschaftlichen Deutung', in C. Brünner (ed.) *Korruption und Kontrolle*, Wien.

Harris, M. (1980) *Cultural Materialism*, New York.

Hirschman, A. (1988) *Engagement und Enttäuschung*, Frankfurt.

Kirsch, G. (1987) 'Karl Marx – Entfremdung: Der Preis der Freiheit?', in M. Timmermann (ed.) *Die ökonomischen Lehren von Marx, Keynes und Schumpeter*, Stuttgart.

Klaveren, J. von (1985) 'Korruption im Ancien Régime', in C. Fleck and H. Kuzmics (eds) *Korruption. Zur Soziologie nicht immer abweichenden Verhaltens*, Königstein, Ts.

Klitgaard, R. (1988) *Controlling Corruption*, Berkeley and Los Angeles.

Lüdtke, H. and Schweitzer, H. (1993) 'Korruptionsneigung bei unterschiedlichen Erwartungskonstellationen in der Handlungssituation. Ein Quasi-Experiment mit Studenten, *Kölner Zeitschrift für Soziologie und Sozialpsychologie*, no. 3.

Merton, R.K. (1968) 'Social Structure and Anomie and Continuities', in R.K. Merton (1968) *The Theory of Social Structure and Anomie*, New York.

Neckel, S. (1990) 'Die Wirkungen politischer Skandale', *Aus Politik und Zeitgeschichte*, 9 February.

Olson, M. (1963) 'Rapid Growth as a Destabilizing Force', *The Journal of Economic History*, vol. 23, pp. 529–52.

Parsons, T. and Shills, E.A., with the assistance of Olds, J. (1951) 'Values, Motives, and

Systems of Action', in T. Parsons and E.A. Shills (eds) *Toward a General Theory of Action*, New York.

Pinto-Duschinsky, M. (1987) 'Corruption', in J. Kuper (ed.) *Political Science and Political Theory*, London.

Schuller, W. (1985) 'Korruption und Staatspolizei im spätrömischen Staat', in C. Fleck and H. Kuzmics (eds) *Korruption. Zur Soziologie nicht immer abweichenden Verhaltens*, Königstein, Ts.

Smelser, N.J. ([1971] 1985) 'Stabilität, Instabilität und die Analyse der politischen Korruption', C. Fleck and H. Kuzmics (eds) *Korruption. Zur Soziologie nicht immer abweichenden Verhaltens*, Königstein, Ts.

Smith, A. (1985) *Die Theorie der ethischen Gefühle*, Hamburg.

Tocqueville, A. de (1988) *Democracy in America*, New York.

Voslensky, M.S. (1984) *Nomenklatura*, München.

Wagner, U. and Phillips, W.L. (1993) 'Variation of out-group presence and evaluation of the in-group', *British Journal of Social Psychology*, vol. 23, pp. 24–51.

Weber, M. (1964) *Wirtschaft und Gesellschaft* (Studienausgabe), Köln and Berlin.

World Bank (1991) 'The International Bank for Reconstruction and Development', in World Development Report, *The Challenge of Development*, Oxford.

Zuma (1983) *ZUMA -Handbuch Sozialwissenschaftlicher Skalen*, Teil 1–3, Bonn: Zentrum für Umfragen, Methoden und Analysen.

3 Why should one trust in corruption?

The linkage between corruption, norms and social capital

Peter Graeff

Introduction

Corruption is always possible in a situation where a person holds an office that involves the disposal of resources and the opportunity to abuse them for private ends. Nye (1967: 966) defines corruption as a behaviour deviating from formal duties of a public role in order to gain financial benefits or status improvements. The advantages of a corruptly behaving public official could be material, symbolic or emotional (Lüdtke and Schweitzer 1993). The following examples illustrate the notion of corruption:

> *Example 1:* A policeman stops a tourist car on a south Italian highway because the driver exceeded the speed limit. The driver offers a 20 Euro note before the policeman is able to ask for his driving licence. The policeman takes the money, thanks the driver and permits the driver to go on.

> *Example 2:* The daughter of a high-ranking public official wants to apply for a job in her father's agency. Unfortunately, she did not pass the job interview. When her father heard about the failing of his daughter he phoned the chief of the personnel department – an old friend of his. Their families regularly have meals together. During the phone call, the chief of the personnel department assures the father that his daughter will be asked to attend a second job interview. He adds that his friend should not worry – he will be around in the second interview.

Why did those people behave this way? If one tries to understand their reasons from a sociological point of view (which is identical to the question: what guided their action during the crucial decision moments?) the principal task is the explanation of the social system, not the behaviour of a single person (Coleman 1990: 2). Therefore my aim is to describe and explain the social phenomenon of corruption, not the corrupt behaviour of a single public official. According to Coleman (1990: 134), systems of social action result from the interests and power of actors. By this means they influence decisions for certain behaviour. In this chapter I will analyse the social system that occurs in a situation of corruption. Thereby, I will elucidate the notion of corruption and try to clarify the principles of corrupt behaviour. Eventually, I will subsume corruption under the social capital concept.

Principles of corruption

In order to explain the principles of corruption it is necessary to look at the relations between the participants of a corrupt exchange. Banfield (1975) sets up a three-actor model that can be used to illustrate their interests and resources.

The actor who abuses his authority for private gain is called the 'agent' and the actor who receives a benefit from this illegal behaviour is called the 'client'. The third actor is called the 'principal' and assigns (decision) power and resources to the agent. The principal can be a person (such as the leader of a department), an authority or department, or the state itself. The agent breaks a rule (given by the principal or by formal law) in order to give the client an illegal benefit.

Corruption involves the breaking of a (formal or informal) contractual relationship between principal and agent. This contract grants the agent a sphere of responsibility and some decision latitude. The agent follows up this leeway on his and the client's behalf without informing the principal. The client pays off the agent for the abuse of his office.

In corrupt exchanges all sorts of people and groups like families, friends, political parties or institutions can be favoured. This must not obscure the fact that corruption always happens between real persons only – corruption is inconceivable between legal persons or organizations. Corruptly behaving people are aware of the illegality of the exchange. Legally, corruption is treated as a voluntary act that involves deliberation. Since corrupt deals are planned, the theoretical analysis of corrupt exchanges should involve decisions, too. This fits the fact that actors voluntarily take part in the illegal exchange. If an actor is forced to participate in an illegal exchange this is blackmail. Corruption differs from such criminal acts in several ways.

My strategy to approach the phenomenon of corruption by analysing the relationship between agents and clients is supported by the characteristics of corruption itself: since corruption is illegal, it can happen only in privacy and corrupt exchanges are limited to the private sphere of the actors. Even if corrupt practices are prevalent in a society and everyone knows about it, corruption is still illegal and involves the risk of prosecution.[1] Corruptly behaving actors expose themselves to the risk of being punished. Furthermore, they have to consider that they cannot bring their case to court in order to get what the corruption partner promised to give.

Special social situations reduce the impact of these aspects on the decisions of the actors (to accept corrupt transactions). The more frequently certain transactions (such as that described in example 1) are conducted (and the more widespread and prevalent they are in a country), the smaller the risk may appear of a corrupt exchange being 'unfair' and only to the advantage of one of the participants. Since corruptly behaving actors cannot indict each other in order to fulfil their illegal promises, the question arises as to which situational aspects assure the fulfilment of the promises (even if the actors are aware of the possibility of getting punished for their deeds).

Every situation of corruption imposes certain general conditions on the actors: they can only interact in privacy, they can be punished for their illegal exchange and they cannot use legal measures to claim what the corruption partner promised. Those general conditions imply a special relationship between the actors. Their relationship is reciprocal under the following circumstances: only if every actor assumes that his partner will accomplish his part of the deal, one is willing to offer or to accept a corrupt exchange.[2]

The utilities of both actors are interdependent.[3] Reciprocity is a necessary condition for an actor to make a corrupt offer. Moreover, it is necessary for the conduction of the corrupt exchanges because the criminal act implies the risk of negative sanctions (Coleman 1990: 147). In principle, every actor could reveal the illegal exchange if his partner did not fulfil his part of the corrupt agreement. Of course, such a revelation depends on the costs for oneself. An actor who unveils corruption admits his own criminal act. Most often, the illegality and arbitrariness of corrupt exchanges imply that corruption has negative external effects for non-participants as in corrupt deals particularistic interests outweigh universalistic interests. The corrupt deeds must be kept secret to prevent the external effects becoming public.

There are two general reasons why actors assume to be in a reciprocal relationship: norms and trust. In order to understand the impact of norms on the perception of reciprocity it seems useful to start from a situation with strangers (as in example 1): the policeman and the tourist do not know each other and it is unlikely that they will ever meet again. Since the actors have not dealt with each other in the past, they do not have any knowledge about each other. The risk decreases if norms structure the situation already.[4] Assume a prevalent 'culture of corruption' in a country in which public officials demand an illegal processing fee (in order to speed up their work). Then there is only a minimal risk if an actor offers or accepts this processing fee because the likelihood of being prosecuted and getting punished is small. The decision to join such a corrupt exchange is easily made. In this way a norm directs corrupt transactions by implying the reciprocity between the actors.

Example 2 describes a different situation, where norms are of less importance because the actors met each other in the past frequently and anticipate that they will deal with each other again. Reciprocity originates from the same background and the shared knowledge about each other which simplifies the decision to make a corrupt offer. The prospect of dealing with each other again adds the opportunity to reinforce or punish a corrupt partner's behaviour. In this situation reciprocity is related to the actors' trust that renders it possible to arrange the corrupt deal individually.

Norms can regulate isolated corrupt exchanges if those norms clearly define what corruptly behaving actors should do. In long-term relations actors are able to organize the corrupt exchange in accordance with their needs and wishes. This implies a strong dependence between them, too. A strong utility interdependence, however, decreases the risk of exchange (Schmid and Robison 1995). In this situation trust gives the opportunity to make the corrupt deal without referring to any norms. If the reciprocity is not challenged during the long-term corrupt exchange, a higher level of trust is achieved (even if the relationship was guided by norms before). 'Fairly' behaving actors reinforce reciprocity. Then, actors regard their criminal acts as beneficial. This increases trust again (Husted 1994: 21).

It depends on the actors' knowledge of each other whether norms (or cultural aspects) or trust matter for corrupt exchanges. Since knowledge is a function of the frequency of corrupt deals, the given level of corruption in a society needs to rely either on trust or on norms. One can be substituted for the other.[5] Figure 3.1 depicts this suggestion.

Norms as a guiding principle

There are many social norms that foster corruption indirectly by implying social ties or obligations (e.g. *guanxi*, see the contributions by Schramm and Taube and by Schweitzer in this volume), and there are corruption norms that directly imply the reciprocity necessary to conduct corrupt deals. To keep to the

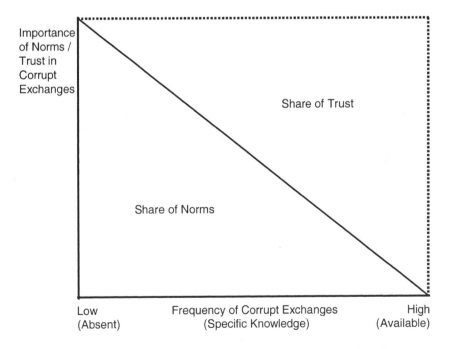

Figure 3.1 Shares of norms and trust as a criterion of corrupt exchanges (as a function of the frequency of corruption).

essentials points I will mainly stick to the emergence and maintenance of corruption norms.

As corruption is a socially evaluated behaviour, it involves the distinction between the public and the private role of public officials. Societies diverge in the degree of differentiating between the private and public role. This becomes clear if one tries to distinguish between gifts and bribes (Rose-Ackerman 1999).[6] In some Asian or African countries, where formal principal–agent relationships or formal agent–client relationships are regarded as unnatural and artificial, gifts are an adequate feedback for services received. However, the general conditions for corrupt exchanges are still valid if a corruption norm exists. I define a corruption norm as the expectation that one can usually offer or accept a corrupt deal in a certain situation. If the corruption norm is a guiding principle of behaviour it has to contradict another already existing norm or law (Schweitzer 2002). Otherwise, the actors could make their corrupt exchange public. Their transaction would no longer count as corruption. A corruption norm involves illegal behaviour. But this does not mean that it is automatically perceived as an illegitimate behaviour. Some corrupt actions correspond to citizens' expectations, such as in those cases where clients gain control over bureaucratic processes. Sometimes corruption provides the opportunity to avoid unreasonable regulations. From a public official's point of view it could be legitimate to charge an additional processing fee (sometimes called 'speed money'). In those cases a corruption norm stands in the way of another norm. This makes it necessary to keep the corrupt transaction secret.

According to Coleman, 'a norm concerning a specific action exists when the socially defined right to control the action is held not by the actor but by others' (Coleman 1990: 243). A mutual consent among the actors exists about who has the right to control a specific action. Norms belong to certain actions which Coleman calls 'focal actions' (Coleman 1990: 246).[7] Norms reduce or increase the likelihood of the appearance of focal actions. Usually, there are laws that are intended to hinder all focal actions concerning corruption. But there are also certain norms that foster corruption (such as 'one has to support family members by all means – even if it is against the law').

Norms arise from individual actions but constitute an entity beyond single individuals (Berger 1998: 65). There are several kinds of norms. Just to give an example I will mention the 'formal manners' by Elias (1969) which modify the behaviour of an actor so that he respects the interests of his interaction partners. Since in corrupt exchanges the actors' interests are interdependent and every actor has to consider the interests of the other (e.g. about the secrecy of the transaction), corruption norms can be taken as negative 'formal manners'.

In principle, the 'aim' of norms is to gain control over rights to act (Berger 1998: 67). The emergence of norms is related to this 'aim'. If corruption norms are taken as negative 'formal manners', they arise because they are beneficial for everybody who obeys them. Such a functionalistic explanation implies that people want this norm to come into being,[8] but it is totally unclear how people get the right to act. Coleman (1990) mentions an important reason for the emergence of norms: the existence of externalities. A norm can emerge if actors are not able to eliminate externalities via market or negotiation activities. In those situations norms can help by providing a rule. Many corruption cases are examples for this, such as the problem of regulatory burden or red tape in public bureaucracies. Civil servants can create and exploit additional regulatory burden. If that is ignored by their superiors the new 'regulatory procedure' becomes a habit of the civil servants and can establish a norm. Sometimes, the superiors intentionally overlook exploiting behaviours of civil servants in order to provide them with an additional income (Klitgaard 1991).

When authors try to define norms, most of them also stress the point that norms include the opportunity to sanction any deviating behaviour (from these norms) (Weede 1992). It is reasonable to assume that corruption norms emerge more often in societies where there are fewer opportunities for sanctioning. According to Coleman (1990), sanctioning is more likely in tight social relationships since the reinforcement or punishment of others is easier. To apply a sanction during corrupt exchanges is a special case. Sanctioning an action against a corruption norm (e.g. by unveiling the corruption) is difficult since the costs of revealing corruption affect both actors. The chance to make the corrupt deal public is an instrument of power for each actor during and after corrupt exchanges. This means that the possibility of sanctioning is part of the actors' decision conditions. Therefore it is possible to sanction behaviour against a corruption norm, but the general conditions of corrupt exchanges make the application of those sanctions unlikely.

Corruption norms create a social scope for actors who want to act in their own particular interest at the expense of others. Actions derived from corruption norms are mostly illegal but seldom illegitimate. One may think of legal 'loopholes' which give actors the opportunity to harmonize particularistic and universalistic interests via corrupt exchanges (Smelser 1971). In this situation corruption serves as a social 'tool', bringing individual and public interests into accordance with each other. But usually, statements about corruption norms are not as positive as those by Smelser (1971).

Corruption norms are part of a bigger system of social norms in a society and they are characterized by the fact that actors strive for their very own interest at the expense of the public. If corruption norms are prevalent in a society a 'systemic corruption' exists, with serious consequences for the political and legal system. Most often the incentive for politicians to overcome these problems is small because they benefit from such a situation. According to Schweitzer (2002) 'systemic corruption' occurs in those societies which are unable to solve conflicts in their normative systems. If universalistic norms do not prevail over particularistic norms people cannot be prevented from realizing private gain at the expense of society as a whole.

If a corruption norm already structures a situation the accomplishment of a corrupt exchange does not depend on a specific corruption partner. This means that the actors expect (due to the reciprocity) that they are not likely to be punished for criminal acts. This way, a corruption norm leads to the investment of trust in other actors, regardless of who the other actor is.

Trust as a guiding principle

If actors do not know each other and their interaction is loosely guided by general suppositions and expectations, a corruption norm can structure the situation and can guide the actors' behaviour. But if an action is based on specific, rather than general, information about the corruption partner, a trustful relationship exists between them because both accept the negative consequences of getting caught or getting punished. The successful repetition of corrupt exchanges increases the actors' trust on each other (Bunker and Cohen 1987; Husted 1994). This is due to the fact that more and more information about the interaction partner becomes available during the repetition process.

The definition of trust depends on an author's theoretical perspective. There are two aspects, however, which belong to almost every definition of trust (Neubauer 1999; Graeff 1998) and which are applied both by authors who use Rational Choice theories (like Coleman 1990) and by authors who use functionalistic theories (like Parsons 1980): a truster places resources at the disposal of another actor or party (the trustee) and this action involves a risk (Deutsch 1973). The concept of risk merely means that the truster faces a loss if his trust is disappointed.

Reciprocity has a special meaning in theories about interpersonal trust (Neubauer 1999: 96ff.). It is – as mentioned before – a characteristic of corrupt exchanges too. Since corrupt transactions are illegal, it is necessary that both actors expect a fair deal. Since every actor offers or accepts a corrupt deal by his own free will, the transaction would not happen if one of the actors suspected his partner of not doing his part of the illegal bargain. Coleman's concept of trust (1990) can be combined with the previously mentioned ideas about corruption because it includes attributes that correspond to those of typical corruption situations:

1   According to Coleman (1990: 97) 'trust allows an action on the part of the trustee that would not have been possible otherwise'. This trust characteristic is directly applicable to corruption: the mutual trust of corruption partners allows an increment in their utility that would not have been gained in legal transactions. Since illegality always involves risk, both actors must accept the risk.
2   The second characteristic of Coleman's (1990: 98) trust concept is the trustee's control over the truster's pay off: 'the person who places trust is better off than if trust were not placed, whereas if the trustee is not trustworthy, the trustor is worse off than if trust were not placed'. Both actors are in control of advantages and losses from corrupt exchanges due to reciprocity. If agent and client act truthfully both are better off. If one of

them does not act trustworthily the other one loses his promised gain, and the risk of being discovered and punished increases for both actors.

3   The third criterion mentioned by Coleman (1990) is the truster's voluntarily placing of resources at the disposal of another actor, without any real commitment from his interaction partner. The link to corrupt exchanges is obvious: no one is able to make recoverable commitments for illegal activities.

4   The fourth and last criterion of Coleman's trust concept is the time lag between the trust-donating action of one actor and the trust-reinforcing action of the other actor. Since trust has to do with future actions, time lags are constituting elements of trust relationships. The same is valid for corrupt exchanges where it can be discovered only a long time after a corrupt deal's termination whether the partners have kept their secrecy.

According to Coleman's Action Theory trust can be taken as a game. The elements of the game are the participants' potential gain (G) or loss (L) and the chance to win (p). Transferred to a corruption situation, G and L are the utility increments compared to legal activities and p is the chance of the trustee's action as expected by the truster. A rational actor will place trust and will accept a corrupt offer if (Coleman 1990: 99).[9]

$$\frac{p}{1-p} > \frac{L}{G}$$

An actor initiates a corrupt exchange if a chance of winning relative to the chance of losing is greater than the amount that he would lose relative to the amount that he would win. The likelihood of winning (p) has a special meaning. It reflects the trustworthiness of a person (Coleman 1990).

What was said about corruption before can be combined with the Coleman approach. On the one hand, Coleman's trust concept stresses gains and losses – crucial decision elements of corrupt exchanges. On the other hand, the p parameter reflects the reciprocity since mutual trust will increase if corrupt exchanges are successfully accomplished.

Coleman's concept of trust refers to an actor's process of deliberation and assessment. This implies trust being a function of risk. Rearranging Coleman's decision condition to $p > L/(L+G)$ yields a trust investment even if the trustworthiness is low (probability of getting disappointed is high), as long as G is sufficiently high. If the expected loss would be great relative to the expected gain, p – the trustworthiness of the trustee – must be big in order to yield a trust investment. Equal gains and losses imply a $p > 50$ per cent. If the potential loss is ten times higher than the potential gain this implies a $p > 90$ per cent (Noteboom 2002: 39). Obviously, under the condition of a secure gain ($p = 1$) there is no risk left and this equation is no longer valid. It does not make sense to associate trust decisions with such situations since actors do not expose themselves to any risk (Deutsch 1978).

For the analysis of corrupt exchanges, p can get more specified since information about the interaction partner and expectations about his 'fair behaviour' are inseparably connected. Corruption decisions due to personal experience and knowledge about the partner must positively correlate with the duration of the relationship. Therefore, p must depend (positively) on time:

$$p = p(t)$$

This conception is due to the observation that people become corrupt over time. Most often people do not enter a career in politics or public institutions intending to use their position for criminal acts. They develop corrupt practices while they get used to the habits in an institution. They see opportunities to hide information that must not come before the public, and they learn to use these opportunities. As incumbents, they meet other people who probably offer illegal deals. After some time in their position they have enough experience to evaluate the risk of those illegal offers. This way, legal relations between public officials and citizens (or between public officials themselves) contribute to the emergence of corruption (Lambsdorff 2002: 238).

Corruption happening due to trust is based on the actors' knowledge about each other. The better the knowledge, the more reliable are the actors' evaluations and the more specific are their expectations. Several aspects foster the actors' trust in each other. Generally, every increase in trust is identical to a reinforcement of reciprocity. As in families, reciprocity is a 'natural' element of social settings, so if corrupt deals include those social settings the likelihood of corrupt exchanges must increase. Rose-Ackerman puts it this way:

> A public official may favour his own relatives in allocating concessions and other public benefits in return for a share of the benefits. He may do this not only because he cares about them, but also they care about him and will be less likely than strangers to reveal the corrupt deal or to renege on the agreement.
>
> (Rose-Ackerman 1999: 98)

Mutual sympathy or perceptions of similarities are fostering aspects of reciprocity too (Graeff 1998).

The conception of trust introduced here is a specific one. It cannot be applied in general to other social phenomena that involve trust since this kind of trust gets activated only in specific situations. Trust of corruptly behaving actors is a cognitive concept; it is 'knowledge-based trust' (Yamagishi and Yamagishi 1994). For its emergence are emotions of little importance. It can neither be treated as dispositional trust – that is, as a consistent tendency to trust across a broad spectrum of situations and persons (Deutsch 1973; Wrightsman 1991) – nor could it pass as a situational concept only. A characteristic of trust in corrupt relationships is the decision of placing or not placing trust as a result of the comparison of potential gains and potential losses. 'The decision to trust another person is essentially *strategic*. Strategic (or knowledge-based) trust pre-supposes risk' (Uslaner 2002b: 17).

There are some techniques used for initiating corrupt deals, such as giving small presents. An accumulation of those gifts makes it (socially) difficult for the actor who received the presents to abandon the relationship. This is exploited by the giver who offers an illegal deal when the other actor feels forced to con-tinue the relationship. But every corruptly behaving actor has a certain goal that he attains by means of the corrupt deal. It can lead to problems, therefore, to claim that corruption situations gather momentum so that one of the actors is forced to continue corruption against his will. Such a conception is likely to confound corruption with blackmail. I do not deny that some public officials get involved into corruption because they do not know what the appropriate behaviour in their position is. Stupidity and greed is a dangerous combination, at least for a public official. But this does not happen often.

Usually, criminal acts like corruption or blackmail do not occur as single delicts. Corruptly behaving actors tend to commit other criminal offences, too, especially if they belong to criminal networks. But for the examination of the principles of corruption it might be misleading to merge this social phenome-non with others.

Both trust and norms facilitate the actions of the exchange partners in cor-ruption. All social mechanisms like trust or norms, providing this facilitation can be taken as social capital. I will turn to that in the next section.

Corruption as negative social capital

A corrupt transaction can be seen as an individual's attempt to invest his resources in the best possible way. The actor's relationships enabling him to achieve additional gains can be perceived as a resource (from the individual's perspective). Loury (1977, 1987) has introduced the term 'social capital' for this kind of resources. The concept has been specified by Coleman (1990), Fukuyama (1995) and Putnam (1993). These authors apply social capital explicitly to certain positive relations between actors and exclude relations that only provide benefits at the expense of others. The productivity of social capital results from the fact that it enables the actors to reach goals that would have been unattainable without it.

Corruption serves a certain purpose – namely, to ameliorate the situation of the actors illegally. Theoretical approaches accentuating the instrumental char-acter of social capital can be used to find a theoretical juncture between corrup-tion and social capital (for a different view see Hirschman 1984). Coleman (1988) illustrates this instrumental character with the role of the interrelations between parents, teachers and pupils to improve learning conditions in school. It was the educational context where the social capital concept was used by Hanifan (1916) for the first time in its contemporary meaning. Rudimentary ideas on the functions of social capital, however, can also be found in the works of Durkheim and Weber.[10]

The theoretical links between trust and social capital are treated differently in the literature. Some authors consider trust as a component of shared values and norms that constitute social capital. Others claim that trust is an outcome of social capital (Woolcock 1998). If one differentiates between trusting behaviour and a person's trustworthiness, the causality problem can get solved. In a transaction without reciprocity (i.e. if an actor cannot be perceived as trustworthy) social capital cannot emerge. People who do not behave as they say cannot facilitate actions of others. The term of social capital should not be used to denote a behaviour which is not in accordance with the attitude.

If social capital is used successfully, then facilitation of certain actions must result. This can lead to the formation of trust. If so, it increases the trustworthiness of the helping person. Therefore, social capital in corrupt exchanges only exists if all actors believe that their partners behave as they say (this feature of corruption was called 'reciprocity' before). This highlights the fact that social capital is always positive for its users, despite the vagueness of whether it will have positive or negative external effects for other people (Portes 1998).

Two conditions must apply if corrupt transactions are to be subsumed under the concept of social capital (Coleman 1990: 302). First, a social structure among the actors must exist. This social structure is defined in corrupt exchanges due to reciprocity.[11] Second, social capital facilitates certain actions of people within a social structure and makes the achievement of certain ends possible that would not be attainable otherwise. Corrupt exchanges reflect this characteristic of social capital because the agent uses his authority in order to provide an action option for the client. This option would not have been attainable for the client otherwise (e.g. legally). This can be seen in both examples, too: legally, the tourist would have had to be punished (if one assumes that he actually drove too fast) and the public official would have had to consider different job opportunities for his daughter (if he had accepted her failure).

The value of social capital depends on the situations and on the actions, respectively. Both situations and actions are clearly defined in corrupt exchanges so that (from an Action Theory's point of view) social capital can be related directly to corrupt exchanges. Since social capital is not completely fungible[12] it is not tradable. Although the corrupt actors use it for very private ends, it is not their 'private property' since it inheres in the structure of their relation.

Generally, norms and trust are special forms of social capital. Norms are powerful but unstable forms of social capital. Concerning corruption this can be explained by the fact that norms provide only unspecific information for actions while trust is based on specific knowledge about other actors. The development of corruption norms used as negative social capital by certain groups depends on the closeness of those groups. The closeness is a necessary condition for the emergence of expectations about certain actions (Coleman 1990).

It depends on the stability of the relations as to how long social capital can be used. Relationships with trusting actors are stable by themselves. In corrupt relationships this stability is improved by the secrecy about the illegal transaction.

If actors violate a social norm by adhering to another social norm, i.e. a corruption norm, they have to put (socially accepted) ethical values aside. The susceptibility to violating norms depends on an actor's position of power. The empirical results by Bailey (1971: 20) and Starr (1978: 59) suggest that powerful people are generally less likely to be sanctioned than others. It is also less likely that powerful people follow rules (which fits the assumption about the p parameter). An explanation might be that non-powerful actors avoid sanctioning them. If the powerful actors notice that, then their (subjective) risk of getting punished for violating social norms decreases. If powerful public officials violate social norms (due to corrupt exchanges), then they jeopardize their position. On the one hand, they have much to lose. On the other hand, the likelihood is small that they will be called to account for their violation by non-powerful colleagues or subordinates. Imagine a low-level public servant discovering the corrupt activities of a high-ranking public official. He will think twice before he whistle-blows. In itself, revealing the corruption provides no advantages. Since the reactions of his colleagues and superiors could be negative, too, because he accuses a member of his own social group, there is not the slightest reason to sanction the high-ranking public official. Moreover, he has to consider that powerful public officials are able to control the information outlets which are used to uncover corruption.

This example raises questions as to under which circumstances do actors generally apply sanctions. Though non-participants can point to the corrupt deal, they must take the social capital of the corrupt actors into consideration (this aspect makes the fight against Mafia-like organized groups so difficult and dangerous). The low-level public servant must take into account that the high-ranking public official will use his social capital to harm him. Most probably the high-ranking public official has better sources of information, and he will bring his influence to bear. His social capital has a deterrent effect – it yields negative externalities. The low-level civil servant could overcome the negative externalities if he holds strong ethical or ideological/religious views. If he had such opinions, and if he did not have any further advantage of announcing the corrupt deal, it would make little sense bringing this information before the public. This example should be sufficient to demonstrate the negative externalities of social capital derived from corrupt exchanges.

Generally, there are two possibilities among free actors to create negative social capital: either intentionally by planning and accumulating or as a 'by-product' of the accidental activities of actors. In the second example mentioned, the father did not generate his social capital intentionally (in order to get a job for his daughter). It developed as a by-product of his working relations. The corruption norm (as a form of negative social capital) in example 1 was not created by the tourist or the policeman intentionally, though they exploited it.

Social capital that is used for corrupt exchanges is sometimes intentionally created by techniques for initiating corrupt exchanges, as mentioned before. A client tests an agent's susceptibility for corrupt deals by offering tiny gifts or tips. This is useful in situations where people lack information about each other, since the accumulation of those small gifts can be taken as social capital if they shape the relation of client and agent. The gifts are a form of social influence anyway. The client's gain increases if the agent perceives their relationship more and more as a situation of mutual exchange. This can result in a situation where the accumulation of the petty gifts sums up to a 'bribe' that makes it difficult for the agent to quit the relationship.

Social capital has a positive impact on a society if it associated to (ethical, ideological or religious) attitudes and rules which encourage people to evaluate their own behaviour by taking the gains or the losses of others into account. Though a corruptly behaving actor considers the gains and losses of his partners, he does not care about disadvantages to non-participants. One major disadvantage is the emergence of distrust among the non-participants whenever a corruption case is unveiled. This is an obstacle to the creation of socially positive social capital.

There are some differences between the ways negative and positive social capital works. Usually positive social capital decreases if the dependence between actors is reduced. This is not true for negative social capital (e.g. corrupt relationships). When negative social capital is considered, the relationships get stabilized when the dependence increases. The social system of corrupt relationships is closed. Therefore, it facilitates the emergence of norms and trust (Coleman 1990).

The impact of changing the numbers of actors has a different effect on positive and negative social capital: positive social capital increases its value for a society if the group of actors' (fostering the social capital) actions becomes larger. An incentive for free-riding emerges. This is different for social systems using negative social capital. If the group of members becomes larger, the coercion becomes bigger to use and foster negative social capital. If one member denies using it he questions his reciprocity to other members. Imagine the boss of a construction company who belongs to a corruption network. One day he starts working in an honest way. His old 'friends' get suspicious when he submits a building application in compliance with the law or if he does not ask them for 'advantages' anymore. Finally, they have to figure out the reasons for his unusual behaviour because defecting from a criminal social system is a threat to the remaining group members.

Discussion

This chapter is an attempt to analyse corruption with a three-actor model (Banfield 1975) by combining ideas from economics and sociology. If corruption is considered under a Rational Choice approach, the actors share a social relationship with strong situational conditions. To focus on the crucial point of corruption only, the chapter deals solely with the agent–client relationship and does not touch upon the role of the principal. This is so because the strong situational conditions of the agent–client relationship are not applicable to the agent–principal relationship. One could try to apply the trust concept here introduced to pinpoint the agent's scope of action: the principal will monitor the agent if he suspects him of exploiting his decision latitude. If the principal decides rationally, the agent's scope of action must depend on the p parameter mentioned before. Assuming constant gains and losses, the agent's scope of action expands if p increases. But these reflections are modified by the fact that trust is only one option for the principal. Reciprocity does not necessarily arise from these situational conditions. Moreover, some contracts substitute trust.

Imagine that a principal and his subordinate conclude a contract for certain services. The subordinate commits himself to work at a predetermined level of quality. The principal must not worry about the fulfilment of this contract because he can sue the subordinate for non-fulfilment. Trust is less necessary in this situation since the principal's risk is reduced.[13] Warranties work the same way. If a car seller gives a warranty for each car then he will increase his reputation and trustworthiness.[14] But the latter is less relevant for the decision of the buyer as he will take a lower risk in buying one of his cars (as long as the contract is valid).

It is difficult to pinpoint the scope of action a principal grants a client, therefore, by analysing their relationship. At least it is true that the agent can develop criminal activities only insofar as he is able to hide his activities (Cartier-Bresson 1997).

Certain 'social' costs caused by corruption emerge because of the principal's losses. Since the corruptly behaving actors have to regard the situational conditions like secrecy or non-suability, transaction costs emerge. Della Porta and Vannucci (1997) argue that the actors have to invest time and resources for hiding their deal and monitoring the partners. But if corruption norms result from externalities or from advantages to actors, then rational decision-makers will accept corrupt deals only if transaction costs are lower than the expected gains. If trust exists between the actors already, transaction costs are less important because trust reduces the (subjective) costs for actors (Rose-Ackerman 1999: 98). 'Social' cost accumulation occurs less because of the expenditures of corruptly behaving actors than because of the negative externalities of corruption for others. The distribution of corruptly traded resources is only due to the advantage of the corruption partners, not due to the principal or due to a social aim. 'Social' costs arise because of the externalities of negative social capital too, exemplified by the influence and power of the Mafia.

I distinguish between negative and positive social capital by its effect on society. A usual objection against such a procedure is the confounding of consequences and prerequisites because the social phenomenon is defined by its outcome. A careful consideration of this argument reveals that it is not true. The basis of my argumentation is Coleman's Action Theory (1990). His theory is a Rational Choice approach that admits the existence of social contexts – it does not deal with social structures itself.

Analysing corruption (or trust/social capital) at a sociological micro level is advantageous because the parameters and influencing factors creating the social phenomenon can be isolated. The causality runs from the decisions of actors to the results of their actions – for example, the establishment of social networks. By this I do not deny the opposite causality: differences between kinds of social networks can affect the level of trust (or corrupt actions) within this network. A socio-cultural context is important for the explanation of decisions and actions. That poses the question: what is necessary for the existence of social capital – trust or network? Must trust occur first, or must a certain network structure exist first, before social capital can come into being? Coleman's Action Theory does not answer this question. It can be answered if negative social capital (derived from corrupt exchanges) is considered. Since corruption depends on decisions, actors need knowledge about gains, losses, the reliability of their partners and the situation. This knowledge sometimes leads to expectations of reciprocity, sometimes not. And those expectations turn the balance to accept or deny a corrupt offer. Reciprocity is the decision criterion, though negative social capital stabilizes the relationship and creates trust among the actors, as long as every actor sticks to the rules. Thus far social capital rests on reciprocity. But this does not contradict the fact that a decision about reciprocity comes first. Since decisions are taken previously, negative social capital is not merely explained by its function. Subsuming corruption to the social capital concept can serve as a theoretical foundation to substantiate empirical questions and its examinations on a micro and macro level of society. Recently, some papers have come up dealing with the empirical link between social capital and corruption (Uslaner 2002a; Bjørnskov 2003), though a complete analysis is still missing.

If one wants to derive practical conclusions for fighting corruption, then one may consider a situation where prevalent corruption norms in a society exist. Then, the identity of the corruption partner does not matter. It may be helpful to increase moral costs of corruption by stressing the importance of anti-corruption norms. Since norms most often emerge from externalities, one has to examine the political and bureaucratic system. Increasing moral costs by building a 'corporate culture' (resting on ethical consents and administered by training programmes to public officials and citizens) is just one aspect (of many) and does not remove the cause.

Anti-corruption laws and norms increase the risk of corrupt exchanges but also increase the stability and closeness of corrupt networks already existing. The concept presented here suggests that it is likely that regular corrupt deals with the same partner create a trustful relationship that is not affected by reshaping the principal–agent–client relations. That is so because (negative) social capital probably continues to exist if civil servants are transferred to other offices. Job rotation might be helpful if the public official loses the disposal over resources or if the reciprocity between the corruption partners is being destroyed.

My approach of analysing corruption includes ideas from sociology and economics. It differs from the latter in several aspects. Recently, New Institutional Economics (e.g. Transaction Cost Theory) has become a popular approach for analysing corruption. The concept here introduced suggests (in contrast to this approach) that it is inaccurate to state that corruption is simply an outcome of an inadequate institutional framework (Dietz 1998). Nevertheless, I use the basic assumptions of Transaction Cost Theory, such as the necessity of secrecy, the possibility of punishment and the loss of the right to sue. While these facts constitute a social situation, they are interpreted in economics usually as costs which disregards the social dynamics related to them. My approach can be seen as an expansion of this concept, filling a theoretical gap about trust and norms that inheres in this approach.

Institutional economists are primary interested in the formal aspects of organizational relationships. Reverting to insights of non-cooperative Game Theory (Fudenberg and Tirole 1991; Osborne and Rubinstein 1994), economists are able to explain social aspects as well. Their principal aim is to consider an institutional framework that reduces corruption. As reciprocity between corruptly behaving actors is one of the main reasons why corruption happens in all offices, it might be useful to expand their analysis to aspects like trust or norms in order to tackle the problem of corruption from its formal and social points of view.

Notes

1 Especially for developing countries, the 'mis-governance' of the state is sometimes called 'public corruption' (for an example, see Biswal 1999). This oxymoron is due to the assessment that people feel badly treated and exploited by government and public administration. Usually, the word is used for forms of endemic corruption associated with structural government and administration problems (e.g. the lack of rule of law, a weak or non-existent jurisdiction, etc.). The term 'corruption' is open to all sorts of interpretation, but in order to focus on the phenomenon properly one should not forget that a prerequisite of a corrupt deal is that all actors voluntarily consent to it. Most measures of 'bad governance' interpreted as corruption include coercion and refer, therefore, more to blackmail or exploitation.

2 Notice that I refer to a special understanding of the term 'reciprocity'. Usually, this term is defined and used for mutual exchanges of deeds, goods and services (Gouldner 1960). But this meaning is insufficient to include the crucial element of corrupt deals: the mutual *expectation* that the corruption partner will play 'fair'. There is another difference: usually, reciprocal relationships are motivated both by selfishness and altruism (Noteboom 2002). It is difficult, however, to read motives of altruism into a corrupt deal. Furthermore, reciprocity as the expectation to play 'fair' can be the result of trust or norms, as will be explained (see pp. 42–3). For the sake of the concept's clarity I do not treat reciprocity as a norm itself.

3 In real-world exchanges it is frequently the case that corruption serves to gain an increment on utility which cannot be achieved otherwise. This kind of interdependence leads to a new question: how do actors distribute their gains? This aspect of the relationship between agent and client is beyond the scope of this chapter (see Della Porta and Vannucci (1999) for some answers from an economic theoretical point of view).

4 Those norms usually include knowledge about the appropriate circumstances for their use. Lambsdorff (2002) correctly annotated this point by stating that some of them must reduce the tourist's risk that the policeman does not denounce his corrupt offer (and the other way round). Since these norms must sustain ideas about cooperation and mutual fairness, the actors should not get into trouble when it comes to negotiate the prices for the corrupt services.

5 Primary I suggested that norms are a good 'breeding-ground' for trustful corruption relationships. Vannucci gave me the hint that it could be the other way round, too: norms can emerge from corrupt relationships as well.

6 Rose-Ackerman (1999: 93) differentiates between bribes and gifts by using two criteria: gifts are offered without the idea of getting something in return (no 'quid pro quo') and are given to the principal only. Bribes always involve a quid pro quo and are given to the agent only. This typical economic conception contradicts the sociological idea that gifts involve not an explicit, but a strong binding, implicit service in return (Mauss 1999; Godelier 1996).

7 Coleman (1990: 246) illustrates his term 'focal actions' with the example of a three-year-old child who drops a cellophane sweet wrapper on a pavement. Any action that has the effect of littering the pavement belongs to the class of focal actions which are opposed to tidiness norms.

8 This functionalistic perspective on the creation of norms corresponds with the fact that many agents (in poor countries particularly) have an interest in the emergence and maintenance of corruption norms. If this is going to happen, they benefit the most from these norms but their gains come at the public's expense.

9 The usefulness of such a trust concept is controversial. Williamson (1996: 250–75) denotes deliberate trust decisions as 'calculative trust'. He takes every moral action to be an end in itself. Moral actions contradict the economic utility maximization principle since they are motivated by unselfish emotions. Therefore, the concept of trust should be reserved for non-calculative personal relations only. Ripperger (1998) shows that Williamson (1996) takes the economic assumption about selfishness falsely for a selfish motive. Thereby, he mingles assumptions about human actions (like the economic principle of selfishness) with action motives and disregards the fact that the utility maximization principle is a methodological conception (which is not limited to serve certain purposes). Every specific aim can be achieved rationally. Selfishness as a moral concept applies to that which an actor maximizes (Ripperger 1998: 248). Conceptions about rational and selfish actions are logically independent (Rowe 1989).

10 Durkheim describes societies being composed of social structures possessing a multitude of social functions. Weber, in contrast, focuses his analyses on individuals and the patterns of their actions and regulations.

11 Coleman's Action Theory does not regard special social structures between actors. Strictly speaking, his theory only deals with rational decisions of actors. The decisions are made regardless of the social context. Here, my corruption approach goes beyond his theory.

12 Social capital is fungible with respect to specific actions. Concerning corruption this is important because sometimes third persons serve as mediators between actors for initiating corrupt deals. The analysis of intermediaries in corrupt exchanges is beyond the scope of this chapter but can be done by applying Coleman's Action Theory to corruption networks. (See also the contribution by John Bray in this volume.)

13 Offe (1999: 66) gives some counter-arguments: 'Institutions are *incomplete* and ambiguous (at least "at the margin"), and they are *contested* ... Both contracts and market competition are known to be *incomplete*, and the same applies to laws and constitutional regimes.' He concludes (1999: 67): 'As a consequence, trust in the anonymous mechanisms of institutions is justified only by trust in the voluntary compliance of those actors who are mandated with the supervision and enforcement of these rules. As there is the risk of violation and breakdown, there is also the need for trust in *persons* which cannot be fully substituted for by trust in institutions.'

   Offe is perfectly right when he claims that the incompleteness of institutions (like laws and contracts) leaves a free space that makes it impossible to rely totally on them. Nonetheless, valid contracts reduce the actors' subjective risk in getting what they want. Trust seldom refers to the objective risk in a situation since in reality an actor is usually unable to anticipate and assess all possible events or assign probabilities to them. This is also true for corruption situations where a lot of intervening factors exist: an actor can fail in doing his part of the corrupt deal – not because he denies fulfilling his promise but because something unexpected happened (Noteboom 2002: 41). The actor's consideration of these unexpected events is part of his assessment about the reliability of his partner (e.g. his trustworthiness). This is the crucial point in every trust decision, as this is the determinant of the subjective risk.

14 Reputation is a prominent concept in economics (Lambsdorff 2002). It is similar to the trust concept introduced here since it denotes relevant knowledge about the interaction partner. In contrast to trust it does not involve risk.

References

Bailey, F.G. (1971) *Gifts and Poisons: The Politics of Reputation*, New York.

Banfield, E.C. (1975) 'Corruption as a Feature of Governmental Organisation', *Journal of Law and Economics*, vol. 18, no. 3.

Berger, J. (1998) 'Das Interesse an Normen und die Normierung von Interessen. Eine Auseinandersetzung mit der Theorie der Normentstehung bei James S. Coleman', in H.P. Müller and M. Schmid (eds) *Norm, Herrschaft und Vertrauen*, Opladen, pp. 64–78.

Biswal, B.P. (1999) 'Private Tutoring and Public Corruption: A Cost-effective Education System for Developing Countries', *The Developing Economies*, vol. 37, no. 2, pp. 222–40.

Bjørnskov, C. (2003) *Corruption and Social Capital*, Mimeo.

Bunker, S.G. and Cohen, L.E. (1983) 'Collaboration and Competition in Two Colonization Projects: Toward a General Theory of Official Corruption', *Human Organization*, vol. 42, pp. 106–14.

Cartier-Bresson, J. (1997) 'Corruption Networks, Transaction Security and Illegal Social Exchange', in P. Heywood (ed.) *Political Corruption*, Oxford, pp. 47–60.

Coleman, J.S. (1988) 'Social Capital in the Creation of Human Capital', *American Journal of Sociology*, vol. 94, pp. 95–120.

Coleman, J.S. (1990) *Foundations of Social Theory*, Cambridge, Mass.

della Porta, D. and Vannucci, A. (1997) 'The "Perverse Effects of Political Corruption"', in P. Heywood (ed.) *Political Corruption*, Oxford, pp. 100–22.

Deutsch, M. (1973) *The Resolution of Conflict*, New Haven.

Dietz, M. (1998) *Korruption – Eine institutionenökonomische Analyse*, Berlin.

Elias, N. (1969) *The History of Manners*, New York.

Fudenberg, D. and Tirole, J. (1991) *Game Theory*, Massachusetts.

Fukuyama, F. (1995) *Trust. The Social Virtues and the Creation of Prosperity*, New York.

Godelier, M. (1996) *Das Rätsel der Gabe. Geld, Geschenke, heilige Objekte*, München.

Gouldner, A.W. (1960) 'The Norm of Reciprocity: A Preliminary Statement', *American Sociological Review*, vol. 25, no. 4, pp. 161–78.

Graeff, P. (1998) *Vertrauen zum Vorgesetzten und zum Unternehmen*, Berlin.

Husted, B.W. (1994) 'Honor among Thieves: A Transaction-cost Interpretation of Corruption in Third World Countries', *Business Ethics Quarterly*, vol. 4, no. 1, pp. 17–27.

Klitgaard, R. (1991) *Controlling Corruption*, Berkeley.

Lambsdorff, J. Graf (2002) 'Making Corrupt Deals: Contracting in the Shadow of Law', *Journal of Economic Behaviour and Organization*, vol. 48, pp. 221–41.

Lambsdorff, J. Graf and Teksoz, S.U. (2002) 'Corrupt Relational Contracting', this volume.

Lüdtke, H. and Schweitzer, H. (1993) 'Korruptionsneigung bei unterschiedlichen Erwartungskonstellationen in der Handlungssituation. Ein Quasi-Experiment mit Studenten', *Kölner Zeitschrift für Soziologie und Sozialpsychologie*, vol. 45, pp. 465–83.

Mauss, M. (1999) *Die Gabe. Form und Funktion des Austausches in archaischen Gesellschaften*, Frankfurt am Main.

Neubauer, W. (1999) 'Zur Entwicklung interpersonalen, interorganisatinalen und interkulturellen Vertrauens durch Führung – Empirische Ergebnisse der sozialpsychologischen Vertrauensforschung', in G. Schreyögg and J. Sydow (eds) *Managementforschung* (9th edn), Berlin, pp. 89–116.

Noteboom, B. (2002) *Trust. Forms, Foundations, Functions, Failures and Figures*, Cheltenham.

Nye, C.J. (1967) 'Corruption and Political Development: A Cost–benefit Analysis', *American Political Science Review*, vol. 61, no. 2, pp. 417–27.

Osborne, M. and Rubinstein, A. (1994) *A Course in Game Theory*, Massachusetts.

Parsons, T. (1980) *Zur Theorie der Interaktionsmedien*, Wiesbaden.

Portes, A. (1998) 'Social Capital: Its Origins and Applications in Modern Sociology', *Annual Review of Sociology*, vol. 24, pp. 1–24.

Putnam, R.D. (1993) *Making Democracy Work: Civic Traditions in Modern Italy*, Princeton.

Richter, R. and Furubotn, E.G. (1996) *Neue Institutionenökonomie*, Tübingen.

Ripperger, T. (1998) *Ökonomik des Vertrauens*, Tübingen.

Rose-Ackerman, S. (1999) *Corruption and Development. Causes, Consequences, and Reform*, Cambridge.

Rowe, N. (1989) *Rules and Institutions*, Ann Arbor.

Schmid, A.A. and Robison, L.J. (1995) 'Applications to Social Capital Theory', *Journal of Agriculture and Applied Economics*, vol. 27, pp. 59–66.

Schweitzer, H. (2002) *Ideas for Developing a Theory of Corruption*, Mimeo.

Smelser, N.J. (1971) 'Stability, Instability and the Analysis of Political Corruption', in B. Barber and A. Inkeles (eds) *Stability and Social Change. In Honor of Talcott Parsons*, Boston, Mass., pp. 7–29.

Starr, J. (1978) *Dispute and Settlement in Rural Turkey*, Leiden.

Uslaner, E. (2002a) *Varieties of Trust*, Mimeo.

Uslaner, E. (2002b) *The Moral Foundations of Trust*, Cambridge.

Weede, E. (1992) *Mensch und Gesellschaft*, Tübingen.

Williamson, O.E. (1996) *The Mechanisms of Governance*, New York.

Woolcock, M. (1998) 'Social Capital and Economic Development: Toward a Theoretical Synthesis and Policy Framework', *Theory and Society*, vol. 27, pp. 151–208.

Wrightsman, L.S. (1991) 'Interpersonal Trust and Attitudes Toward Human Nature', in J.P. Robinson, P.R. Shaver and L.S. Wrightsman (eds) *Measures of Personality and Social Psychological Attitudes*, New York, pp. 373–412.

Yamagishi, T. and Yamagishi, M. (1994) *Trust and Commitment in the United States and Japan*. Vol. 18: *Motivation and Emotion*, pp. 129–66.

4 Corruption trends

Christian Bjørnskov and Martin Paldam

Introduction

Transparency International has now posted the κ-index on perceived corruption for the last eight years.[1] At the outset, few observations were available, but more than a hundred countries are now covered. The κ-index is compiled from a total of 17 primary indices to give an aggregate measure of the highest reliability available, which allows researchers to study the cross-country levels of corruption. The result is a new empirical literature on (a) the sources of corruption, and (b) the consequences of corruption; the literature is surveyed in Lambsdorff (1998) and Jain (2001).

With respect to the determinants of corruption, a consensus is emerging that (at least) the four factors A1–A4 of Table 4.1 influence corruption (see Husted 1999; Treisman 2000; Paldam 2001, 2002). Below, a new factor, A5, is added: corruption is strongly connected to social capital. The effects of corruption are analysed by, for example, Mauro (1995), Olson *et al.* (2000), Mo (2001) and Le *et al.* (2003). Regarding the consequences, the two main results are that factors B1 and B2 are influenced by corruption.

In principle, cross-country regressions can neither control for country-fixed effects nor for the dynamics of the relationship. These problems can only be fully addressed in studies using panel data; but panel estimates make sense only if the time series contain 'meaningful' information. We first use the time series

Table 4.1 Main factors in the cross-country studies of corruption

---

Explaining corruption: A $\rightarrow \kappa$

A1	The transition from a poor LDC to a rich DC decreases corruption strongly
A2	Inflation waves rapidly increase corruption
A3	Corruption increases with the complexity of the regulatory system and decreases with the quality of the legal system
A4	Various cultural-religious factors affect corruption – especially Protestantism
A5	When social capital, measured as generalised trust, increases, corruption decreases

Corruption as the explanation: $\kappa \rightarrow$ B

B1	Corruption decreases investment and hence growth
B2	Corruption decreases political stability

---

to calculate a non-parametric trend score, ψ, which disregards the levels. It turns out that significant ψ's appear in the corruption data for 30 countries and three main groups of countries. These trends turn out to be almost independent of all the main variables mentioned above. However, some of the variation in the trends can be explained by the trends in social capital.

The chapter is structured as follows. The second section defines the trend score and surveys the results of applying the measure. The third looks at the relation between the ψ's and indicators of social capital and economic freedom. The fourth concludes by considering the policy implications.

The trend scores: definition and results

In this section, we first argue that trends may be relatively well determined. Then a distribution-free trend score is defined and applied to the κ-index.

The variation in the κ-index across the primary series and over time

The κ-index is scaled from 1 to 10 with one decimal point. However, the 17 primary indices used in the construction of the κ-index cover different country samples; hence, only six indices are used to construct κ for the median country. The standard deviation of these indices is also given for each country and year. On average it is almost one, so the standard error is $1/\sqrt{6} \approx 0.41$. As a crude rule, we thus know that two observations have to differ by about one to be significantly different, i.e. to have a t-ratio above 2. By this crude rule, 44 countries have a significant range across the eight years, suggesting that the data contains many trends.

However, if we surround each observation with a significance band of two (i.e. twice the standard deviation), it appears that in virtually every case the observations over time remain within this band. Even after some refinement of the calculation method, it is clear that few trends are significant by this method. In addition, the most different observations ought to be at both ends of the distribution; that is, when a parametric approach is used, very few countries have significant trends in their κ-scores.

From the descriptions of the way the individual indices are constructed, it nevertheless seems likely that year-to-year changes may be better determined than the standard deviations of the observations suggest.[2] Hence, analysing corruption trends based on these data should make sense after all.

As the mix of primary indices changes over time the use of the different sources can overshadow the actual trends in the data. Trends detected may therefore arise (1) due to changes in the perception provided by sources that consistently enter in the index, or (2) as random effects due to sources dropping in and out. When detecting steady and significant trends there is a high likelihood that this is generated by the first influence, because these trends are observed for a larger period of time.

Ideally we want to delete singular large random variations that might arise by changing sources, and to concentrate on the steady impact that arises from sources consistently entering into the index. We have therefore chosen to disregard the numerical information and calculate trends using a distribution-free test.

Defining the Kendall trend score, ψ

Consider N observations of corruption $(n_1, n_2, \ldots, n_N)$ available from a hypothetical country, for example the numbers $Ex = (4.5, 4.7, 5.3, 5.4)$. As the standard deviation of each observation is about 1 and the range is only 0.9, there is no significant parametric trend in the series, but κ is rising each and every year. To test for the trend, we therefore calculate Kendall's τ between the data series and a simple trend $T_n = (1, \ldots, N)$ with the same number of observations as the observed series – for Ex we compare with $T_4 = (1, 2, 3, 4)$. The N observations give a total of $(N(N-1))/2$ pairs: pair 1 is (n_1, n_2), pair 2 (n_1, n_3) up to pair $(N(N-1))/2$ which is (n_{N-1}, n_N). We now separate the pairs into three categories and count the members in each category, $N(+)$, $N(-)$ and $N(0)$ according to the following rule: Consider pair j, (n_a, n_b), where $a < b$. If $n_a < n_b$ add 1 (one) to $N(+)$, if $n_a > n_b$ add 1 (one) to $N(-)$, and if $n_a = n_b$ add 1 (one) to $N(0)$. Only the $n = N(+) + N(-)$ pairs allow a comparison, i.e. the $N(0)$ ties have to be disregarded. Therefore, the trends, ψ, between the n observations are:

$$\psi = k/n, \text{ where } k = N(+) - N(-) \text{ and } n = N(+) + N(-) \tag{1}$$

Kendall originally calculated the distribution of τ where both series are random. We consider a case where only one series is random (and hence use a different Greek letter), which is distributed as a cumulative binominal distribution with the assumption that the probability is random ($p = 0.5$) for the trend-score of each pair. Table 4.2 shows the points of significance of this

Table 4.2 Binominal tests

Annual observations N	Pairs generated $N(N-1)/2$	Significance points for net number of signs, k					
		10%		5%		1%	
		k	ψ	k	ψ	k	ψ
4	6	0	±1	0	±1	n/a	n/a
5	10	±2	±0.8	±1	±0.9	0	±1
6	15	±4	±0.73	±3	±0.8	±1	±0.93
7	21	±7	±0.67	±6	±0.71	±4	±0.81
8	28	±10	±0.64	±9	±0.61	±7	±0.75

Note
The significance limits for ψ are calculated for no ties. The net number of signs is $k = N(+) - N(-)$.

distribution. The table shows that the hypothetical example is significant at the 5 per cent level of probability, while five observations (4.3, 4.7, 5.1, 4.9, 6.0), which have one falling pair, also show a positive trend at the 5 per cent level.

The trend scores have three important properties: (1) since the test is based on pairs across time, it is independent of gaps in the observations; (2) hence it is relatively robust to changes in the mix of the primary indices; (3) if we compare countries in a group we can add the counts for $N(+)$ and $N(-)$ for all countries of the group and hereby obtain a high number of pairs (n) in the test.

The corruption trends calculated

Table 4.6 in the Appendix (see p. 71) reports the results of using this method for all countries where the κ-values are available. Table 4.3 shows the average corruption level, κ, and the trend scores, ψ, for six country groups, as well as some average indications of the significance of these average scores.

Transparency International calibrates the data to give every year the same average, so by construction there can be no trend for corruption in the world. We therefore look at *relative* trends for different country groups. The first point to note in Table 4.3 is that the world shows no tendency of either falling or rising corruption, as it should. However, if the average reached for each group based on the available observations is typical for the trend in the group, it is easy to make a *standard calculation* (see Table 4.4), which assumes that all countries have observations of κ for all eight years. In this calculation, the number of pairs increases from 1,700 to an imputed number of 4,228, and the average ψ-score becomes -0.074, which is significant (for 1,700 observations) even at the 1 per cent level. This means that the calibration might as well have added a trend as calculated or deleted an unknown trend. The calibration used by TI is thus somewhat arbitrary. This arbitrariness, it seems, is unavoidable because inferences about trends of countries where insufficient data is available are naturally not robust. All trends discussed from now are thus *relative* trends.

A first look at the relative trends: the main country groups

At the country level, a total of 30 countries have significant corruption trends: 14 have decreasing corruption (κ rises), while 16 have increasing corruption (κ falls).[3] We have found no obvious characteristic for the countries in either group. The trends in the major country groups are reported in Tables 4.3 and 4.4.

The strongest negative trend appears in Africa, where the number of observations is small relative to the number of countries, and there are thus few significant trends in the individual countries. However, when all observations are merged, a sadly negative trend appears.[4] The other clearly negative trend appears in the post-communist countries. This group has few observations per country as well, yet countries like Poland, Romania and the Czech Republic,

Table 4.3 Data for the main groups of countries

Group of countries	Number in group	Corruption measures		Calculation of trend				Countries with significant ψ's		Relative number*	
		κ-level	ψ-trend	Up	Down	Tied	All	Down	Up	(a)	(b)
				N(+)	N(−)	N(0)					
Africa	19	3.11	**−0.293**	59	108	20	187	–	3	88	57
Latin America	18	3.46	0.060	133	118	21	272	4	4	160	160
Orient (Far East)	11	4.70	**0.178**	152	106	30	288	3	1	76	131
Post-communist	24	3.33	−0.102	84	103	23	210	2	3	130	75
West	22	7.91	0.021	264	253	68	585	4	4	75	131
Residual	15	3.87	−0.054	70	78	10	158	1	1	69	48
All countries	109	4.45	−0.002	762	766	172	1,700	14	16	100	100

Notes
The data used are the Transparency International data set, scaled as in the original. A high κ-score thus means low corruption, and a positive trend means that corruption goes down. The trend score is shown in bold if it is significant at the 1 per cent level, and in italics if it is significant at the 5 per cent level.
* The last two columns show the relative number of significant trends: (a) relative to 'All' ($\times 1{,}000$), and (b) relative to the number of countries ($\times 100$). Both columns are scaled to have an average of 100.

Table 4.4 Standard calculation extending the data to all countries

Country group	ψ-trend	Sample, as Table 4.1		World Bank list added	
	From Table 4.1	Number	Available pairs	Full number	Potential pairs
Africa	−0.293	19	187	38	1,064
Latin America	0.060	18	272	20	560
Orient (Far East)	0.178	11	288	15	420
Post-communist	−0.102	24	210	28	784
West	0.021	22	585	22	616
Residual	−0.054	15	158	28	784
All countries		109	1,700	151	4,228
Average ψ as weighted sum		−0.003		−0.074	

Note
The World Bank list is the one used in the 2002 World Development Indicators. It excludes very small countries, of which Luxembourg and Iceland are included in the TI list, which also includes Taiwan. The potential number of pairs per country is 28. The trend score is shown in bold if it is significant at the 1 per cent level, and in italics if it is significant at the 5 per cent level.

where the series cover 6–7 years, have significantly negative trends. Fortunately, other post-communist countries such as Bulgaria have positive trends.

The most positive trends appear in the Orient, where corruption is decreasing significantly throughout the region and particularly strongly in the three countries of the Chinese area: China, Hong Kong and Taiwan. It is interesting that Singapore, with a standard of living above the average Western country, has a higher κ-score than most Western countries as well. So basically we note that this country group has a κ-development very much in line with the transition hypothesis for corruption mentioned as item A1 in Table 4.1. Note also that China still has a high level of corruption despite its positive trend.

The remaining groups have unclear trends. The data sets are almost complete for Latin America and the West. However, both country groups have as many countries with positive as negative trends.

No convergence of corruption in the world, but in the West

With increasing globalisation corruption should converge. The usual test for convergence is: $\partial\psi\partial/\partial\kappa < 0$, a deterioration in the score should arise the higher the level. However, the data given in Table 4.6 show no connection between trends and levels. Figure 4.1 rather shows a positive slope, indicating a weak, but insignificant divergence of corruption in the world. Within the West, we note that especially Latin Europe has a clear upward trend (i.e. clearly falling corruption).

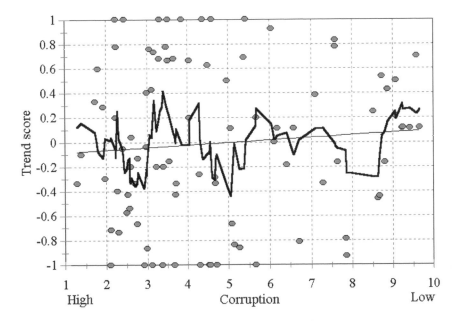

Figure 4.1 Relation between trends and levels of corruption for 94 countries.

Note
The grey dots are the 94 observations given in the Appendix (pp. 71–3), where a trend has been calculated. The bold black line is an MA(7) process through the points (sorted by level), and finally the
thin black line gives the linear regression line – it is far from significance, and a number of experiments dividing the points in various ways gave no significant slopes either.

Explaining corruption trends

Table 4.1 suggests a set of variables, A1 to A4, that ought to work in the
first difference explaining corruption trends. However, we have been unable
to establish any significant association with the ψ scores and these variables.
Clearly the time horizon is too short to capture the effect of A1, the transition
of corruption; nor do we have enough high inflation rates in the data to
show the effect of A2; neither institutions nor culture change fast enough
to give first differences of any use explaining the trend scores. This is obviously
one of the reasons why the literature still refrains from using panel-data
methods.

A missing variable

For the sake of exposition, Figure 4.2 plots corruption levels against the residuals from the standard model; that is, where κ is explained by economic development, inflation and property protection.[5] The figure shows an obvious
linear relationship between the residuals from the model and κ. The correlation

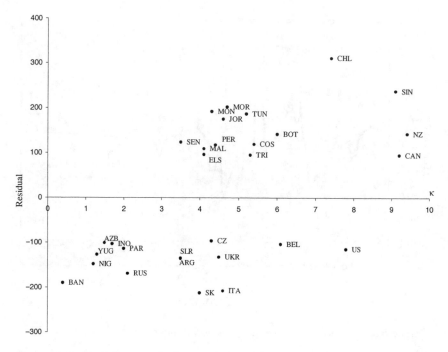

Figure 4.2 Residuals from standard corruption models.

is 0.40 and the trend is significant at the 1 per cent level. Such heterogeneity suggests at least one important unobserved variable or a model misspecification.

A look at the figure already suggests what the problem might be. The countries placed in the upper right-hand corner are Chile, Singapore, New Zealand and Canada. These appear to be countries with strong formal and informal institutions. Those placed in the reverse corner include Bangladesh, Nigeria, Azerbaijan and Yugoslavia, and are countries with weak institutions (especially as regards civic institutions) and strong ethnic divisions – and even a recent history of violence, military coups, etc. Recent advances in social capital theory suggest the former countries to be relatively proficient in social capital while the latter should be deficient.[6] Hence, social capital might be the missing variable (Paldam and Svendsen 2001; Uslaner 2001; Bjørnskov 2003).

Data for social capital: the use of generalised trust

Several incongruent definitions exist of social capital, although they fall in a number of related families outlined in Paldam (2000). However, for most of the definitions cross-country data do not exist. The best available cross-country data are the ones for *generalised trust*, which we have found to be one of the best variables measuring social capital.[7] In our Sample I these data are from the World Values Survey's (WVS) second wave in 1990 and the European Values

Survey (EVS) in 1999 (Inglehart *et al.* 1998; van Schaik 2002).[8] These data give social capital trends for 22 countries, for which ψ-scores are also available.

Figure 4.3 shows the association between trends in corruption and social capital. The correlation between trends in corruption, ψ, and social capital in Figure 4.3 is 0.38 and is depicted by the linear trend line.[9] While the figure is suggestive, it is nevertheless far from conclusive.

A slightly larger data set – Sample II – is reached by supplementing the second-wave data with the third wave of the WVS (1993–95) and employing the average yearly social capital trend in the data when comparing with the 1999 EVS scores. However, the time span in Sample II is shorter and the period may be less relevant to compare with the available ψ-scores covering the following 5–8 years. The varying, and on average shorter, time span also increases the measurement error due to common regional or global economic fluctuations. Only the results reached by Sample I will be presented, but rather similar results are reached when Sample II is used.

In the modelling we include three additional data sets, both as trends and levels:

1 civil liberties from Freedom House, which is broadly used as measure of institutional quality (e.g. Scully 1988);[10]
2 economic development (average GDP per capita 1995 and GDP growth per capita 1995–99); and
3 average inflation rates 1995–99 from World Bank (2002).

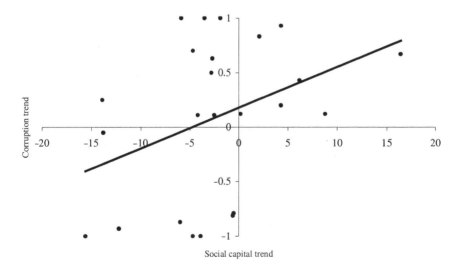

Figure 4.3 Trends in corruption and social capital.

Model and causality

We use Model 2 estimated in first differences to allow us to ignore persistent national features such as openness, culture and religion that are often found to be determinants of corruption levels. The variables of equation (2) are social capital, ω, initial corruption, κ_0, a vector of control variables, X, a constant α, and the error term, ε.

$$\kappa_t - \kappa_{t-1} \approx \psi_t = \alpha + \beta\kappa_0 + \gamma\omega_0 + \varphi(\omega_t - \omega_{t-1}) + \chi X + \varepsilon \qquad (2)$$

The model is presented in more detail in Bjørnskov (2003), which also explores the causal mechanisms connecting social capital and corruption and rejects reverse causality – as does Uslaner (2001, 2002). The relation from trust to corruption appears much more robust than the relation the other way. Hence, we choose not to instrument for trends in social capital.[11]

Theoretically, this may be an artefact of the concept of trustworthiness, because this concept is likely to stand between corruption and trust. Increasing corruption may be interpreted as a signal of decreasing trustworthiness of the average agent *vis-à-vis* his principal, which in turn will also lower generalised trust. Thus, the reverse relation might be less easy to catch when we have no data for the intermediate variable of trustworthiness. However, while the causal pattern shown is intuitively appealing regarding trust in formal institutions such as the government, it is perhaps less clear with respect to interpersonal trust, which is measured by the generalised trust scores. People might react by relying more on horizontal interactions as formal institutions and impersonal business transactions grow increasingly corrupt, which would create the opposite reaction and destroy the causal relation from corruption to trust thereby explaining the empirics.[12]

The model estimates

The results of estimating equation (2) by ordinary least squares are shown in Table 4.5. The estimate in column one is controlling for starting point – the level of corruption in 1996 and the generalised trust score in the 1990 wave of the World Values Survey. This causes the ψ's to follow the national social capital trend. The findings thus support the model and confirm Uslaner's (2001) result that to a large degree corruption trends are caused by movements in national social capital. In other words, we find some evidence that the unobserved variable apparent in Figure 4.2 is social capital. Yet, while the results indicate that low levels of initial corruption result in higher ψ's and thus faster elimination of corruption, the system also contains implicit see-saw dynamics, as higher initial levels of social capital lead to higher corruption trends. In other words, there is conditional convergence with respect to corruption, but conditional divergence with respect to social capital. As such, this is congruent with the picture in Figure 4.1, showing that there is neither convergence nor divergence on a global level.

Table 4.5 Trends in corruption and social capital

	Dependent variable: ψ-scores						
	1	2	3	4	5	6	7
Corruption 1996	−0.62	**−0.93**	−0.66	−0.91	−0.68	−0.58	**−1.09**
	(−2.27)	(−3.07)	(−2.31)	(−2.41)	(−2.20)	(−1.85)	(−3.34)
Generalised trust 1990	0.57	0.55	0.57	0.57	0.57	0.57	0.50
	(2.11)	(2.16)	(2.06)	(2.09)	(1.99)	(2.00)	(1.97)
Trust change	0.46	0.45	0.55	0.44	0.48	0.45	0.42
	(2.46)	(2.56)	(2.31)	(2.35)	(2.23)	(2.23)	(2.38)
Civil liberties		−0.47					−0.39
		(−1.90)					(−1.60)
Trend in civil liberties			0.15				
			(0.62)				
Transition country							−0.33
							(−1.23)
Log GDP				0.36			
				(1.11)			
Economic growth					0.05		
					(0.24)		
Inflation						0.05	
						(0.23)	
Constant	0.18	1.55	0.30	−3.69	0.31	0.11	2.03
	(0.67)	(1.89)	(0.65)	(−1.05)	(0.64)	(0.21)	(2.26)
Observations	22	22	22	22	22	22	22
Adjusted R-squared	0.27	0.36	0.24	0.28	0.21	0.23	0.38
F-value	3.58	3.97	2.69	3.02	2.31	2.56	3.58

Note
t-statistics are in parentheses. Variables are shown in bold when significant at the 1 per cent level, and in italics when significant at the 5 per cent level.

Columns two to seven present a modest sensitivity analysis showing that the estimates on initial corruption (β), initial social capital (γ) and social capital trends (ϕ) appear to be quite robust to the inclusion of additional control variables; ϕ remains significant at the 5 per cent level throughout, while γ is significant at or very close to 5 per cent in all specifications. Only β falls short of significance at 5 per cent in column six in which we add average inflation rates. Its size also varies substantially, but the data lack substantial variation in that series. Our preferred specification is nevertheless column two, which includes the initial level of civil liberties that is often used as a measure of legal protection. This specification explains roughly one-third of the variation in the data, although the civil liberties index is only significant at 8 per cent. Columns three to six show that no other variable attains significance while β, γ and ϕ remain unaffected at the same time as the results in column seven seem to suggest that some of this effect is due to the substantial institutional advances in post-communist Europe in the period. The results are also relatively robust to other tests.[13]

The order of magnitudes of the effects found can be assessed from an example. Consider the Czech Republic, which has a perfect negative trend ($\psi = -1$), and imagine that the Czech 1990–99 trend in social capital differed upward by one-half the standard deviation, corresponding to approximately 8 percentage points on the generalised trust scale. This corresponds to a 4 percentage point increase in social capital instead of the realised 4 percentage point decrease. The estimates in Table 4.5 imply that this change would have cut the negative Czech corruption trend in half. To obtain a comparable effect, the Czech Republic had to have started with an institutional standard roughly equal to that of the Scandinavian countries, or from an unrealistically low level of social capital. Only the joint effect of having advanced to the social capital level of Scandinavia, but with German institutions, yields a comparable effect. In other words, our results suggest that social capital trends seem to have driven corruption trends in Europe in the 1990s to a larger extent than most other variables often mentioned in the cross-country literature.

Conclusions

This chapter examines corruption trends in a sample of more than a hundred countries. First, we document that approximately 30 countries and three regions have significant corruption trends, measured by Kendall's τ. Regarding the main regions in the world, corruption is increasing in Africa and in post-communist Europe as well, while the countries in the Orient are becoming less corrupt.

The residuals from a standard corruption model show systematic variation that corresponds to the meagre information available on social capital. For a sub-sample of 22 European countries some social capital data are available, measured as generalised trust scores. We document that the main force driving the variation in corruption trends is in fact underlying trends in social capital. What has caused the increasing corruption in many post-communist countries thus seems to be a combination of the destruction of social capital in the communist era and the subsequent additional decline of the transition period. For example, it is interesting to note that while Slovenia has been able to raise its level of generalised trust and keep corruption in check, other post-communist countries such as Poland and Romania have experienced rapidly declining rates of trust and are now fighting increasing corruption problems.

Whether these conclusions apply to the rest of the world must await future research. They do, however, suggest that an effective long-term method to combat corruption could be not to invest extensively in control and monitoring schemes but instead to direct part of the resources towards building social capital. Recent advances in social capital research, for example, imply that curbing income inequality and investing in education, overall institutional quality and political stability could result in more trusting populations. Such investments also have the additional benefits of being conducive to growth and welfare.

Appendix

Table 4.6 Corruption levels and trends

	Country	1995	1996	1997	1998	1999	2000	2001	2002	Level	Trend
1	Denmark*	9.3	9.3	9.9	10.0	10.0	9.8	9.5	9.5	9.66	0.12
2	Finland*	9.1	9.1	9.5	9.6	9.8	10.0	9.9	9.7	9.59	**0.70**
3	New Zealand	9.6	9.4	9.2	9.4	9.4	9.4	9.4	9.5	9.41	0.11
4	Sweden*	8.9	9.1	9.4	9.5	9.4	9.4	9.0	9.3	9.25	0.12
5	Iceland*				9.3	9.2	9.1	9.2	9.4	9.24	0.11
6	Singapore	9.3	8.8	8.7	9.1	9.1	9.1	9.2	9.3	9.08	0.50
7	Canada	8.9	9.0	9.1	9.2	9.2	9.2	8.9	9.0	9.06	0.22
8	Netherlands*	8.7	8.7	9.0	9.0	9.0	8.9	8.8	9.0	8.89	0.43
9	Norway	8.6	8.9	8.9	9.0	8.9	9.1	8.6	8.5	8.81	−0.17
10	Luxembourg			8.6	8.7	8.8	8.6	8.7	9.0	8.73	0.54
11	Switzerland	8.8	8.8	8.6	8.9	8.9	8.6	8.4	8.5	8.69	−0.44
12	Australia	8.8	8.6	8.9	8.7	8.7	8.3	8.5	8.6	8.64	*−0.46*
13	United Kingdom*	8.6	8.4	8.2	8.7	8.6	8.7	8.3	8.7	8.53	0.25
14	Ireland*	8.6	8.5	8.3	8.2	7.7	7.2	7.5	6.9	7.86	**−0.93**
15	Germany*	8.1	8.3	8.2	7.9	8.0	7.6	7.4	7.3	7.85	**−0.79**
16	USA	7.8	7.7	7.6	7.5	7.5	7.8	7.6	7.7	7.65	−0.17
17	Hong Kong	7.1	7.0	7.3	7.8	7.7	7.7	7.9	8.2	7.59	**0.78**
18	Austria*	7.1	7.6	7.6	7.5	7.6	7.7	7.8	7.8	7.59	**0.83**
19	Israel		7.7	8.0	7.1	6.8	6.6	7.6	7.3	7.30	−0.33
20	Chile	7.9	6.8	6.1	6.8	6.9	7.4	7.5	7.5	7.11	0.38
21	France*	7.0	7.0	6.7	6.7	6.6	6.7	6.7	6.3	6.71	*−0.81*
22	Japan	6.7	7.0	6.6	5.8	6.0	6.4	7.1	7.1	6.59	0.11
23	Portugal	5.6	6.5	7.0	6.5	6.7	6.4	6.3	6.3	6.41	−0.19
24	Belgium*	6.9	6.8	5.3	5.4	5.3	6.1	6.6	7.1	6.19	0.11
25	Botswana				6.1	6.1	6.0	6.0	6.4	6.12	0.00
26	Spain*	4.4	4.3	5.9	6.1	6.6	7.0	7.0	7.1	6.05	**0.93**
27	Slovenia*					6.0	5.5	5.2	6.0	5.68	0.20
28	Estonia*				5.7	5.7	5.7	5.6	5.6	5.66	−1.00
29	Namibia				5.3	5.3	5.4	5.4	5.7	5.42	1.00
30	Taiwan	5.1	5.0	5.0	5.3	5.6	5.5	5.9	5.6	5.38	**0.69**
31	Costa Rica			6.5	5.6	5.1	5.4	4.5	4.5	5.27	*−0.86*
32	South Africa	5.6	5.7	5.0	5.2	5.0	5.0	4.8	4.8	5.14	**−0.83**
33	Trinidad and Tobago							5.3	4.9	5.10	
34	Malaysia	5.3	5.3	5.0	5.3	5.1	4.8	5.0	4.9	5.09	*−0.67*
35	Tunisia				5.0	5.0	5.2	5.3	4.8	5.06	0.11
36	Hungary*	4.1	4.9	5.2	5.0	5.2	5.2	5.3	4.9	4.98	0.50
37	Mauritius				5.0	4.9	4.7	4.5	4.5	4.72	*−1.00*
38	Greece	4.0	5.0	5.4	4.9	4.9	4.9	4.2	4.2	4.69	−0.33
39	Jordan		4.9		4.7	4.4	4.6	4.9	4.5	4.67	−0.29
40	Uruguay			4.1	4.3	4.4		5.1	5.1	4.60	*1.00*
41	Czech Republic*		5.4	5.2	4.8	4.6	4.3	3.9	3.7	4.56	**−1.00**
42	Poland*		5.6	5.1	4.6	4.2	4.1	4.1	4.0	4.53	**−1.00**
43	Italy*	3.0	3.4	5.0	4.6	4.7	4.6	5.5	5.2	4.50	**0.63**

continued

Table 4.6 Continued

	Country	1995	1996	1997	1998	1999	2000	2001	2002	Level	Trend
44	Lithuania*					3.8	4.1	4.8	4.8	4.38	1.00
45	Mongolia					4.3				4.30	
46	Peru				4.5	4.5	4.4	4.1	4.0	4.30	*−1.00*
47	South Korea	4.3	5.0	4.3	4.2	3.8	4.0	4.2	4.5	4.29	−0.26
48	Belarus*				3.9	3.4	4.1		4.8	4.05	0.67
49	Morocco				3.7	4.1	4.7		3.7	4.05	0.20
50	Jamaica				3.8	3.8			4.0	3.87	1.00
51	El Salvador				3.6	3.9	4.1	3.6	3.4	3.72	−0.33
52	Sri Lanka								3.7	3.70	
53	Slovak Republic				3.9	3.7	3.5	3.7	3.7	3.70	−0.43
54	Malawi				4.1	4.1	4.1	3.2	2.9	3.68	−1.00
55	Brazil	2.7	3.0	3.6	4.0	4.1	3.9	4.0	4.0	3.66	**0.68**
56	Ethiopia						3.7		3.5	3.60	
57	Turkey	4.1	3.5	3.2	3.4	3.6	3.8	3.6	3.2	3.55	−0.15
58	Croatia					2.7	3.7	3.9	3.8	3.53	0.67
59	Bulgaria*				2.9	3.3	3.5	3.9	4.0	3.52	**1.00**
60	Ghana				3.3	3.3	3.5	3.4	3.9	3.48	0.78
61	Argentina	5.2	3.4	2.8	3.0	3.0	3.5	3.5	2.8	3.40	−0.20
62	Zimbabwe				4.2	4.1	3.0	2.9	2.7	3.38	**−1.00**
63	Panama						3.7	3.0		3.35	
64	Latvia*				2.7	3.4	3.4	3.4	3.7	3.32	1.00
65	Mexico	3.2	3.3	2.7	3.3	3.4	3.3	3.7	3.6	3.31	**0.68**
66	Dominican Republic							3.1	3.5	3.30	
67	Macedonia					3.3				3.30	
68	Senegal				3.3	3.4	3.5	2.9	3.1	3.24	−0.20
69	Egypt		2.8		2.9	3.3	3.1	3.6	3.4	3.18	*0.73*
70	Thailand	2.8	3.3	3.1	3.0	3.2	3.2	3.2	3.2	3.13	0.43
71	Zambia				3.5	3.5	3.4	2.6	2.6	3.12	−1.00
72	China	2.2	2.4	2.9	3.5	3.4	3.1	3.5	3.5	3.06	**0.76**
73	Romania*			3.4	3.0	3.3	2.9	2.8	2.6	3.00	**−0.87**
74	Colombia	3.4	2.7	2.2	2.2	2.9	3.2	3.8	3.6	3.00	*0.41*
75	Burkina Faso						3.0			3.00	
76	Philippines	2.8	2.7	3.1	3.3	3.6	2.8	2.9	2.6	2.98	0.00
77	Guatemala				3.1	3.2		2.9	2.5	2.93	*−1.00*
78	Mozambique					3.5	2.2			2.85	
79	India	2.8	2.6	2.8	2.9	2.9	2.8	2.7	2.7	2.78	−0.13
80	Nicaragua				3.0	3.1		2.4	2.5	2.75	−0.67
81	Cote d'Ivoire				3.1	2.6	2.7	2.4	2.7	2.70	−0.33
82	Venezuela	2.7	2.5	2.8	2.3	2.6	2.7	2.8	2.5	2.61	0.00
83	Moldova					2.6	2.6	3.1	2.1	2.60	−0.20
84	Kazakhstan					2.3	3.0	2.7	2.3	2.58	−0.20
85	Vietnam			2.8	2.5	2.6	2.5	2.6	2.4	2.57	−0.50
86	Bolivia		3.4	2.1	2.8	2.5	2.7	2.0	2.2	2.53	*−0.40*
87	Armenia					2.5	2.5			2.50	
88	Ecuador		3.2		2.3	2.4	2.6	2.3	2.2	2.50	−0.60
89	Uzbekistan					1.8	2.4	2.7	2.9	2.45	*1.00*
90	Russia*		2.6	2.3	2.4	2.4	2.1	2.3	2.7	2.40	0.00

Table 4.6 Continued

	Country	1995	1996	1997	1998	1999	2000	2001	2002	Level	Trend
91	Albania					2.3			2.5	2.40	
92	Georgia					2.3			2.4	2.35	
93	Uganda		2.7		2.6	2.2	2.3	1.9	2.1	2.30	−0.70
94	Ukraine				2.8	2.6	1.5	2.1	2.4	2.28	−0.40
95	Tanzania				1.9	1.9	2.5	2.2	2.7	2.24	0.78
96	Pakistan	2.3	1.0	2.5	2.7	2.2		2.3	2.6	2.23	0.20
97	Honduras				1.7	1.8		2.7	2.7	2.23	1.00
98	Haiti								2.2	2.20	
99	Kyrgyzstan					2.2				2.20	
100	Kenya		2.2		2.5	2.0	2.1	2.0	1.9	2.12	−0.70
101	Yugoslavia				3.0	2.0	1.3			2.10	−1.00
102	Indonesia	1.9		2.7	2.0	1.7	1.7	1.9	1.9	1.97	−0.30
103	Cameroon		2.5		1.4	1.5	2.0	2.0	2.2	1.93	0.29
104	Azerbaijan					1.7	1.5	2.0	2.0	1.80	0.60
105	Paraguay				1.5	2.0			1.7	1.73	0.33
106	Angola						1.7		1.7	1.70	
107	Madagascar								1.7	1.70	
108	Nigeria		0.7	1.8	1.9	1.6	1.2	1.0	1.6	1.40	−0.10
109	Bangladesh		2.3					0.4	1.2	1.30	−0.30

Notes

All data are from the Transparency International home page; countries are sorted by level; the number in the first column gives the rank according to the level, which is the average of all available observations. Trends are calculated using the trend-score ψ. Significant ψ-scores at the 1 per cent level are shown in bold, and at the 5 per cent level in italics.

* Denotes that the country is included in the European sub-sample employed in section 3 'Explaining Corruption Trends' (pp. 65–70).

Acknowledgements

We are grateful for comments and suggestions from Karsten Bjerring Olsen, Gert Tinggaard Svendsen and participants at the conference. We also thank Susan Stilling and Gerda Christophersen for correcting our draft text, and Johann Graf Lambsdorff for careful editing. All remaining errors are entirely ours.

Notes

1 The home page of the NGO is <http://www.transparency.org>, where the data are posted. Table 4.6 in the Appendix reports the κ-data. The reader should note that if the index *rises*, it means that corruption *declines*.
2 People who are interviewed about corruption are often asked in ways that put special emphasis on trends, and not just levels, as the questions imply comparisons.
3 The former group consists of Colombia, Italy, Brazil, Mexico, Taiwan, Finland, Egypt, China, Hong Kong, Austria, Spain, Bulgaria, Uzbekistan and Uruguay; the latter group consists of Zimbabwe, Mauritius, Peru, Guatemala, Poland, the Czech Republic, Ireland, Romania, Costa Rica, South Africa, France, Germany, Uganda, Malaysia, Australia and Bolivia. The Appendix reports all the data, including the trend

scores for each in the six country groups. The groups in Tables 4.2 and 4.3 are the same as in Paldam (2002).

4 The explanation is probably that the colonial powers managed to reduce the corruption level temporarily, but now as the colonial heritage is vanishing, corruption reverts.

5 This regression, which includes a constant term, GDP per capita in linear and squared terms, and the Freedom House index of civil liberties, explains about 80 per cent of the variation in the data. Full results can be obtained from the authors. Countries with residuals of less than ± 1 standard deviation have been deleted from the figure for clarity.

6 The generalised trust scores used in this chapter as measures of social capital for some of these countries can be obtained from the third wave of the World Values Survey. They are: 19.2 (Nigeria), 19.4 (Azerbaijan), 20.5 (Bangladesh), 20.9 (Chile), 47.4 (New Zealand) and 53.1 (Canada). Given a social capital explanation, only Chile seems out of place. In addition, Uslaner (2002) and Bjørnskov (2003) both show that social capital, measured as generalised trust, is a strong determinant of corruption levels.

7 Svendsen; Nannestad and the two authors are presently engaged in a major social capital project involving generation of new cross-country data for 15 countries using all the main social capital definitions; at present only working papers are available from the project.

8 Generalised trust is the national proportion of people answering yes to the following question: In general, do you think that most people can be trusted, or can't you be too careful? As such, it measures the trust radius of the average citizen. The 1990 data are split between East and West Germany; we therefore use a population-weighted average for the entire country.

9 It is suggestive that the correlation is almost exactly the same as that between the levels of corruption and residuals in Figure 4.2.

10 The Freedom House indices are constructed on a discrete scale from one to seven where low ratings imply good institutions. They can be downloaded at <http://www.freedomhouse.org>.

11 It should be noted that this was tried. Trends in the overall Freedom House index were identified as a proper instrument for social capital trends, but proved to create severe multicollinearity problems, as the instrument was strongly correlated with initial levels of social capital. The main findings nevertheless survive our attempts at instrumentation.

12 The empirical results are reached for generalised trust. For special trust the results are likely to be different.

13 The findings are not substantially altered if we use only significant corruption trends and set the insignificant trends at zero. They are also robust to weighting the observations according to the number of years for which we have data on the κ index. In addition, we test our preferred specification by excluding the two observations with the largest or smallest value of any variable in the specification. In general, most results remain significant. The least robust variable is once more civil liberties, our measure of the quality of formal institutions. The initial level of corruption is significant at the 5 per cent level or better in all specifications and the social capital trend is significant in seven out of nine specifications. Finally, quite similar results are obtained using absolute changes in κ-levels from start of period to end of period, although the estimates are slightly less precise.

References

Bjørnskov, C. (2003) 'Corruption and Social Capital', *Working Paper* 03-13, Aarhus School of Business.

Husted, B.W. (1999) 'Wealth, Culture and Corruption', *Journal of International Business Studies*, vol. 30, no. 2, pp. 339–60.

Inglehart, R., Basañez, M. and Moreno, A. (1998) *Human Values and Beliefs. A Cross-Cultural Sourcebook*, Ann Arbor.

Jain, A.K. (2001) 'Corruption: A Review', *Journal of Economic Surveys*, vol. 15, pp. 71–121.

Lambsdorff, J. Graf (1998) 'Corruption in Comparative Perception', in A.K. Jain (ed.) *Economics of Corruption*, Dordrecht.

Le, Q., Mehlkop, G. and Graeff, P. (2003) 'The Mechanics of Corruption and Political Instability', Paper presented at the Annual Meeting of the European Public Choice Society in Aarhus, April.

Mauro, P. (1995) 'Corruption and Growth', *Quarterly Journal of Economics*, vol. 110, no. 3, pp. 681–712.

Mo, P.H. (2001) 'Corruption and Economic Growth', *Journal of Comparative Economics*, vol. 29, no. 1, pp. 66–79.

Olson, M., Sarna, N. and Swamy, A.V. (2000) 'Governance and Growth: A Simple Hypothesis Explaining Cross-Country Differences in Productivity Growth', *Public Choice*, vol. 102, no. 3–4, pp. 341–64.

Paldam, M. (2000) 'Social Capital: One or Many? Definition and Measurement', *Journal of Economic Surveys*, vol. 14, no. 5, pp. 629–53.

Paldam, M. (2001) 'Corruption and Religion. Adding to the Economic Model', *Kyklos*, vol. 54, no. 2/3, pp. 383–414.

Paldam, M. (2002) 'The Cross-Country Pattern of Corruption: Economics, Culture and the Seesaw Dynamics', *European Journal of Political Economy*, vol. 18, no. 2, pp. 215–40.

Paldam, M. and Svendsen, G.T. (2001) 'Missing Social Capital and the Transition in Eastern Europe', *Journal for Institutional Innovation, Development and Transition*, vol. 5, pp. 21–33.

Schaik, T. van (2002) 'Social Capital in the European Values Surveys', Paper presented at the OECD–ONS International Conference on Social Capital Measurement in London, September.

Scully, G. (1988) 'The Institutional Framework and Economic Development', *Journal of Political Economy*, vol. 96, no. 3, pp. 652–62.

Treisman, D. (2000) 'The Causes of Corruption: A Cross-National Study', *Journal of Public Economics*, vol. 76, no. 3, pp. 399–457.

Uslaner, E.M. (2001) 'Trust and Corruption', Paper presented at the Conference on Political Scandals, Past and Present at the University of Salford, 21–23 June.

Uslaner, E.M. (2002) *The Moral Foundations of Trust*, Princeton, N.J.

World Bank (2002) *World Development Indicators*, CD-ROM and online database, Washington, DC.

5 Trust and corruption*

Eric M. Uslaner

Introduction

Willie Sutton, one of America's most famous criminals, was asked by a judge at one of his trials why he robbed banks. 'That's where they keep the money,' he replied. That's one man's story, based firmly in rational choice theory. Why do others rob banks, refuse to pay their taxes, or flout the law more generally? My concern here is *not* about why individuals pay little heed to the law, but rather why respect for the law is greater in some countries compared to others – and why this matters.

I shall investigate the relationship between corruption and trust. Corruption is illegal (or barely legal) behaviour by political elites to manipulate the affairs of state for private gain. Trust is a value expressing the belief that others are part of your moral community. It lays the basis for cooperation with people who are different from yourself (Fukayama 1995: 153; Uslaner 2002: chapter 2). Trusting societies have less corruption.[1] People who have faith in others are more likely to endorse strong standards of moral and legal behaviour (Uslaner 1999a, 1999b). Alternatively, people who believe that the legal system is fair and impartial are more likely to trust their fellow citizens (Rothstein 2000).

Societies with more generalized trust and less corruption have better governance, stronger economic growth, spend more on redistribution, and have greater respect for the law among the citizenry. If we want to achieve any or all of these goals (or policies), where do we begin? Do we start with trust or with corruption? Can we simply put the rascals who loot the public purse in jail or must we work to increase trust in society, an arguably much tougher task? How might we reduce corruption or increase trust?

My message is not one of optimism. My initial cross-section results suggest that the connection between trust and corruption is indeed reciprocal – and that the effect of corruption on trust is greater than the opposite causal claim (trust begets an honest political system). It seems that there is considerable support for the old Chinese maxim, 'The fish rots from the head down.' Corrupt leaders breed distrust throughout society. However, an analysis of *changes* in trust and corruption leads to a different and more pessimistic conclusion: as societies become less corrupt, they do *not* become more trusting. Yet, as countries become more trusting, they become less corrupt. When I turn to the consequences of trust and corruption, I shall show that the causal connection is from trust to corruption, not the other way around. So simply rounding up the usual suspects among the elite and tossing them in the clink will not produce better economic performance or lead to better governance.

The scourge of corruption

Trust leads us to give of ourselves, in both time (volunteering) and money (giving to charity; see Uslaner 2002: chapter 7). Trust is based upon an optimistic view of the world. Trusters believe that the world is a good place, will continue to get better, and that they can make it better (Seligman 1991; Uslaner 2002: chapter 4). Corruption involves expropriating what rightfully belongs to others. Trust rests on a foundation of openness – accepting others for what they are, rather than for what you would like them to be. Transparency is the enemy of corruption. Corruption is systematic and involves *trust among the conspirators*. But this is a very different type of trust from the faith in others I have been describing. There are two dimensions of trust. First is the distinction between moralistic and strategic trust and the second is between generalized and particularized trust. Trust as an alternative to corruption reflects moralistic trust (the belief that people of different backgrounds may still constitute a 'moral community') and generalized trust (the belief that most people can be trusted). Corruption rests on strategic trust (trust based upon experience rather than values) and particularized trust (trust only in people like yourself). Strategic trust is based upon our day-to-day experience with specific people: we trust someone to repay a loan or to live up to their end of a bargain based upon our experience or information we receive from other people we know. Particularized trust is faith only in people like ourselves (as opposed to people in general). Entrance into a corruption network is not easy. Members of a conspiracy of graft cannot simply assume that others are trustworthy (as moralistic trusters do). Treating strangers *as if* they were trustworthy (also as moralistic trusters do) can be hazardous at best. And believing that people without any ties to the conspiracy are trustworthy (as generalized trusters do) threatens the integrity of the cabal.

The difference between generalized and particularized trust is similar to the distinction Putnam (2000: 22) draws between 'bonding' and 'bridging' social capital. *The central idea distinguishing generalized from particularized trust is how inclusive your moral community is.*

The roots of graft

The boss of New York City's Tammany Hall Democratic party machine in the nineteenth century, George Washington Plunkitt, explained his ill-gotten wealth: 'I seen my opportunities and I took 'em' (Riordan 1948: 4). Corruption transfers resources from the mass public to the elites – and generally from the poor to the rich (see especially Onishi and Banerjee 2001). It acts as an extra tax on citizens, leaving less money for public expenditures (Mauro 1997: 7; Tanzi 1998: 582–3). Corrupt governments have less money to spend on their own governments, pushing down the salaries of public employees. In turn, these lower-level staffers will be more likely to extort funds from the public purse. Government employees in corrupt societies will thus spend more time lining their own pockets than serving the public. Corruption thus leads to ineffective government (Mauro 1997: 5; LaPorta *et al.* 1998: 32). Businesses may also bribe politicians to gain restrictions on trade and to make it more difficult and expensive for foreign companies to enter domestic markets. Corruption thus closes markets (Leite and Weidmann 1999: 20, 23; Mauro 1997: 4). In each instance corruption harms the economy by transferring funds from public purposes to private gain, and slows economic growth.

Generalized trust is predicated on the notion of a common bond between classes and races and on egalitarian values (Putnam 1993: 88, 174; Seligman 1997: 36–7, 41). Faith in others leads to empathy for those who do not fare well, and ultimately to a redistribution of resources from the well-off to the poor. If we believe that we have a shared fate with others, and especially people who are different from ourselves, then gross inequalities in wealth and status will seem to violate norms of fairness. Trusting people will thus feel an obligation to support programmes that will benefit the disadvantaged. And trusting societies are more likely to spend more on social programmes, to have more effective governments, to more open economies, lower crime rates, and higher economic growth (LaPorta *et al.* 1997: 335; Uslaner 2002: chapter 8).

Trickle down or bubble up?

Does corruption simply reflect venal leaders or does it have a cultural foundation? If we can control corruption by strengthening legal institutions from above we might be able to increase the stock of trust in society. If corruption rests upon the level of trust in a society (or other cutural values; cf. Husted 1999), it will not be so easy to control graft.

Mauro offers a top-down view of corruption (in what I shall call the 'rotting fish' account):

> You live in a society where everybody steals. Do you choose to steal? The probability that you will be caught is low, because the police are very busy chasing other thieves, and, even if you do get caught, the chances of your being punished severely for a crime that is so common are low. Therefore, you too steal. By contrast, if you live in a society where theft is rare, the chances of your being caught and punished are high, so you choose not to steal.
>
> (Mauro 1998a: 12)

An honest government, one that enforces the law fairly and provides little opportunity for private gain, can lead people to have greater faith in each other

(Levi 1998; Misztal 1996: 251; Offe 1996: 27; Seligman 1997: 37). Rothstein finds a stronger correlation between trust in people and confidence in the legal system in Sweden than for any other political institution. He argues that we can create trust from above:

> Political and legal institutions that are perceived as fair, just and (reasonably) efficient, increase the likelihood that citizens will overcome social dilemmas ... In a civilized society, institutions of law and order have one particularly important task: to detect and punish people who are 'traitors', that is, those who break contracts, steal, murder, and do other such non-cooperative things and therefore should not be trusted. Thus, if you think that particular institutions do what they are supposed to do in a fair and efficient manner, then you also have reason to believe ... that people will refrain from acting in a treacherous manner and you therefore believe that 'most people can be trusted'.
>
> (Rothstein 2000: 19–21)

Tyler (1990: chapters 4, 5) argues that people respect the law because they believe that the justice system is fair and that they have been treated fairly. The key to less corruption – and more trust – then, is an effective system of property rights and the rule of law (Lambsdorff 1999; Leite and Weidmann 1999: 20, 23; Treisman 2000).

The 'rotting fish' account sees corruption as a plague on the ordinary citizen imposed by selfish and unaccountable leaders. The 'rotting fish' account stresses empowering the people, through free elections, independent media, and structural reforms to bring government closer to the people (Adsera, Boix and Payne 2000; Brunetti and Weder 1999; Fisman and Gatti 2000; Treisman 2000).

In contrast to the 'rotting fish' argument, the *'raccomandazione'* thesis emphasizes how corruption is part of the larger culture. *Raccomandazione* is the Italian practice of soliciting favours from people in high places (what Plunkitt would call 'honest graft'). In October 2000 the director of a civil court in Southern Italy received 88 pounds of fish in return for helping to expedite the case of a plaintiff. A lower court convicted the director of corruption, but a higher court overruled the verdict. The director could only be convicted of *pretending* to influence higher authorities; punishment would be warranted only if the official *couldn't* deliver. Even direct evidence of pay-offs (what *New York Times* reporter Stanley [2001], called 'squid pro quo') was insufficient to convict.

This case is surely exceptional. Courts do not generally (if ever) enforce corrupt deals. The case was not unique: *Raccomandazione* 'is by now so deeply rooted in our culture that most people believe it is an indispensable tool when seeking even that to which they are entitled', a court wrote in 1992 as it overturned yet another conviction for influence peddling (Stanley 2001). Yet, courts don't need to ratify agreements. Turning a blind eye may be sufficient:

Former Italian Prime Minister Giulio Andreotti was acquitted in 1999 of the charge that he tried to influence the Mafia; a judge in Palermo postponed a new trial, arguing that the court had more important business. And the curse of corruption in Central and Eastern Europe is the moral ambivalence that ordinary citizens develop towards those who exploit them. When doctors demand 'gift payments' for basic medical treatment, as most do, Hungarians shrug their shoulders and cast no moral judgement (Kornai 2000: 3, 7, 9).

The *raccomandazione* account emphasizes that corruption is ingrained into the political culture of a society. Italian society has traditionally been marked by low levels of generalized trust (Almond and Verba 1960) and high levels of particularized trust, and these strong in-group ties are the foundation for the Mafia's ring of corruption (Gambetta 1993). These strong ties among an in-group establish bonds of reciprocity that help to sustain a corrupt regime: corrupt officials need to be sure that their 'partners' *will deliver* on their promises (Lambsdorff 2002a, 2002b). Lambsdorff (2002a) argues: 'if corrupt deals cannot be enforced, this can act as a deterrent to corruption itself'. So particularized trust may create the same bond among corrupt officials that generalized trust does in the larger society – but with the opposite consequences.

The message of *raccomandazione* (as well as 'gift payments') is that you can't cleanse a polity by replacing its leaders – or even its laws. Laws may set out fierce punishments, as in Italy, yet most bad deeds go unpunished (Tanzi 1998: 574). We can tinker with institutional design and even restructure entire political systems. We can put political leaders in jail. But cultures of corruption will not wither away. An Indian journalist commented on the sharp cleavages that led to a cycle of unstable coalitions, none of which could form a government: 'We have the hardware of democracy, but not the software, and that can't be borrowed or mimicked' (Constable 1999: A19).

The history of Paterson, New Jersey and its surrounding county of Passaic points to the futility of reform efforts.[2] Paterson and its surrounding county, as most Northeastern industrial areas, for many years was dominated by a corrupt Democratic machine. Reformers in New Jersey sought to 'cleanse' Paterson's political system early in the twentieth century:

> when the working class did start to build a power base, it was unceremoniously cut off. By 1907 the longtime practice of city aldermen's selling jobs on the municipal payroll was so blatant that the New Jersey Legislature established a special form of government solely for the city of Paterson. It revoked the aldermen's power and left them with only such insignificant duties as licensing dogs, peddlers, and junkyards. The mayor became the single elected official with authority.
>
> (Norwood 1974: 52–3)

By the middle of the century Republicans alternated with the Democrats in power. Both the city and the county have restructured their electoral systems. Yet, six major government or party officeholders and more than a handful of police officers have either been convicted of or face indictment for receiving or demanding kickbacks (*The Record* 2001). In 1988 the state of New Jersey took control of the Paterson school system, charging rampant corruption (Lindsay 1998). Paterson's history provides little support for a 'rotting fish' explanation; as in Italy, corruption seems ingrained into Paterson's culture.

Confidence in the legal system depends upon trust (my view), and not the other way around (as argued by Rothstein [2000] and others). Countries with more trusting populations display higher support for the legal system. In trusting nations, elites are also more likely to say that the legal system is fair. Yet, there is no corresponding causal link between support for the law and trust in people (Uslaner 2002: chapter 8).[3]

So we should expect the same dynamic between trust and corruption. It would be nice if we could clean up corruption and thereby boost trust in our fellow citizens. If the roots of corruption lie in a culture of mistrust, then the task becomes much more daunting.

The roots of corruption and trust

What, then, are the roots of corruption and trust? Does corruption lead to less trust, or does mistrust of others lead to less corruption?

Trust is easy to measure. There is a standard question: 'Generally speaking, do you believe that most people can be trusted, or can't you be too careful in dealing with people?' In Uslaner (2002: chapter 3) I show that this question *does* reflect moral trust, especially trust in strangers. I used the most recent value available in the World Values Surveys for 1981, 1990 and 1995 (see Uslaner 2002: 225, n.6 for a discussion of the surveys, and 230 for the rationale for excluding countries with communist legacies from much of the analysis below).

I primarily employ the Transparency International estimate of corruption for 1998.[4] Each country's score comes from a 'poll of polls' business executives and the public, as well as rankings by risk analysts and experts on the politics and economics of each country (Treisman 2000). The ratings range from zero (most corrupt) to 10 (least corrupt).

I estimated statistical models for trust and corruption to examine the roots of each – and to see in particular what the interaction between the two is. I employed two-stage least squares, which permits me to examine reciprocal causation. The model for trust is based upon the arguments in Uslaner (2002: chapter 8).

The model for trust is simple: it includes corruption, the percentage Catholic, and the level of economic inequality. Inglehart (1997: 95) has found that countries with large shares of Catholics are less trusting, perhaps attributable to the hierarchical structure of authority in the Church. I have argued above that trust depends upon an equitable distribution of wealth, so I use the Gini indices reported in Deininger and Squire (1996).

The model for corruption includes five independent variables, some of which have not been investigated in previous studies. The motivating force behind this model is to put the 'rotting fish' and *raccomandazione* models to the test. Does corruption lead to less trust, or does trust lead to less corruption? Is there an institutional fix to the problem of corruption? Does democratization lead to greater honesty in government? Or is democracy merely a shell into which the raw stuff of political culture must be moulded?

My model for corruption does not include many variables in the literature; I tested for them, but none were significant once I entered trust and other predictors in my estimations. Once trust entered the equation for corruption I did not find significant relationships for the level of public sector wages (LaPorta *et al.* 1998; Mauro 1997: 5; Tanzi 1998: 573; Treisman 2000; but cf. Rose-Ackerman 1978: 90–1), per capita income or gross domestic product (Lambsdorff 1999: 7; Mauro 1995: 701, and 1998b: 13; Paldam 2000: 9); the size of the unofficial economy (Lambsdorff 1999); the level of newspaper readership (Adsera, Boix and Payne 2000); federal versus unitary governments or the share of government revenues spent at the local level (Treisman 1998; Fisman and Gatti 2000); ethnolinguistic diversity (Treisman 2000); or the level of political stability (Leite and Weidmann 1999: 20; Treisman 2000).

Generalized trust is the main variable of interest in the model. Also in the model are the level of tariffs (from the Barro-Lee data set); a measure of how extensive property rights are in a country (from LaPorta *et al.* 1997); the Freedom House index summarizing the level of democratic freedoms in a country;[5] and the average score from the World Values Survey measuring how strongly people believe that the devil exists.

Closed markets present great opportunities for corruption. Countries that maintain open markets will limit the opportunities for corruption (Leite and Weidmann 1999: 20; Treisman 2000). Free societies give citizens more power to monitor governments and to hold them accountable. Societies with a free press, for example, make it more difficult for elites to get away with corrupt behaviour (Adsera, Boix and Payne 2000; Brunetti and Weder 1999; Treisman 2000). A strong system of property rights makes it difficult for politicians to expropriate people's wealth (Leite and Weidmann 1999: 20). Belief in the devil is the religiosity variable with the most robust connections to corruption.

The trust and religiosity variables reflect the *raccomandazione* argument. Trust and religiosity are values that shape the underlying culture of a society (cf. Husted 1999). If corruption largely depends upon cultural values, then there is little that we can do to reduce malfeasance, at least in the short run. On the other hand, freedom, property rights and tariffs are more malleable. So it may be possible to reduce corruption through appropriate reforms in the constitutional or political structure of a country – or even by reshaping policies.

The estimates for both trust and corruption in Table 5.1 suggest that corruption has both cultural and structural roots. *The most powerful effects are for the cultural variables.* The countries in this sample have corruption scores ranging from 1.9 (most corrupt) to 10 (least corrupt). Moving from the least to the most trusting society changes trust by 4.278 points, according to the corruption regression – more than half the total distance in this sample. Belief in

Table 5.1 Simultaneous equation estimation for trust and corruption

	Coefficient	Standard error	t ratio
Trust equation			
Corruption	3.393****	0.803	4.23
Gini coefficient	−31.894*	23.855	−1.33
Percentage Catholic	−0.126***	0.043	−2.92
Constant	32.363**	11.519	2.81
Corruption equation			
Trust	0.069**	0.029	2.39
Freedom	−0.198**	0.108	−1.83
Property rights	1.250**	0.464	2.69
Belief in devil	0.851**	0.340	2.50
Tariffs	−21.127**	11.687	−1.81
Constant	0.715	2.160	0.33

Notes
For trust equation: RMSE = 7.769; F = 16.051, estimated R^2 = 0.725.
For corruption equation: RMSE = 1.033; F = 21.206, estimated R^2 = 0.863.
**** $p < 0.0001$.
*** $p < 0.001$.
** $p < 0.05$.
* $p < 0.01$ (N = 23).

the devil has the same general effect, moving corruption 4.298 points. The structural/policy variables have weaker effects. Moving from the least to the most free country leads less corruption (by 2.376 points on the scale), while countries with the greatest protection for property rights have substantially less corruption (by 3.75 points). More open markets do lead to less corruption, but the effect is modest. Following Treisman (2000), I find only a minuscule effect for free trade on corruption.

Societies with more economic inequality and with larger shares of Catholics are less trusting. However, the biggest impact on trust comes from corruption. The roots of corruption stem from below, but those of trust may be top-down. Corrupt officials may indeed lead people to believe that other ordinary citizens cannot be trusted.

Or does it? The results in Table 5.1 come from a cross-sectional analysis that is static. The big impact of freedom on corruption occurs for the countries with strong democratic traditions (scores below 4.0 on the Freedom House scale). *But these are already the least-corrupt countries.* The most-corrupt countries also are the least free (mean corruption score = 6.7 for countries scoring 4 or above). But across these countries, including many recent democracies, there is virtually no correlation between corruption and freedom.

The situation doesn't look much better when I examine the relationship between corruption and *change in the Freedom House scores from 1978–98.* If we are to seek to rid countries of corruption we need to know which factors produce change. There are two ways in which one can overcome this problem. First, I shall focus on changes in the potential causes of corruption: is there less corruption in countries that have become more democratic? Second, I focus on changes in corruption *and* changes in the potential causes of democracy.

Focusing on change leads to difficult estimations. Countries that already rank very highly on freedom have little room to move further. For the advanced industrial nations,[6] 70 per cent already had the rating of most free and the remaining 30 per cent were at the next level (scores of 2 and 3 respectively). The first group of countries (the United States, Canada and most of Western Europe) *cannot* become more democratic; the second group cannot become *much more democratic*. To ensure that I do not confound the already free countries with those where structural reforms might do some good, I restrict the analysis to the 14 countries ranking above 4 on the Freedom House scale in 1998.

There is a very weak correlation ($r^2 = 0.119$) between the 1998 corruption score from TI and change in the level of democratization. So the long march to democracy did not seem to produce less corruption over the past two decades. And virtually the entire positive relationship between honesty in government and democratization is traceable to one country – Chile. When I plot the relationship without Chile, the correlation drops to virtually zero. Making countries more democratic does not seem to make them less corrupt. And we see a similar dynamic for countries below the mean in trust.

For the countries that have surveys on trust in both the first (1981) and second (1990–95) waves of the World Values Survey, I computed change in trust scores. The logic here is that countries with low levels of trust that became more trusting should also become less corrupt. Yet there is relatively little change in trust over time. The correlation of trust indicators across the 22 nations for which we have data in both the first and second waves is 0.906 and the regression coefficient for 1981 trust on 1990 trust is 1.022 – indicating only the slightest upward blip over time. Second, for the small number of countries with low trust in 1981 (N = 10), there is no relationship ($r^2 = 0.000$) between change in trust and the corruption index.

Corruption is stable as well, but not quite as uniform over time as trust. The simple correlation between corruption in the 1980–85 measure and the 1998 estimate is 0.816, and the regression coefficient is 0.825, indicating a trend towards less corruption over time.

In Figure 5.1 I plot the relationship between changes in trust and corruption for the 18 countries for which there are data on both variables over time. Countries that became more trusting (Mexico and Italy in particular) became less corrupt and countries that became less trusting showed an increase in corruption (Argentina, South Africa and France in particular). The relationship is moderate ($r^2 = 0.227$), but it is robust (see p. 85).

There is more variation in the Freedom House measures of democratization over time: the correlation between the 1978 and 1998 scores is just 0.463 (N = 64). Yet democratization does not go hand in hand with more honesty. The plot of change in corruption and change in democratization is rather weak ($r^2 = 0.022$). Hungary, Poland, and the Philippines have all become more

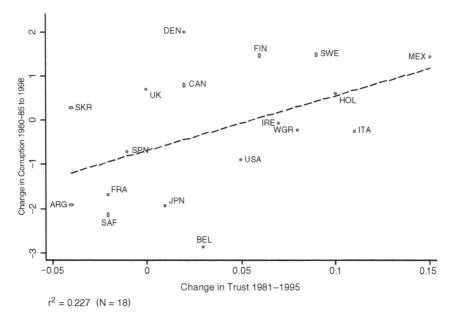

Figure 5.1 Changes in corruption and trust.

democratic and less corrupt, but democratization only seems to have heightened the lack of transparency in Russia, South Africa and the Czech Republic.

I examine the reciprocal relationship between change in trust and change in corruption in Table 5.2. Note again that the number of cases is very small, but the results are stable. I am strongly constrained in the choice of variables that might be theoretically relevant because the dependent variables are changes. I am not trying to explain *trust* or *corruption*, but changes in trust and changes in corruption. What seems theoretically relevant for the simple aggregate levels may not be so important for changes.

The equation for trust includes change in corruption, growth in trade from 1970–90, and change in the gross domestic product (GDP) from 1980–90 (from the Penn World Tables). The change in corruption equation includes changes in trust and freedom as well as the change in imports from 1980–90 (from the Penn World Tables), and ethnolinguistic diversity. The estimates in Table 5.2 exclude Hungary, the only country with a legacy of communism that had values on trust in both 1981 and 1990. There may be good reason to include changes in GDP in the change in corruption equation as well: when countries become richer, their citizens may feel less need to seek gains through corruption. I did not include changes in GDP for two reasons: first, with such a small number of cases, adding extra variables is hazardous; more critically, adding changes in GDP to the corruption change equation induces considerable collinearity with the other predictors.

Table 5.2 Simultaneous equation estimation for changes in trust and corruption for countries without a legacy of communism

	Coefficient	Standard error	t ratio
Change in trust equation			
Change in corruption	−0.002	0.017	−0.11
Growth in trade	0.043**	0.018	2.36
Change in GDP 1980–90	−0.148	0.106	−1.39
Constant	0.099**	0.033	3.01
Change in corruption equation			
Change in trust	14.233**	7.543	1.89
Change in freedom	0.285**	0.150	1.90
Change in imports	0.084**	0.047	1.78
Ethnolinguistic diversity	−2.984**	1.709	−1.75
Constant	−1.064	0.680	−1.57

Notes

For change in trust equation: RMSE = 0.043; F = 4.616, estimated R^2 = 0.490.

For change in corruption equation: RMSE = 1.187; F = 3.020, estimated R^2 = 0.488.

**** $p<0.0001$.

*** $p<0.001$.

** $p<0.05$.

* $p<0.01$ (N = 18).

Two things stand out from the results in Table 5.2. First, there seem to be many paths to reducing corruption. There are significant relationships between change in corruption for change in trust, change in freedom, change in the level of imports and ethnolinguistic diversity.

Expanding markets and democratization seem to bring less corruption. Countries with more diverse populations became more corrupt: each ethnic group might look out for its own welfare, reinforcing particularizing trust. And, of course, change in trust matters. The overall impacts are roughly equal for each variable, though the largest seems to be for democratization. Now this seems rather curious. The relationship between change in corruption and democratization is very weak in simple bivariate relationships (without Hungary, the simple r^2 falls to 0.007).

The significant coefficients in the corruption equation seem to stem from collinearity among change in freedom, change in imports and ethnolinguistic diversity. When I eliminate any of these three variables, the others fall to insignificance, leaving only change in trust as a significant predictor of changes in corruption.

Second, change in corruption is *not* a significant predictor of change in trust. Increases in trade modestly increases trust, while there is a weak *negative* relationship between change in GDP and trust. Yet the direction of the relationship between trust and corruption goes one way – from trust to corruption. This is strong support for the bottom-up thesis. You can't get rid of corruption by structural change or even by replacing one elite with another. The strongest determinant of change in corruption is change in trust. Neither changes very readily, and this makes assaults on corruption more difficult. Practices such as *raccomandazione* rest upon a set of cultural norms.

The consequences of corruption

Students of corruption have compiled a laundry list of the negative consequences of corruption. Corrupt countries should have higher rates of theft and tax evasion (cf. LaPorta *et al.*, 1998). Corruption should also lead to higher rates of business regulation; regulations can serve to restrict markets and extract extra legal payments from investors. Dishonest governments might also need to have higher marginal tax rates to compensate for revenues extracted by the leadership. Corruption should also slow economic growth (Leite and Weidmann 1999; Mauro 1995: 701; Tanzi 1998: 585; but cf. Poirson 1998: 14). Corruption reduces the amount of money available for various government programmes, including the government's share of the gross domestic product and expenditures on the public sector, for education, and transfers from the rich to the poor (Mauro 1998a: 269; Tanzi 1998: 582–6). Corrupt governments also tend to be less efficient and less stable (see Mauro 1995; LaPorta *et al.* 1998; Treisman 2000). And they should especially be less responsive to the public will (Adsera, Boix and Payne 2000).

So what shapes respect for the law and good governance? Is it honesty or trust? It is difficult to separate the effects of the two variables, since they are highly correlated ($r = 0.724$, $N = 47$). Nevertheless, I shall try to do so. In Table 5.3, I present estimates of the effects of trust and corruption for 14 measures of social and governmental performance and public policies. I estimated the equations by two-stage least squares with three equations for each performance measure: one for trust, one for corruption, and the third for the indicator in question. Corruption and trust were included as endogenous variables separately in each performance measure equation. The other two equations (for trust and corruption are identical to those in Table 5.1). The other variables in the performance measures were the 1998 Freedom House score, 1990 per capita income (from the Penn World Tables), and Vanhanen's (1997) measure of knowledge diversity, a generalized indicator of the scope of education in a society. I seek to answer whether corruption or trust has an impact on these measures of performance. Then, recognizing that multicollinearity can depress or inflate the effects of both predictors, and even change signs, I include both trust and corruption as predictors of performance. The performance measures and their sources are listed in Table 5.3.[7] The entries in the table are the significance levels of the regression coefficients.

Clearly Mauro and Rothstein are on to something. Countries with high levels of corruption also have high rates of theft and tax evasion. Trust is marginally significant for tax evasion, while tax evasion very strongly tracks the level of corruption in society. People see corrupt regimes and believe that it is acceptable to steal and especially to withhold their taxes. Otherwise their hard-earned money would go directly into the pockets of the politicians.

Table 5.3 Effects of trust and corruption on political and economic performance

Indicator (source)	Corruption	Trust	Corruption vs. trust	Freedom	Significant variables	N
Theft rate (Lederman)	**				1990 per capita income	14
Tax evasion (LaPorta)	***	*	Corrupt**		1990 per capita income knowledge diversity	22
Business regulations (LaPorta)	**		Corrupt**		Knowledge diversity	23
Top marginal tax rate (LaPorta)				**		23
GDP growth rate (Diener)			Trust**	**		22
Mean yearly GDP growth 1980–90 (Fedderke)	**			****	Knowledge diversity	23
Government share of GDP (LaPorta)	**	***	Trust**	**		22
Public sector expenditures (LaPorta)	**	**	Trust**			21
Education expenditures (LaPorta)	**	**	Trust*			23
Transfer expenditures (LaPorta)	*				1990 per capita income	
Political stability (Mauro)	***	**				
Judicial efficiency (Mauro)	****	****	Trust**			22
Red tape in bureaucracy (Mauro)	*	**	Corrupt***		Knowledge diversity	22
Government responds to will of people (Gallup survey)					Knowledge diversity	21

Notes

**** $p < 0.0001$.

*** $p < 0.001$.

** $p < 0.05$.

* $p < 0.01$.

Corruption does shape one measure of the growth rate (mean yearly GDP growth), but not another. It does lead to fewer public expenditures on the public sector or on education, to less political stability, a less-efficient judiciary, more red tape in the bureaucracy, and to a less-responsive government. But neither trust nor corruption has any effect on the top marginal tax rate, the government's share of the gross domestic product, or on transfer expenditures (though see LaPorta *et al.* 1997; Uslaner 2002: chapter 8).

Trust does not seem to affect obedience to the law in the aggregate analyses, although there is a weak connection to tax evasion. There are no significant ties between trust and tax rates or bureaucratic regulations. Nor does trust seem to lead to greater growth (but see LaPorta *et al.* 1997; Uslaner 2002: chapter 8). Yet trust does seem to matter, generally more than corruption, for governmental expenditures, for political stability and for the overall quality of government.

When I put trust and corruption in the same equation, corruption seems to matter more for adherence to the law and for red tape in the bureaucracy. Most of the time it is trust that matters most. Trusting governments, more than honest governments, spend a greater share of their gross domestic product on government, spend more for education and on the public sector more generally, and have better functioning judiciaries and greater political stability.

Reprise

Some of these findings are not very surprising. Since trust links us to others in society who are different from ourselves, we might expect that trusting societies would spend more on government programmes that raise standards of living for the less well-off. Putnam (1993: 111–15), LaPorta *et al.* (1997) and Uslaner (2002: chapter 8) have also linked social trust to governments that perform well and redistribute resources from the rich to the poor, as well to higher economic growth. Cooperative societies will have better performing economies (cf. Knack and Keefer 1997). Trust, not honesty, seems to produce better government performance, more redistribution and economic growth.

Corruption, rather than mistrust, seems to lead people to break or evade the law. Corrupt bureaucracies get mired in red tape. Yet judicial efficiency seems more rooted in trust than in corruption.

To reduce corruption you need to increase trust. Trust changes slowly in most countries. Trust depends upon an egalitarian distribution of wealth in a society, and economic inequality is almost as stubbornly stable as trust (the correlation between the Gini indices for 1980 and 1990 is 0.827 for a sample of 47 nations). You can't increase trust by removing dishonest leaders and replacing them with a new set of elites, as the case of Paterson, New Jersey indicates. Reforming the institutions of a corrupt political system did not lead to less corruption almost a century later. As the American baseball player, Berra, once said: 'It's déjà vu all over again.'[8] Culture, including the culture of corruption, changes slowly, if at all.

Notes

* This chapter is based upon many of the ideas in Uslaner (2002) and reflects extensive conversations with Bo Rothstein and Martin Paldam, as well as comments by Johan Graf Lambsdorff, Markus Taube and other participants at the Conference on 'Corrupt Transactions Exploring the Analytical Capacity of Institutional Economics', University of Göttingen, Göttingen, Germany, 15–16 November 2002. I am particularly grateful to the Center for International Development and Conflict Management at the University of Maryland, the General Research Board of the University of Maryland, the Russell Sage Foundation, the Carnegie Corporation and the American Academy of Political and Social Sciences for support for writing this chapter. I am also grateful to Johannes Fedderke, Ronald Inglehart, Rafael LaPorta and Daniel Treisman for providing me with data. Some of the data I employ were made possible by the Inter-University Consortium for Political and Social Research, which is not responsible for any interpretations I have made.

1 I shall discuss the measures of trust and corruption below. For now it is sufficient to note that the simple correlation between the two aggregated measures across 47 countries is 724.

2 The choice of Paterson, New Jersey is not accidental. I was born and raised there and my father lived and breathed its politics. An alderman is the equivalent of a city council member.

3 The data were estimated by two-stage least squares using aggregated measures of trust in people and confidence in the legal system from the World Values Surveys (see p. 81) and a measure of fairness of the legal system. The latter measure was developed by the Institute for Management Development in Lausanne, Switzerland surveys business executives on their 'confidence in the fair administration of justice in society' (published in the Institute's *World Competitiveness Yearbook* and reported in Treisman 1999: 18).

4 The data on corruption (for 1998) come from the global organization Transparency International and are found on its website at <http://www.transparency.de/documents/cpi/index.html>.

5 The Freedom House scores are for 1998 and are taken from: <http://www.freedomhouse.org/rankings.pdf>. The Freedom House website contains scores for both political and civil liberties. They were very highly correlated, so I summed the two (cf. Inglehart 1997: 357).

6 As determined by the log of GDP per capita adjusted for comparative purchasing power (PPP) in the Penn World Tables. Advanced industrial countries (N = 20) had scores above 4.0.

7 Sources from LaPorta are reported in LaPorta *et al.* (1997, 1998) and provided by LaPorta; the source from Lederman is provided by Lederman of the World Bank; Diener is from Diener (1995), Mauro from Mauro (1995); Fedderke from Fedderke; and Gallup survey from Treisman.

8 See <http://www.yogi-berra.com/yogiisms.html> (accessed 23 May 2001).

References

Adsera, A., Boix, C. and Payne, M. (2000) 'Are You Being Served? Political Accountability and Quality of Government', *Inter-American Development Bank Research Department Working Paper*, no. 438, Washington.

Almond, G. and Verba, S. (1960) *The Civic Culture*, Princeton.

Brunetti, A. and Weder, B. (1999) 'A Free Press Is Bad News for Corruption', Unpublished paper, University of Basel, Switzerland.

Constable, P. (1999) 'India's Democracy in Uncertain Health', *Washington Post*, 21 April, A17, A19.

Deininger, K. and Squire, L. (1996) 'A New Data Set: Measuring Economic Income Inequality', *World Bank Economic Review*, vol. 10, pp. 565–92.

Diener, E. (1995) 'A Value Based Index for Measuring National Quality of Life', *Social Indicators Research*, vol. 36, pp. 107–27.

Fisman, R. and Gatti, R. (2000) *Decentralization and Corruption: Evidence Across Countries*, Washington, DC.

Fukayama, F. (1995) *Trust: The Social Virtues and the Creation of Prosperity*, New York.

Gambetta, D. (1993) *The Sicilian Mafia: The Business of Private Protection*, Cambridge.

Husted, B.W. (1999) 'Wealth, Culture, and Corruption', *Journal of International Business Studies*, vol. 30, pp. 339–60.

Inglehart, R. (1997) *Modernization and Postmodernization*, Princeton.

Knack, S. and Keefer, P. (1997) 'Does Social Capital Have An Economic Payoff? A Cross-Country Investigation', *Quarterly Journal of Economics*, vol. 112, pp. 1251–88.

Kornai, J. (2000) 'Hidden in an Envelope: Gratitude Payments to Medical Doctors in Hungary', <http://www.colbud.hu/honesty-trust/kornai/pub01.PDF>.

Lambsdorff, J. Graf (1999) 'Corruption in Empirical Research – A Review', *Transparency International Working Paper*, <http://www.transparencyde/working-papershtml/lambsdorff_eresearchhtml> (accessed 23 March 2001).

Lambsdorff, J. Graf (2002a) 'What Nurtures Corrupt Deals? On the Role of Confidence and Transaction Costs', in D. Della Porta and S. Rose-Ackerman (eds) (2002) *Corrupt Exchanges*, Baden-Baden.

Lambsdorff, J. Graf (2002b) 'How Confidence Facilitates Illegal Transactions', *American Journal of Economics and Sociology*, vol. 61, no. 4, pp. 829–54.

Lancaster, T.D. and Montinola, G.R. (2001) 'Comparative Political Corruption: Issues of Operationalization and Measurement', *Studies in Comparative International Development*, vol. 36, pp. 3–28.

LaPorta, R., Lopez-Silanes, F., Schleifer, A. and Vishney, R.W. (1997) 'Trust in Large Organizations', *American Economic Review Papers and Proceedings*, vol. 87, pp. 333–8.

LaPorta, R., Lopez-Silanes, F., Schleifer, A. and Vishney, R.W. (1998) 'The Quality of Government', Unpublished manuscript, Harvard University.

Leite, C. and Weidmann, J. (1999) 'Does Mother Nature Corrupt? Natural Resources, Corruption, and Economic Growth?', *International Monetary Fund Working Paper*, WP/99/85, Washington.

Levi, M. (1998) 'A State of Trust', in M. Levi and V. Braithwaite (eds) *Trust and Governance*, New York.

Lindsay, D. (1998) 'After a Lengthy Court Fight, There's Still No Sign of a Consensus on How to Improve Urban Schools', <http://www.edweek.org/sreports/qc98/states/nj-n2.htm> (accessed 19 May 2001).

Macaulay, S. (1963) 'Non-Contractual Relations in Business: A Preliminary Study', *American Sociological Review*, vol. 28, pp. 55–67.

Mauro, P. (1995) 'Corruption and Growth', *Quarterly Journal of Economics*, vol. 110, pp. 681–712.

Mauro, P. (1997) *Why Worry About Corruption?*, Washington.

Mauro, P. (1998a) 'Corruption and the Composition of Government Expenditure', *Journal of Public Economics*, vol. 69, pp. 263–79.

Mauro, P. (1998b) 'Corruption: Causes, Consequences, and Agenda for Further Research', *Finance and Development* (International Monetary Fund), March, pp. 11–14.

Misztal, B.A. (1996) *Trust in Modern Societies*, Cambridge.

Norwood, C. (1974) *About Paterson*, New York.

Offe, C. (1996) 'Social Capital: Concepts and Hypotheses', Unpublished manuscript, Humboldt University (Germany).

Onishi, N. with Banerjee, N. (2001) 'Chad's Wait for Its Oil Riches May Be Long', *New York Times*, 16 May, <http://www.nytimes.com/2001/05/16/world/16CHAD.html> (accessed 17 May 2001).

Paldam, M. (2000) 'The Cross-Country Pattern of Corruption', Unpublished manuscript, University of Aarhus.

Poirson, H. (1998) 'Economic Security, Private Investment, and Growth in Developing Countries', *International Monetary Fund Working Paper, WP/98/4*, Washington.

Putnam, R.D. (1993) *Making Democracy Work: Civic Traditions in Modern Italy*, Princeton.

The Record (2001) 'Fava's Big Challenge: Wanted: A New Type of Passaic County Sheriff, editorial', <http://www.bergen.com/editorials/fava200103292.htm> (accessed 19 May 2001).

Riordan, W. (1948) *Plunkitt of Tammany Hall*, New York.

Rose-Ackerman, S. (1978) *Corruption: A Study in Political Economy*, New York.

Rothstein, B. (2000) 'Trust, Social Dilemmas, and Collective Memories: On the Rise and Decline of the Swedish Model', *Journal of Theoretical Politics*, vol. 12, pp. 477–99.

Rothstein, B. (2001) 'Creating Trust from Above: Social Capital and Institutional Legitimacy', Presented at the European Consortium for Political Research Joint Sessions of Workshops, Grenoble, April.

Seligman, A.B. (1997) *The Problem of Trust*, Princeton.

Seligman, M.E.P. (1991) *Learned Optimism*, New York.

Stanley, A. (2001) 'Rome Journal: Official Favors: Oil That Makes Italy Go Round', *New York Times*, A4.

Tanzi, V. (1998) 'Corruption Around the World: Causes, Consequences, Scope and Cures', *IMF Staff Papers*, vol. 45, pp. 559–94.

Treisman, D. (1999) 'Decentralization and Corruption: Why Are Federal States Perceived to Be More Corrupt?', Presented at the Annual Meeting of the American Political Science Association, September, Atlanta.

Treisman, D. (2000) 'The Causes of Corruption: A Cross-National Study', *Journal of Public Economics*, vol. 76, pp. 399–457.

Tyler, T.R. (1990) *Why People Obey the Law*, New Haven.

Uslaner, E.M. (1999a) 'Trust But Verify: Social Capital and Moral Behavior', *Social Science Information*, vol. 38, pp. 29–56.

Uslaner, E.M. (1999b) 'Morality Plays: Social Capital and Moral Behavior in Anglo-American Democracies', in J.V. Deth, M. Maraffi, K. Newton and P. Whiteley (eds) *Social Capital and European Democracy*, London.

Uslaner, E.M. (2002) *The Moral Foundations of Trust*, New York.

Vanhanen, T. (1997) *Prospects of Democracy*, New York.

6 Self-enforcing corruption

Information transmission and organizational response

Lambros Pechlivanos

Introduction

Organizations usually consist of individuals who share neither the same goals nor the same information. In such an environment, motivational issues are far from trivial problems to resolve. The principal–agent model is the simplest framework used to analyse such situations (e.g. Holmström 1979; Grossman and Hart 1983). As the number of members in an organization increases, however, the design of the optimal grand contract becomes more complicated. A number of them may collude, thus creating a new set of restrictions to be dealt with. A plethora of different results about optimal contract designs have been reached, depending on whether these side-contracts lead to actions that may be beneficial or detrimental to the organization, or whether information transmission is facilitated or not (Holmström and Milgrom 1990; Itoh 1993; Tirole 1986).[1]

Collusion does not occur only between members of an organization. Some members may also collude with outside parties, possibly at the expense of the organization as a whole. However, the principal does not necessarily have power over non-members. Her[2] ability to discipline outside parties may be restricted. In this case the principal can design policies that affect only her agents. A full-blown mechanism design approach might not be appropriate, and therefore a more circumstantial analysis of potential policy instruments is needed. As a consequence, collusion usually occurs in equilibrium. This is the situation this chapter concentrates on.

A common feature of the literature is the assumption that all parties have the ability to write enforceable contracts.[3] This assumption is not innocuous when analysing side-contracts. Departing from this approach, this chapter attempts to explain explicitly the procedures under which such side-contracts may be enforced. The mechanism that is used to enforce the desirable behaviour is persuasion through manipulation of future returns. If the parties involved interact repeatedly, an implicit threat of retaliatory behaviour in the future may be sufficient to deter any deviation from collusion.

Examples of collusion among members of an organization and outside parties are numerous. Interest groups lobbying members of legislative bodies, criminals offering kickbacks to policemen or citizens bribing low-rank administrators to bypass red tape are just a few common examples of corrupt activities. Although these phenomena are far more pervasive in the public sector, private institutions are not immune.

The framework employed to analyse such phenomena is a principal–agent–client model. Consider the following situation. A clientele needs the services of an organization to accomplish a task. The organization is structured as a two-tier hierarchy, in which a principal oversees a group of agents. Each client is randomly assigned to an agent with whom she has to deal indefinitely and who is the only one that can provide this service to her. Assume that there is an incentive for the client to persuade the agent to bypass regulations and that she is willing to reward him for the favour. To help the client, the agent must undertake a costly action which is not observable by the client. Such side-contracts are assumed to be prohibited by the contract governing the principal–agent relationship. This implies that corrupt side-contracts are not enforceable by an external authority and therefore, for illicit trade to take place, the client must rely on the agent's goodwill to return the favour.

Before any transaction takes place, the principal designs the policy instruments she will have at her discretion to control her agents and to deter corruption.[4] Being conscious of the self-enforcing nature of the client–agent relationship, the principal would like to manipulate the information the client collects about the agent's behaviour. It is in the interest of the principal to implement policies that garble the information that reaches the client. As has been shown in the literature of repeated games (Kandori 1992a), the worse the informativeness[5] of the signals observed by the players, the lower the degree of cooperation that can be sustained. The reasoning goes as follows. Collusion is sustainable only if the client and the agent can punish non-conforming behaviour. Threats of punishments, though, are effective only if the players can infer that such behaviour has occurred. Obviously, the effectiveness of such arrangements depends on the precision of the inferences made, which in turn depends on the information the two players receive about each other's actions.[6]

The premise of this chapter is that the reliance of self-enforcing relationships on informational flows is important when evaluating the effectiveness of the principal's policies. The goal is to characterize the principal's optimal policies when facing self-enforcing client–agent relationships – in contradistinction to the optimal policies had the same relationships been enforceable. Hence, the analysis concentrates on instruments that affect the informational flows between the client and the agent. These instruments include (a) the auditing of the agents' performance, and (b) the imposition of penalties on the agents.[7]

It should be stressed that the term 'auditing' does not refer to an *ex post* evaluation of the agent's behaviour, but rather to a proactive monitoring of the agent's decisions. The principal, acting as a monitor, has the authority to review her agents' decisions. She can either rubber-stamp what her agents have decided (i.e. choose not to audit), or thoroughly review and then accept it or reverse it. Within this framework, auditing serves a double role. First, it is useful because it allows the principal to intercept corrupt activities and negate them. Hence, clients may have less of an incentive to bribe for services they may never receive. But, additionally, and more interestingly for the purpose of this chapter, even if auditing is not observed by the client it is also useful because it garbles the information the client receives about the agent's behaviour.

The following example illustrates this point. Consider a real estate developer (the client) whose business is concentrated in a certain region and who must acquire a permit from the zoning authorities in order to build on each property she wants to develop. Of course, it is in the client's interest to build in excess of the established regulations, and she is willing to bribe a bureaucrat in the zoning office to bring this about. The bureaucrat (the agent) has the discretion to give the permit or to stop the project, depending on its compliance with regulations. If he decides to help the developer and accept the project, he has to undertake costly actions to support his decision (find loopholes, fabricate documents, etc.). His decisions, however, are subject to review from his superior (the principal). In the end, the developer either receives the permit or is asked to make changes to comply with the regulations. When receiving a negative response, the developer is not able to infer with certainty whether the bureaucrat attempted to help but was audited, or did not bother to support the proposal even though he was bribed.

The imposition of penalties has two countervailing effects. Obviously, an agent is less willing to consent to his client's wishes if he knows that he would be punished when caught. On the other hand, if penalties are observable by the client, their imposition increases the client's information about the agent's performance and facilitates collusion.[8] There exists a trade off between the deterrent power of the punitive measures inflicted upon the agent and the additional information they provide the client with respect to the agent's past behaviour. It looks plausible that there is a positive correlation between the severity of penalties and their observability by outsiders. In most judicial systems, the more ambitious the prosecution's goal the more concrete must be the proof of guilt, and thus the more visible the whole process becomes. Hence, the principal might prefer to impose mild penalties at the expense of deterring fewer agents in order to decrease the observability of the penalties, thus retaining the enforceability problems in the remaining corrupt relationships.[9]

Since punishment entails no direct cost to the organization, it seems plausible that the principal should set the penalties high enough to deter such agents completely. In that case, there would be no ongoing collusion to worry about. However, in practice we rarely observe prompt and severe punishment in cases of detected corruption (Klitgaard 1988). In most administrations, the procedures are convoluted and usually end up being resolved in courts. Moreover, several theoretical justifications have been put forth for the non-optimality of infinite penalties, ranging from the inducement of marginal deterrence to the presence of imperfections in detection technology (an innocent could be found guilty) coupled with risk-averse agents.

In addition, we find that penalties have another effect: they differentiate between deterred and undeterred agents, thus creating a new source of uncertainty for the client. Moreover, this type of uncertainty, which depends on agent characteristics, may facilitate collusion. The undeterred agents want to build a 'reputation' for being corrupt, and this extra incentive increases their eagerness to abide by their side-arrangements.

In this chapter, the second section (pp. 96–100) models and characterizes the repeated client–agent relationship under auditing. The third section (pp. 100–1) describes the optimal intensity of auditing. The fourth section (pp. 102–6) introduces heterogeneity among agents and describes the effects of penalties on the relationship. The fifth section (pp. 106–7) discusses the optimal severity of penalties. Finally, conclusions are presented (pp. 107–8).

Client–agent relationship

Before clients and agents start interacting, the principal announces her policies and commits to following them. Specifically, she sets the probability that she will audit her agents and the penalty she will inflict upon corrupt ones. Subsequently, each client is randomly assigned to an agent, with whom she will interact thereafter. In the current section, the focus is on the effects of auditing. The characterization of the effects of the imposition of penalties is deferred until the fourth section (pp. 102–6). This allows us to separate the effects of the two policies.

Stage game

There are two active players, the client and the agent, each of whom takes an action. Since the principal acts before the client–agent relationship begins, her actions are taken as given by both the client and the agent. This allows us to represent auditing as a random variable. Given the realization of the auditing event, payoffs are distributed. The official aspects of client–agent interaction are not modelled explicitly; neither are the payoffs accrued to all players because of them. For simplicity, the net benefits resulting from the official activity are normalized to zero. Hence, all benefits or costs of corruption described below are above and beyond the official ones.

The exact timing of the game is as follows. First, both players simultaneously choose their actions. The client decides whether to pay a 'bribe' to the agent ($a^C \in \{b, nb\}$), and the agent decides whether to deliver the 'favour' to the client ($\alpha^A \in \{d, nd\}$). Afterwards, the agent observes whether auditing occurred (s_A) or not (s_N) ($\omega \in \{s_N, s_A\}$), with $p = Prob(\omega = s_N)$. Finally, as a result of the agent's action and of the realization of the random variable, the client observes whether she received the favour ($y \in \{f, nf\}$), and, as a result of the client's action alone, the agent observes whether he was bribed. The metaphor of reciprocal trade to represent this situation will often be used. Consider that a bribe is traded for a favour:

client chooses a^C;	ω is observed by	client observes y;
agent chooses α^A	the agent	agent observes a^C

It is assumed that the client's decision to bribe and the agent's decision to deliver the favour are costly to them (where the cost is denoted by K). Nevertheless, the benefit enjoyed by the recipient (denoted by B) is larger, thus allowing for mutual gains from trade.[10] If auditing occurs, the client does not receive her favour, although the agent may have taken the necessary action and has already incurred the cost. The payoffs to the players are represented by the normal form presented in Figure 6.1. This figure helps us understand the nature of the imperfect monitoring of the agent's action by the client. When the client finds that she did not receive the favour, she cannot be certain whether the agent defected or was cooperating but audited.[11] In contrast, the agent has full information throughout the game.

It can be seen clearly that the stage game has a unique equilibrium under which the agent cannot be trusted by the client, and therefore the equilibrium strategies are, for the client, not to bribe and, for the agent, not to deliver the favour. Hence, the maxima value sustained in equilibrium is $v = (0,0)$.

If no auditing

Agent Client	Deliver	Not deliver
Bribe	$B–K, B–K$	$-K, B$
Not bribe	$B, -K$	$0, 0$

If auditing

Agent Client	Deliver	Not deliver
Bribe	$-K, B–K$	$-K, B$
Not bribe	$0, K$	$0, 0$

Figure 6.1 Stage-game normal form representation.

Repeated game

In the infinitely repeated game, after every period, both players accumulate their observations and form a history of the way the game is played. As was argued in the previous section, the agent observes all actions and realizations of outcomes, and therefore he has information about the whole history of the game.[12] In contrast, having observed only her own actions and reception of favours, the client's information is partial. Formally, strategy profiles (s_C, s_A) are pairs of infinite sequences of mappings from histories to actions. In each period, a pure action profile $\alpha = (\alpha_C, \alpha_A)$ induces a probability distribution over the reception of favours $\pi(y \mid \alpha^A, \omega)$. The observational reception of favours is compounded with past observations to form the history of the game. The players' actual per period payoffs are denoted by the pair $r = (r_C, r_A)$. Hence, expected per period payoffs can be computed as $g(\alpha) = \sum_y \sum_\omega r(\alpha, \omega) \pi(y \mid \alpha^A, \omega)$. If needed, mixed strategy profiles (σ_C, σ_A) can be equivalently defined. When mixed action profiles $\alpha(\alpha)$ are considered, the induced probability distribution over outcomes can be easily computed as $\pi(y \mid \alpha^A, \omega) = \pi(y \mid \alpha^A, \omega) \alpha^A(\alpha^A)$ and expected per period payoffs can be defined as $g(\alpha) = \sum_y \sum_\omega \sum_{\alpha(\alpha)} r(\alpha, \omega) \pi(y \mid \alpha^A, \omega)$. Finally, it is assumed that both players discount payoffs between periods at a rate of $\delta E(0, 1)$.

The objective of the players is to maximize their normalized present value:

$$\max_{\{a^i_t\}_{t=1}^\infty} v_i = (1 - \delta)\, E_{a^i_t} \left\{ \sum_{t=1}^\infty \delta^{t-1} g_i(a_t) \right\}, \quad i = \text{A, C}$$

The goal of the exercise is to find the maximum payoff that can be supported by a perfect public equilibrium, given the environment created by the principal, parameterized by p, and the discount rate.

Repeated game equilibria analysis

To solve for the equilibrium of the repeated game, in principle, one should consider all possible strategies, which may be highly non-stationary. Nonetheless, as the game is characterized by imperfect public information, the self-generation and factorization properties of Abreu, Pearce and Stacchetti (1986, 1990) can be employed, and it can be shown that all attainable equilibrium payoffs can be derived using strategies that follow a first order Markov process. Moreover, because the game has the special feature of having only one-sided imperfect monitoring, attention can be further restricted, without loss of generality, on public strategies.[13] Hence, the strategy space can be parameterized by the following eight probabilities:[14]

For the client: $\beta_{f,b} = Prob(b \mid f, b)$ $\beta_{f,nb} = Prob(b \mid f, nb)$
                   $\beta_{nf,b} = Prob(b \mid nf, b)$ $\beta_{nf,nb} = Prob(b \mid nf, nb)$

For the agent: $\gamma_{f,b} = Prob(d \mid f, b)$ $\gamma_{f,nb} = Prob(d \mid f, nb)$
                   $\gamma_{nf,b} = Prob(d \mid nf, b)$ $\gamma_{nf,nb} = Prob(d \mid nf, nb)$

Obviously, the stage game equilibria continue to survive in the repeated game. Hence, the myopic repetition of the unique stage game equilibrium constitutes an equilibrium of the repeated game. This equilibrium, however, does not exploit the gains possible from cooperation. The goal is to characterize the most collusive equilibrium, given the environment within which the players interact.

According to the bang-bang rewards property, it is possible to span the entire equilibrium payoff set by considering only extreme values for the continuation payoffs (Abreu, Pearce and Stacchetti 1990). Behind this property, though, is the implicit assumption that the 'public signal space' is continuous. When the signal space is continuous, one can keep the values of the 'reward' and 'punishment' continuations at their extreme values (i.e. use only extreme continuation payoffs) and trace the whole equilibrium payoff set by altering the partition of the signal space. Hence, the largest value of the equilibrium payoff set can be attained by fine-tuning the partition of the public signal space. In essence, the goal is to concentrate the 'punishment phase' in the region that is as informationally efficient as possible (Pearce 1992). In this model the public signal space is discrete (it is the bribing decision cum the reception of favour), and hence the preceding argument does not, literally, apply. Generically, it is impossible to attain the largest equilibrium payoff in this way because the 'punishment phase' cannot be concentrated in the most informationally efficient region. Therefore, what one should do to increase the value of the attainable equilibrium payoff is to make the 'punishment' continuation payoff as large as possible, so long as it does not destroy the players' incentives to behave cooperatively.

The following proposition characterizes the equilibrium strategies that sustain the most collusive equilibrium outcome. This proposition, as well as the subsequent ones in the chapter, will not be proved here; interested readers are referred to Pechlivanos (1997).

Proposition 1
There exist two cut-off values $p^* = K/\delta B$ *and* $\underline{\delta} = K/B$, *such that for all* $p \geq p^*$ *and* $\delta \geq \underline{\delta}$, *the following strategies construct a mixed strategy equilibrium which is more collusive than any of the pure strategy equilibria of the game:*

$$\beta^m_{f,b} = \beta^m_{f,nb} = 1 \qquad\qquad \gamma^m_{f,b} = \gamma^m_{nf,b} = 1$$

$$\beta^m_{f,nb} = \beta^m_{nf,nb} = \frac{\delta pB - K}{\delta pB} \qquad\qquad \gamma^m_{nf,b} = \gamma^m_{nf,nb} = \frac{\delta pB - K}{\delta pB}$$

Essentially this equilibrium prescribes that the players take cooperative action as long as the public signal they observed in the preceding period is beneficial to them.[15] On the other hand, if the two players did not observe a beneficial public signal, they take an action that hinders cooperation (as they may take the non-cooperative action with positive probability). The probability with which they take the non-cooperative action is computed such that the players are simply indifferent with regard to being interested in continuing their cooperation in the future or not.[16]

Conducting comparative statics on the equilibrium strategies, we find that at the most collusive equilibrium all probabilities are weakly increasing in p. This means that, as auditing becomes less frequent, the right incentives can be given to the players even with less-intensive schemes. This is possible because as p increases, reception of favour is a more accurate signal of delivery, and hence the client can punish the agent in an informationally more efficient region. This reduces the probability of entering into a 'punishment phase' along the equilibrium path. Since the incentives are provided in terms of expected payoff differentials, when punishment becomes less ubiquitous, the same incentives can be provided with less intensive punishment.

The same comparative statics results carry on with respect to equilibrium payoffs. Given equilibrium strategies, the largest normalized equilibrium payoff for each of the two players is readily calculated: $v_C^m = pB - K$ and $v_A^m = B - 1/pK$. Summing up the two payoffs, one can find that the largest value of corruption that can be sustained using a self-enforcing arrangement is

$$ v^m = (1 + p)B - \frac{1+p}{p} K. $$

Clearly, v^m is increasing in p. Moreover, it is less than the first best payoff for all p. This result can be summarized with the following proposition:[17]

Proposition 2
The maximum perfect public equilibrium payoffs that can be supported by mixed strategies are strictly decreasing in the probability of auditing.

Optimal auditing

Auditing is costly to the principal. It requires that she spend resources and time to monitor transactions.[18] To ensure that the principal is not able to shut down the whole activity, it is assumed that the cost of auditing all activities is prohibitive. More rigorously, let the cost of auditing be denoted as C. An interior solution is ensured by the following Inada-like conditions:

$$ C'(p) < 0, \ C''(p) > 0, \ C'(1) = 0, \ C'(p^\star) = -\infty \text{ and } C(p^\star) > 2(B - K). $$

Before discussing the principal's optimal auditing decision, one should analyse, as a benchmark, the case in which client and agent can write enforceable contracts. In this case, the two players are able to consummate all potential gains from trade. To see this, consider the following side-contract, enforceable by a third party, between the client and the agent:

At the beginning of each period the client must take action 'b' and the agent action 'd'. Then, the client expects to observe 'f' and the client 'b'. In case 'b' is observed while 'f' is not, the agent must pay a fine F_A to the client, where $F_A \in (K/p, B)$. In all other cases, the transaction is considered complete.

The above contract induces the client to bribe and the agent to deliver every period, and hence the first best outcome can be attained. Therefore, given the probability of auditing, the normalized expected sum of payoffs is $v^e = (1 + p)B - 2K$.

The principal's objective is to minimize the total costs of corruption. These include the direct costs corruption imposes on the organization,[19] as well as the auditing costs. Hence, the principal's problem is to choose a p that minimizes $v^e(p) + C(p)$. This is a standard convex programme, and it has a unique solution p^e, which can be computed by the following first order condition: $-C'(p) = B$.

As was shown in the previous section, when client–agent side-contracts must be self-enforcing, a continuum of different strategies constitutes perfect public equilibria of the game. Strictly speaking, one should be agnostic about the specific strategies that may be played. In the literature, however, attention is frequently focused on the most collusive equilibria. This is the approach followed here too.

When side-contracts must be self-enforcing, the principal has stronger incentives to audit. In this case, auditing garbles the information the client gets about the agent's actions, and hence it reduces the efficacy of the attainable cooperative behaviour. Clearly, the solution to the minimization programme $v^m(p) + C(p)$, denoted by p^m, can be computed by the following first order condition: $-C'(p) = B + 1/p^2 K$. Clearly, p^m is smaller than p^e.[20]

Proposition 3
Due to the non-contractibility of corruption, the principal audits her agents 'excessively' compared to the case in which corrupt activities can be contracted upon.

It should be stressed that the additional disruptive effect auditing brings into the picture is not due to the fact that the two parties are deterred by the decreased profitability of having successful transactions. By construction, the client is not deterred in equilibrium since the principal never chooses to monitor adequately. Along the equilibrium path, both client and agent cooperate. Auditing reduces corruption by making it more costly for the two players to self-police their agreement. In order to give the right incentives to the agent, the client must alter her behaviour depending on the reception of favour. The more intense auditing is, the weaker the correlation between the agent's action and the reception of favour, and, therefore, the higher the probability of entering into a 'punishment phase' along the equilibrium path. Moreover, during 'punishment phases' the degree of punishment is also harsher. Because the incentives are provided in terms of expected payoff differentials, when punishment becomes more ubiquitous the right incentives can be provided only with more powerful incentive schemes.

Agent heterogeneity and imposition of penalties

Agent heterogeneity

The effects of the imposition of penalties on the relationship have not been modelled yet. As has been argued, penalties, if harsh enough, can deter agents. They come, however, at the cost of offering extra information to the client. To be able to analyse the trade-offs between these two conflicting effects, heterogeneity among agents is introduced. Different agents have different tolerance levels towards the penalties inflicted upon them.[21]

There are three categories of agents: easily deterred, normal agents, and tough to deter. Each group is represented in the general population according to the following proportions: N_e, N_n and N_t. The characteristic of each agent is private information, while the population proportions are assumed to be common knowledge.

There are two kinds of penalties the principal can impose on the agents. The first is harsh, and its imposition requires hearings that draw the attention of clients. The second is mild, and it can be imposed unilaterally by the principal behind closed doors. Let the cost to the agents of the two penalties be such that the easily deterred agents are deterred by both penalties, the normal ones are deterred only by the harsh penalty, while the tough ones are never deterred.

Client–agent relationship revisited

In such a model, penalties turn the client–agent relationship into one of incomplete information. When penalties are imposed, a number of agents become deterred. The deterred agents' payoff is such that no delivery is the dominant strategy.[22] The rest of the agents, who remain undeterred, continue to have the same payoff structure as before. In this situation the client's problem is more complicated. She has to deal with an agent whose type she does not know.

The new game is one of incomplete information in the sense of Harsanyi (1967). The uncertainty about each agent's payoff structure is identified by his 'type' $\theta \in \{D, ND\}$ (i.e. whether he is deterred and non-deterred). Depending on the punishment, clients form identical prior beliefs about the types of agents they face. Let μ be the client's belief that the agent is non-deterred. When harsh punishments are imposed, $\mu_0^{harsh} = N_t$, while when moderate punishments are used, $\mu_0^{mild} = N_n + N_t$. Under this specification, we can define the agent's strategy as a sequence of mappings from histories and types to actions.

The motivation behind the introduction of incomplete information in this model differs from the one of the standard paradigm of repeated games with incomplete information (e.g. Kreps and Wilson 1982; Milgrom and Roberts 1982). Here, the non-deterred ('normal type') agents do not want to mimic the deterred ('commitment type') ones. On the contrary, they would like to separate themselves in order to persuade clients that they should be trusted as partners. However, they face the problem that their attempts to deliver may be negated by the occurrence of auditing. Therefore, the non-deterred agents want to separate themselves and to build a 'reputation' for being cooperative in an adverse environment.

Harsh punishment

When the principal employs harsh punishments, the client can observe their realization. Therefore, the client has additional information which allows her to infer with certainty the action taken by the agent. Whether the client receives the favour or does not but observes that the agent was punished, she knows with certainty that the agent attempted to deliver. Thus the game is now one of perfect information, and, given the players' strategies, the evolution of the beliefs is deterministic.

Using Bayes' rule, given an arbitrary non-deterred agent's strategy γ, the evolution of the beliefs is as follows:

1 If the client can infer from public signals that the agent attempted to deliver and μ^+ denotes updated belief in that event, then $\mu_{t+1}^+ = Prob(\theta =$

$$ND|\ either\ y_t = f\ or\ \omega_t = s_A) = \frac{\gamma\mu_t}{\gamma\mu_t + 0(1 - \mu_t)} = 1.$$

2 If the client can infer that the agent did not attempt to deliver and μ^- denotes updated belief in that event, then $\mu_{t+1}^- = Prob(\theta = ND|y_t = nf\ and$

$$\omega_t = s_N) = \frac{(1 - \gamma)\mu_t}{(1 - \mu)\mu_t + 0(1 - \mu_t)}.\ \text{Clearly, if } \gamma = 1, \mu_1^- = 0.\ \text{Hence, if } \gamma = 1_2$$

constitutes an equilibrium strategy for the non-deterred type, the learning process lasts only one period.

From the literature we know that in the case of perfect monitoring a Friedman-type (Friedman 1971) pair of strategies with Nash reversion threats constitutes a sequential equilibrium, where payoffs that lie on the efficiency frontier are attainable. A similar result is found to hold in this perturbed version of the game.

Proposition 4
If p≥p* *and* δ≥δ, *the following pure strategies constitute the most collusive sequential equilibrium of the game under harsh punishment:*

1 The client bribes if, and only if, she received the favour in the previous period. In the first period, the client bribes the agent if, and only if

$$\mu_0 \geq \mu \equiv \frac{(1 - \delta)K}{pB - \delta K}.$$

2   The non-deterred agent delivers the favour if, and only if, he was bribed in the previous period. In the first period he always delivers the favour.
3   The deterred agent never delivers the favour.

To understand the logic behind the proposition one should consider the following. Given these strategies, the agent's type is revealed after the first period. Therefore, the strategies above, which are Friedman-type strategies with threats of permanent reversion to the non-cooperative stage game equilibrium, constitute a sequential equilibrium of the game from the second period on. Moreover, given the agent's type, both players take their most cooperative actions, and thus the payoffs lie on the efficiency frontier.

Let us concentrate now on the first period. The deterred agent plays his dominant strategy. The non-deterred agent has incentives to deliver since by deviating he triggers perpetual non-cooperation. The client also has incentives to bribe in order to generate cooperation, but is uncertain about her agent's type. If her prior regarding non-deterrance of her agent is large enough (i.e. $\mu_0 \geq \underline{\mu}$), she bribes. Otherwise, she prefers not to bribe, because it is not profitable for her to experiment by trying to initiate cooperation with an agent who is most probably deterred. She prefers to wait for the agent to initiate cooperation.

Mild punishment

Mild punishments are not observable by the client. This means we are back to a game with imperfect monitoring. The main difference, compared to the game analysed in the second section (pp. 96–100), is that now, depending on reception of favour, the client updates her belief about the type of agent she faces. The updating process continues until the client learns the agent's type with certainty. Thereafter, the game reverts to its above-described repeated form.

To analyse the game we separate it into two "stages". In the first stage, which may last forever, the agent's type is not fully revealed. The second stage, which starts after the first reception of favour, corresponds to the game already analysed in the second section. To solve for the equilibria strategies of the first stage, we assume that in the second stage the game will be played according to the most collusive equilibrium.

Because there is uncertainty about the agent's type, the first stage should not be approached as a standard repeated game. Although the physical environment is the same in every period, the mere fact that the client is learning something about the agent's type by observing past trade realizations makes every period unique. Nevertheless, a number of features make the analysis tractable. First, reception of favour continues to be determined exclusively by the agent's action. Moreover, since the beliefs depend only on the history of reception of favours, their evolution also depends exclusively on the agent's actions. This means that the beliefs held by the client every period constitute a sufficient statistic of the history of the game. Hence, a recursive structure can be developed, allowing us to use dynamic programming methods where current belief will serve as a state variable.

Therefore, to characterize an equilibrium one has to be able to track the evolution of beliefs $\{\mu\}$ along the game and define the players' strategies for every possible belief that may arise after some realization. The client's strategy can be parameterized by $\beta_{nf}(\mu)$, for every μ.[23] Similarly, the agent's strategy is parameterized by the conjecture he makes about the client's beliefs, i.e. $\{\gamma_b(\mu), \gamma_{nb}(\mu)\}$.

Using Bayes' rule, a sequence of favour receptions, given an arbitrary agent's strategy, determines the evolution of the beliefs. Therefore, by employing the same notation as in the harsh punishment case, the updated beliefs can be computed in the following way:

1   $\mu_{t+1}^{+} = Prob(\theta = ND | y_t = f) = \dfrac{p\gamma\mu_t}{p\gamma\mu_t + 0(1 - \mu_t)} = 1.$ As in the harsh punish-

ment case, a single reception of the favour is sufficient to persuade the client that she confronts a non-deterred agent.

2   $\mu_{t+1}^{-} = Prob(\theta = ND | y_t = nf) = \dfrac{(1 - p\gamma)\mu_t}{(1 - p\gamma)\mu_t + (1 - \mu_t)}.$ Note that there is a

positive probability that the client may not receive the favour regardless of the agent's action. Thus, with positive probability, learning lasts for more than a period. Actually, every period the client does not receive a favour, her belief about the agent's type decreases even further. Hence, for all histories in which no single reception of favour has occurred, the beliefs form a strictly decreasing sequence.

The fact that, irrespective of the current client's belief, the non-deterred agent can persuade the client of his type with a single reception of the favour creates a constant incentive for the agent to deliver the favour. As a consequence, the client's strategy can prescribe the same action irrespective of the belief she holds without compromising the agent's incentives to deliver the favour. Therefore, if the non-deterred agent's incentives to separate are strong enough (i.e. his second-stage continuation payoff is large enough), it would be optimal for him constantly to attempt to deliver the favour, even if the client does not reward him before the uncertainty about his type is resolved. The following proposition shows more rigorously how, due to this effect, we find a surprisingly simple first stage equilibrium.

Proposition 5
Given that the most collusive equilibrium will be played in the second stage, $\forall p \geq p^*$ and $\delta \geq \underline{\delta}$, the unique generic first-stage pure strategy equilibrium is the following: the deterred agent never delivers, the non-deterred agent always delivers, and the client never bribes as long as she has never received a favour in the past. These equilibrium strategies are supported by the following sequence of beliefs:

$$\mu_t = \begin{cases} \dfrac{(1-p)^t \mu_0}{1-[1-(1-p)^t]\mu_0} & \text{if } \gamma_\tau = nf \text{ for all } \tau < t \\[2mm] 1 & \text{if } \gamma_t = f \text{ for some } \tau. \end{cases}$$

In other words, the non-deterred agent is eager to signal his type to the client. The expectation of receiving bribes in the future, after persuading the client of his type, is sufficient to induce cooperative behaviour. On the other hand, the client has no incentive to deviate from the 'I'm not bribing until I'm sure you are non-deterred' strategy, since that way she takes her most profitable action while the agent is already taking his most cooperative one.

Agent behaviour and 'subjective uncertainty'

By comparing the non-deterred agent's equilibrium strategies before and after the resolution of the uncertainty about his type, one can see that the agent is more inclined to cooperate when his client is still uncertain about his type.

The intuition behind this result is simple. The non-deterred agent understands that, had his client known she was dealing with an agent who is willing to deliver the favours he is asked for, she would value a cooperative relationship with him more. This makes him eager to separate himself, and to build a reputation for being non-deterred. Therefore, the principal's policy of punishing her corrupt agents creates an adverse side-effect even in cases in which the act of punishment is unobservable by the client.

Proposition 6
Policies that introduce 'subjective uncertainty' to the client–agent relationship (i.e. uncertainty that depends on unobservable agent characteristics) increase the non-deterred agent's incentive to behave cooperatively.

Optimal severity of penalties

Law enforcement literature deals extensively with the optimal severity of punishment. Becker (1968) argued that penalties should be set at their maximum severity. Subsequently, however, a whole discussion began on whether, depending on the seriousness of the crime, a progressive pattern of punishments is needed in order to induce marginal deterrence (Stigler 1970; Posner 1992; Mookherjee and Png 1992). In another strand, the optimal severity of punishment was linked to the credibility of the enforcement mechanisms. It was found that excessive penalties may not be optimal either because judges and jurors may be reluctant to carry them out or because communities may hesitate to cooperate with police authorities in uncovering criminals if they believe the punishment does not fit the crime (Andreoni 1991; Akerlof and Yellen 1994).

The focus here is on a different aspect – namely, on the fact that the act of punishment may transmit information previously unknown about the actions of the person being prosecuted. A common characteristic of most judicial systems is the fact that the more ambitious the prosecution's goal is, the more concrete the proof of guilt must be. As a result, the whole process becomes more visible. Therefore, disciplinary procedures may actually facilitate the transmission of information between parties engaging in self-enforcing relationships, and they may consequently mitigate the enforceability problems that arise in such relationships. It could actually be argued that the fact that penalties often take the form of internal organizational measures may imply that the principal is concerned about the information transmitted by this action and is trying to minimize the consequences.

Therefore, the imposition of penalties has two conflicting effects on the client–agent relationship. First, penalties increase the cost to the agent of being corrupt, and thus they deter some agents. Second, they can increase the flow of information received by the client and facilitate ongoing corrupt relationships. If more severe penalties are associated with a higher degree of observability of the disciplinary procedure for the client, there might be a trade-off that can limit the optimal severity of punishment.

The trade-off faced by the principal is clear. If the more severe penalty, which is observable, does not deter many more agents than the mild penalty (here parameterized by N_n), the benefits of retaining the enforceability problems in the remaining corrupt relationships may dominate, and the principal may decide to limit the severity of her punitive measures. Of course, if numerous agents are deterred, the weighting goes in the other direction, and the principal will choose to impose the severe penalty. The next proposition states this result.

Proposition 7
There exists a threshold $N_n^* > 0$, such that mild penalties are optimal if and only if the proportion of the normal agents in the population are less than this threshold, i.e. $N_n \leq N_n^*$.
This result highlights the fact that the principal may be willing to allow a strictly positive number of agents who could be otherwise deterred to engage in corrupt activities in order to keep the enforceability problems in the relationships of the tough-to-deter agents.

Conclusions

Parties involved in corrupt relationships do not have the ability to rely on enforceable contracts, and hence they have to devise self-enforcing mechanisms to safeguard their relationships. This chapter considers situations in which self-enforcing corrupt relationships can be sustained because the parties involved interact repeatedly. In this case, the desirable behaviour can be enforced through manipulation of future returns – that is, via implicit threats of retaliatory behaviour in the future. Of course, such threats are effective only if the parties involved are able to infer any deviant behaviour. Obviously, the precision of these inferences depends crucially on the flow of information between the corrupt parties.

A principal determined to fight corruption in the organization she oversees should take into consideration the fact that informational flows between the corrupt parties greatly affect the sustainability and efficiency of corrupt relationships. It is, therefore, in her interest to implement policies that garble the information transmitted from one party to the other. To the extent that auditing her agents and reversing their actions adds uncertainty to the environment in which her agents and their respective clients interact, the principal would prefer to audit her agents 'excessively' as opposed to the case where collusive contracts are enforceable.

Nonetheless, it is worth noting that the effects of the introduction of additional uncertainty on such self-enforcing relationships differ depending on the source of uncertainty. If uncertainty is 'objective' – i.e. it is due to the auditing activity of the principal – it reduces the scope for cooperation. In contrast, if uncertainty is 'subjective' – i.e. it depends on the agents' tolerance of punishment – it increases the incentives of the 'cooperative' types to abide by the agreement, thus inducing a higher degree of cooperation.

In addition, the chapter provides an alternative framework within which it is possible to evaluate the optimal severity of penalties. If the severity of punitive measures is positively related to the observability of the disciplinary processes by outsiders, the principal, by trading off the deterrence power of the penalties with the additional flow of information they provide, may prefer to use moderate penalties even though harsher forms of punishment are available.

Acknowledgements

Comments and suggestions by Johann GrafLambsdorff, and by the participants at the workshop on corrupt transactions in Göttingen, are gratefully acknowledged.

Notes

1 A characteristic of most analyses in which collusion is detrimental to the organization is that, by appealing to the direct revelation principle, they allow all information to be provided truthfully to the principal, thus making the grand contract collusion-proof (e.g. Laffont and Martimort 1997). Kofman and Lawarrée (1996) showed that even in such cases it may be too costly for the principal to implement the collusion-proof contract and may optimally allow for collusion.
2 Throughout the chapter the female pronoun will refer to the client or to the principal, and the male one to the agent.
3 Noted exceptions are Acemoglu (1997), Martimort (1996) and Tirole (1986).
4 The principal is represented as being determined to fight corruption, instead of colluding with the agent to maximize the bribe that can be extracted by the client. This might be the case either because corrupt activities reduce returns to legal activities the principal may care about (Murphy, Shleifer and Vishny 1993), or because the agent's corrupt activity may be competing with complementary illicit services the principal could be offering (Shleifer and Vishny 1993).
5 In Blackwell's sense of quasi-garbling.
6 The assumption that clients are matched with agents for an indefinite time seems

strong. Given that the principal is conscious of the self-enforcing nature of corruption, she could rotate her agents frequently and on predetermined dates. Besides the fact that rotation might be costly if agents acquire job-specific skills over time, such an arrangement does not necessarily destroy the possibility of sustaining collusion. One can show that cooperation can be sustained between members of two groups when there is random matching every period among the members of these groups even if informational transmission is decentralized (Kandori 1992b).

7 Obviously, one can envision other instruments that can be employed to influence an agent's behaviour. The level of wages is a natural choice and has been analysed by many authors (e.g. Carrillo 2000). It is ignored here because it does not affect the information flow between agent and client.

8 The argument made here is similar in nature to the one used in auction theory to support that the auctioneer in sealed-bid auctions should not disclose *ex post* information about the bids received, because this would facilitate bid rigging among contestants.

9 To illustrate the point better consider the following scenario. A freshman Republican representative has been elected to the 108th Congress, representing the upper east side of Manhattan, New York. A segment of her constituency comprises a large part of what is labelled by the media as the 'cultural elite'. The representative, coming from a well-known family, and being an active socialite for most of her life (member of the boards of the Guggenheim and the Metropolitan museums etc.), got a lot of support and contributions from these 'elitists'. The time comes, and the House votes on the abolition of the National Endowment for the Arts. Let us assume that the rules call for a secret vote (though clearly this is rarely the case), and she votes 'no'. In a close call, NEA/NEH is abolished. (Of course, the reader understands that her constituents' uncertainty about her performance does not come from an auditing of any sort, but from the fact that they do not know how the other representatives voted.) Let us assume that the Speaker of the House and the Majority Whip found out that she disobeyed the party line and voted 'no'. They can either make this public and make her the pariah of the party, or they can keep quiet and just cut her out from other deals. With the first option, at next elections she would have no fund-raising problems since she has proven to be a loyal 'benefactor' of the arts. If the second option is chosen, she would have to prove to her constituency that she was not an 'elephant' on this issue.

10 The fact that the cost and benefit of bribing are not the same should be understood as a generalization of the form of bribing. Often, bribes are not just monetary transfers. Consider, for example, a municipal fire-safety inspector being entertained in restaurants, the safety standards of which he is supposed to inspect. Clearly, the cost to the restaurant owner is much smaller than the bill the inspector forgoes. More generally, as in any other contracts, here too corrupt parties will try to economize on transaction costs. Barter often helps in this direction, either because it makes the transactions ethically more acceptable or because it reduces the threat of detection by veiling the quid pro quo.

11 It is obvious that when the client receives $(B - K)$ she is able to infer with certainty that the agent delivered the favour. Hence, we do not impose the standard in the literature common support assumption.

12 Realizations of random audits are known to the agent, but can be suppressed since they can be recovered through trading outcomes and his own actions.

13 For a formal argument, see Pechlivanos (1997).

14 Strictly speaking, the preceding argument shows that one needs to consider only stationary equilibrium strategies. Nonetheless, because the game exhibits continuity at infinity, it is sufficient to check that one-shot deviations are not profitable after every history – that is, to require the strategies to be unimprovable. Hence, it is sufficient to consider only stationary strategies.

15 The beneficial public signal for the agent is that he was bribed, and for the client that she received the favour.
16 Any probability lower than this one would result in a strictly smaller continuation payoff, without at the same time resulting in any benefit in terms of offering better incentives to cooperate. On the other hand, had this probability been greater the players would not have the appropriate incentives to sustain cooperation.
17 This result is closely related to Kandori (1992a), who has shown that, as the public signal becomes more informative, the equilibrium payoff set expands.
18 An alternative, less costly method of manipulating the flow of information between agent and client is the random reversion of the agents' decisions. The advantage of this method is that the principal does not have to spend resources in checking her agents. But, on the other hand, this process is bound to reverse non-corrupt decisions and thereby disrupt the beneficial services provided by the organization. If the principal greatly values the official services, such mindless audits are dominated by educated ones.
19 The simplifying assumption that the costs imposed to the organization by the corrupt activities are equal to the private benefits accrued to the corrupt parties is made for tractability. Any convex function of them could be considered without altering much.
20 Notice that $v^m(p)$ is discontinuous at p^*. The assumptions imposed on $C(p)$, though, ensures the existence of a unique interior solution that lies at the right of p^*.
21 For instance, in the presence of limited liability, agents of different wealth will behave differently. Alternatively, if penalties take the form of administrative measures, like blacklisting, agents with different employment aspirations are affected differently; ambitious administrators may care a lot about their image.
22 This does not mean that they do not accept bribes. Bribes are not observable by the principal, who can detect only whether her agents took inappropriate actions. In any case, according to the specification of the model, the agents do not have the choice of accepting or rejecting bribes.
23 Because the reception of one favour is sufficient to resolve the uncertainty, a first-stage client's equilibrium strategy does not prescribe an action after such event has occurred.

References

Abreu, D., Pearce, D. and Stacchetti, E. (1986) 'Optimal Cartel Equilibria with Imperfect Monitoring', *Journal of Economic Theory*, vol. 39, no. 1, pp. 251–69.
Abreu, D., Pearce, D. and Stacchetti, E. (1990) 'Toward a Theory of Discounted Repeated Games with Imperfect Monitoring', *Econometrica*, vol. 58, no. 5, pp. 1041–64.
Acemoglu, D. (1997) *Career Concerns and Cover-ups: A Dynamic Model of Collusion*, mimeo, MIT.
Akerlof, G. and Yellen, J. (1994) 'Gang Behavior, Law Enforcement, and Community Values', in H.J. Aaron, T.E. Mann and T. Taylor (eds) *Values and Public Policy*, Washington, DC.
Andreoni, J. (1991) 'Reasonable Doubt and the Optimal Magnitude of Fines: Should the Penalty Fit the Crime?', *Rand Journal of Economics*, vol. 22, no. 3, pp. 385–95.
Becker, G. (1968) 'Crime and Punishment: An Economic Approach', *Journal of Political Economy*, vol. 76, no. 2, pp. 169–217.
Carrillo, J. (2000) 'Grafts, Bribes and the Practice of Corruption', *Journal of Economics and Management Strategy*, vol. 9, pp. 257–86.
Friedman, J. (1971) 'A Non-cooperative Equilibrium for Supergames', *Review of Economic Studies*, vol. 38, issue 113, pp. 1–12.

Grossman, S.J. and Hart, O. (1983) 'An Analysis of the Principal–Agent Problem', *Econometrica*, vol. 51, no. 1, pp. 7–45.

Harsanyi, J. (1967) 'Games with Incomplete Information Played by Bayesian Players', *Management Science*, vol. 14, pp. 159–82, 320–34.

Holmström, B. (1979) 'Moral Hazard and Observability', *Bell Journal of Economics*, vol. 10, no. 1, pp. 74–91.

Holmström, B. and Milgrom, P. (1990) 'Regulating Trade Among Agents', *Journal of Institutional and Theoretical Economics*, vol. 146, no. 1, pp. 85–105.

Itoh, H. (1993) 'Coalitions, Incentives, and Risk Sharing', *Journal of Economic Theory*, vol. 60, pp. 410–27.

Kandori, M. (1992a) 'The Use of Information in Repeated Games with Imperfect Monitoring', *Review of Economic Studies*, vol. 59, no. 3, pp. 581–93.

Kandori, M. (1992b) 'Social Norms and Community Enforcement', *Review of Economic Studies*, vol. 59, no. 1, pp. 63–80.

Klitgaard, R. (1988) *Controlling Corruption*, Berkeley.

Kofman, F. and Lawarrée, P. (1996) 'On the Optimality of Allowing Collusion', *Journal of Public Economics*, vol. 61, pp. 383–407.

Kreps, D. and Wilson, R. (1982) 'Reputation and Imperfect Information', *Journal of Economic Theory*, vol. 27, pp. 253–79.

Laffont, J.J. and Martimort, D. (1997) 'Collusion under Asymmetric Information', *Econometrica*, vol. 65, no. 4, pp. 875–912.

Martimort, D. (1996) *Theory of Self-Enforceable Collusion in Organizations*, mimeo, IDEI, Toulouse.

Milgrom, P. and Roberts, J. (1982) 'Predation, Reputation, and Entry Deterrence', *Journal of Economic Theory*, vol. 27, pp. 280–312.

Mookherjee, D. and Png, I.P.L. (1992) 'Monitoring vis-à-vis Investigation in Enforcement of Law', *American Economic Review*, vol. 82, no. 3, pp. 556–65.

Murphy, K., Shleifer, A. and Vishny, R.W. (1993) 'Why is Rent-Seeking so Costly to Growth?', *American Economic Review*, vol. 83, no. 2, pp. 409–14.

Pearce, D. (1992) 'Repeated Games: Cooperation and Rationality', in J.J. Laffont (ed.) *Advances in Economic Theory: Sixth World Congress*, Cambridge.

Pechlivanos, L. (1997) 'Self-Enforcing Corruption and Optimal Deterrence', *GREMAQ Working Paper Series 97.18.460*, Toulouse.

Posner, R. (1992) *Economic Analysis of Law* (4th edn), Boston.

Shleifer, A. and Vishny, R.W. (1993) 'Corruption', *Quarterly Journal of Economics*, vol. 108, no. 3, pp. 599–617.

Stigler, G. (1970) 'The Optimum Enforcement of Laws', *Journal of Political Economy*, vol. 78, no. 3, pp. 526–36.

Tirole, J. (1986) 'Hierarchies and Bureaucracies: On the Role of Collusion in Organizations', *Journal of Law, Economics and Organization*, vol. 2, no. 2, pp. 181–214.

7 The use of intermediaries and other 'alternatives' to bribery

John Bray

Introduction

Corruption regularly features in the international press, and there is now greater awareness of the damage that it inflicts both on companies' reputations and on national economies. Since 1997, OECD member states have introduced new laws, similar to the US Foreign Corrupt Practices Act (FCPA), making it possible to prosecute companies in their home countries for paying bribes abroad. However, despite this apparent progress, international business people frequently express scepticism about the prospects for genuine change. As one US executive commented in response to a recent Control Risks' survey:

> On the surface we seem to be beating it [corruption], but underneath it's like Internet security. People make it better. Then other people find ways to sneak through.
>
> (Control Risks Group 2002a: 15)

The use of intermediaries is one of the most common strategies used to 'sneak through' in large-scale international business transactions. By employing a local agent or a representative, companies can cut down the time needed to get to know new markets, and thus reduce the transaction costs of operating there. Intermediaries may also act as a 'buffer' against demands for bribes: they can make their own decisions whether or not to pay, according to local custom. Foreign employers or partners do not know and – according to conventional business wisdom – do not need to know about payments made on their behalf. However, such practices also involve significant risks even when anti-bribery laws are poorly enforced, and still more in the current era of international legal reform. This chapter analyses the changing nature of those risks and the responses of international companies.

It draws on three main sources. The first is Control Risks' 2002 survey of international business attitudes to corruption, which involved 250 companies in six jurisdictions, and points to important differences in perception between different nationalities and sectors.[1] The second source is information derived from legal cases involving companies accused of corruption. Third, the chapter makes use of illustrative examples drawn from the author's experience as a consultant advising international companies on best practice in difficult environments.[2] The chapter draws heavily on research conducted in the preparation of Control Risks' 2002 report (2002b) on anti-corruption best practice.

The chapter begins with a review of companies' perceptions, showing that a significant number of companies regularly lose business to corrupt competitors, and that levels of corruption in host countries are an important influence on investment decisions. It then examines the legitimate and illegitimate uses of intermediaries in greater detail. In order to evade legal responsibility, companies deny precise knowledge of their representatives' activities. However, plausible deniability implies loss of control, which in turn leads to higher financial costs and an increased risk that the employer will be cheated. In any case, recent legal reforms mean that there is now a higher risk that companies employing intermediaries to pay bribes will be prosecuted. The chapter reviews recent legal cases, and analyses companies' responses. Finally, it reviews other possible 'alternatives' to bribery, including the use of charitable donations and political pressure to gain commercial advantage.

Corruption and competition

Companies operate in the world as it is, not the world as it should be. No one relishes paying bribes, but business people may be tempted to pay when this seems to be an accepted part of the 'system' and there is no apparent alternative. The temptations are particularly severe when companies believe that their competitors are themselves paying bribes.

The Control Risks' survey showed that companies take the pressures of corrupt competition seriously. A significant proportion of respondents in the survey believed that they had lost business in the previous year or the previous five years because a competitor had paid a bribe. However, as Table 7.1 shows, there were wide variations by country of origin, sector and size of company.

A majority of Hong Kong (56 per cent) and Singaporean (52 per cent) companies believed that they had lost business in the last year because a competitor paid a bribe. By contrast, US and British companies, which are the leaders in implementing anti-corruption best practice (see pp. 125–9), were the least likely

Table 7.1 Companies that lost business because a competitor paid a bribe, by country

Country	In the last 12 months (%)	In the last 5 years (%)
Hong Kong	56.0	60.0
Singapore	52.0	64.0
Netherlands	24.0	40.0
Germany	24.0	36.0
US	18.0	32.0
UK	16.0	26.0
Average	27.2	39.2

to have lost business to bribe-paying competitors. In part that may be because they were the most likely to withhold investment from regions with a high risk of corruption: the survey showed that 48 per cent of British companies and 42 per cent of US companies had been deterred from markets with high corruption risks, compared with only 28 per cent of Hong Kong and Singaporean companies.

The figures from Table 7.2 show that public works/construction companies were more likely to have lost business to a bribe-paying competitor than firms in other sectors. Construction companies are particularly exposed because the size of contracts is frequently very large, and this increases the temptations and rewards of bribery. Moreover, public officials often have a high degree of personal influence over the award of construction contracts, which means that they are in a stronger position to seek payment in return for favouring particular firms.

Companies operating in environments where there is a high incidence of corruption face serious dilemmas. They can go along with the system and pay, thus risking blackmail, exposure and legal action. Alternatively, they can refuse to pay, in which case they may find it hard to find business. Or they can refuse to invest in the country at all. Table 7.3 shows that a significant proportion of companies had chosen this option, though there was a wide variation between different sectors.

The two sectors at the top of the list are among those most likely to have lost

Table 7.2 Companies that lost business because a competitor paid a bribe, by sector

Sector	In the last 12 months (%)	In the last 5 years (%)
Public works/construction	40.4	55.8
Pharmaceuticals/medical care	28.6	35.7
Telecommunications	27.3	40.9
Oil, gas and mining	26.1	43.5
Banking and finance	24.1	34.2
Retail	21.4	28.6
Defence	20.0	30.0
Power generation and transmission	18.8	31.3

Table 7.3 Companies deterred from an otherwise attractive investment on account of a country's reputation for corruption, by sector

Sector	Percentage
Oil, gas and mining	52.2
Public works, construction	44.2
Retail	42.9
Banking and finance	39.2
Power generation/transmission	37.5
Pharmaceuticals/medical care	35.7
Arms and defence	30.0
Telecommunications	27.3

business because of bribery: evidently they have been stung by their experiences. Oil, gas and mining companies face particularly acute dilemmas because the most attractive new opportunities are often in countries with poor standards of governance. The survey suggests that in many cases they decided that the corruption risk was simply too high in spite of favourable geological and commercial prospects. The low ranking of the telecommunications industry is striking, and may reflect intense competition among telecommunication companies to establish themselves in emerging markets ahead of their rivals.

Staying away is the ultimate form of risk avoidance, but it also means missing opportunities. Since this is not an attractive option, many try to find an alternative approach to manage corruption-related risks. Employing an intermediary is one of the most popular strategies.

The uses of intermediaries

If international companies are to compete successfully in unfamiliar countries they need local knowledge, and this is all the more important in regions where the administration of contracts lacks transparency. Companies therefore typically use a variety of intermediaries who are better acquainted with local norms – what actually happens as well as what is supposed to happen. Commercial agents are one example; others include consultants, joint venture partners and local subsidiary companies. The employment of such intermediaries is legitimate, and in some jurisdictions essential. By making use of their services, foreign companies cut back the time and effort that would otherwise be necessary to get to know a new market, and therefore reduce the transaction costs of operating there.

Companies typically choose agents and joint venture partners because of their personal connections as well as their professional expertise. In many cases, agents are former employees of government departments, and have friends and former colleagues who are still in office. In Chinese terms (see Schramm and Taube, Chapter 10, this volume), they have good *guanxi*. This enhances their value: if they know key local figures personally, they are more likely to be able to win business. They can get things done.

However, such intermediaries may pay bribes on their employers' behalf, either because they are poorly supervised or because this is the intention of their employers – whether overtly expressed or not. In the Control Risks' survey, respondents gave their views on how far companies from the US and other OECD countries used middlemen – such as agents, consultants and joint venture partners – to get round anti-corruption laws. Table 7.4 points to a widespread perception that they do so 'occasionally' or 'regularly'.

Market corruption

Lambsdorff (2002: 222, citing Husted [1994] and Scott [1972]) refers to two forms of corruption involving middlemen: *market corruption* and *parochial corruption*. Market corruption is a 'competitive form of corruption with a high

Table 7.4 In your opinion, do US or other OECD-based companies circumvent anti-corruption laws using middlemen?

	Never (%)	Occasionally (%)	Regularly (%)	Nearly always (%)	Don't know (%)
US	6.8	47.2	20.0	2.8	23.2
Companies from other OECD countries	5.6	55.6	21.6	–	17.2

degree of transparency'. Lambsdorff cites the examples of *coyotes* who facilitate applications for drivers' licences in Mexico, and *tramitadores* who deal with cumbersome bureaucracies in El Salvador. Another example comes from Brazil where *despachantes* or 'fixers' specialise in obtaining driving licences or sorting out visa problems.[3]

Despachantes know the bureaucratic ropes, and can work their way round difficulties. It is generally understood that they may make payments to ensure that their clients' papers move swiftly from desk to desk, but the amounts paid are low. This is partly because of the competition that they face from rival *despachantes*, which means that they operate in a competitive market. Competition is reinforced by the routine nature of the transactions they handle, which means that it is usually possible for clients to seek similar services elsewhere.

The role of *despachantes* is socially recognised in Brazil: many operate from offices where their profession is openly proclaimed by their name-plates. This does not necessarily mean that market corruption as represented by such fixers is socially desirable. Paradoxically, the practice of paying 'speed money' slows down government transactions because it gives officials an incentive to create delays in the hope of receiving payment for removing them. The people who have to pay extra for government services are often those who are least able to afford the money.

Many international companies tolerate the dynamics of market corruption, often on the grounds that small payments – whether paid directly or via an intermediary – are part of the 'local culture'. The US FCPA does not cover 'facilitating payments', which are defined as those intended to speed up 'routine governmental actions' such as the installation of telephones. However, companies that tolerate facilitating payments may find it more difficult to resist demands for more substantial payments – for example, when bidding for contracts.[4] This leads to a discussion of the second form of corruption involving intermediaries – parochial corruption – which is the main focus of this chapter.

Parochial corruption

Lambsdorff defines parochial corruption as a 'transaction with few potential contractors and, thus, restricted competition'. Since there is limited competition, contractors are often in a position to seek high fees.

A typical example would be a case where a company employs a commercial agent to help it win a government contract. The agent is paid a commission based on a percentage of the contract fee. Often, the agent passes on part of that commission to a government official or a politician in return for confidential information or for favourable treatment in the bidding process. Such payments can amount to significant amounts of money. As former businessman Moody-Stuart points out:

> Five per cent of $200,000 will be interesting to a senior official below the top rank; 5 per cent of $2m is in the top official's area; 5 per cent of $20m is real money for a minister and his key staff; 5 per cent of $200m justifies the serious attention of the head of state.
>
> (Moody-Stuart 1997: 13)

The beneficiaries of such transactions are, first, the companies who win contracts that would otherwise go to competitors, second, the intermediaries who charge high fees, and third, the officials who receive kickbacks. However, there are high social costs. First, bribe payments increase the overall price, which means that there is less money available for other projects. The host government, and the taxpayer, therefore lose out. Second, contractors often recover the costs of bribes through sub-standard performance, or by using cheaper materials. This is particularly dangerous in the case of construction. Turkey's recent experience illustrates the hazards. The country is full of *kacak* or 'contraband' structures whose builders paid bribes to avoid official regulations and tendering procedures. In the 1999 earthquake, such buildings were the first to collapse. The daily *Hurriyet* summed up the problem succinctly, 'Corruption kills people, not earthquakes.'[5]

Trust and deniability

International business people often comment that middlemen provide a 'buffer' or a 'cushion' between them and corrupt officials. It is conceivable that the middleman may have to pay bribes on his foreign employer's behalf. However, it is widely supposed that the latter does not need to know what is going on. Indeed, as one senior UK-based businessman in the defence sector argued to Control Risks, it might even be regarded as intrusive to enquire too deeply into the agent's personal affairs.

If this relationship is to work, the representative needs to be someone whom both sides can trust (on the importance of trust, see Lambsdorff 2002; Lambsdorff and Teksoz, Chapter 8, this volume). As Moody-Stuart points out:

> It is no doubt because confidence and trust are their stock-in-trade that representatives as a class are almost always solid and respectable citizens. Those who have not met – or do not know that they have met – any of these people should set aside images of second-hand car dealers or confidence tricksters. If these men cannot talk comfortably with ministers and

even heads of state on the one hand and mix socially with chief executives and chairmen of large companies on the other, they are incapable of doing their job.

(Moody-Stuart 1997: 31)

The bribe-taker may trust the intermediary because he or she is a former colleague. However, the middleman is just as likely to be a well-connected 'outsider' – either a member of an ethnic minority or a non-citizen – rather than a member of the dominant group. Well-connected individuals of South Asian origin are said to play this role in East Africa, as are Chinese in parts of South-East Asia. Paradoxically, the social vulnerability of these semi-outsiders makes them more trustworthy to officials and politicians belonging to the majority group because it creates a degree of mutual dependence. Ethnic minority 'fixers' are in no position to seek political power on their own account.

For the foreign partner, an element of deniability is crucial because – at least in theory – it mitigates legal risks. He or she will therefore give general instructions to agents, and typically pays by commission rather than asking for detailed activity reports or itemised bills. If the intermediary is found to have paid a bribe, the company can try to deny responsibility, arguing that the middleman acted on his own initiative. Such claims played an important part in the attempted – but ultimately unsuccessful – defence of the Canadian company Acres in the Lesotho Highlands Water Project case (see pp. 122–5).

There may be an element of denial in companies' internal relationships as well as their external ones. In the Control Risks' survey, respondents were asked where corruption was most likely to occur. As Table 7.5 shows, nearly half pointed to senior management. However, a total of 67 per cent pointed to locally based country managers and middle managers.

Middle managers are on the commercial front line. They are often keenly aware of the competition, and they are typically under pressure to deliver quick results. They know that they will be rewarded for success rather than virtuous failure: an inability to win contracts because a competitor is paying bribes is unlikely to win them promotion. As a result, middle managers – like external intermediaries – often hear mixed messages: 'By the way, our code tells you not to pay bribes, but the main thing is to win business.'

These mixed messages can lead to cynicism. A Japanese company has

Table 7.5 Where corruption occurs, which sections of a company are most likely to be involved?

Section	Percentage
Senior management such as divisional directors	47.2
Locally based country managers	41.2
Middle managers	25.6
Junior staff	9.2
Don't know	7.2

recently adopted the US practice of requiring managers to sign annual compliance statements, swearing that they have paid no bribes. One executive told Control Risks that he believed his company's compliance policy was intended to protect senior management, not its middle-ranking employees. His bosses still expected him to win business by whatever means necessary – including bribery. If he were discovered to have paid a bribe, the company would use the annual compliance statement as an excuse for denying responsibility, and would leave him to his fate.

Such cynicism can rebound on the company. If employees do not trust the company to look after their interests they are more likely to 'blow the whistle', giving evidence of the company's past lapses in return for protection from the authorities. Alternatively, they may resort to blackmail. In one case known to Control Risks, an employee tried to blackmail her company by threatening to publicise evidence of tax-related corruption in the Middle East unless she was promoted.

Uncontrolled risks

Deniability is supposed to provide the company with a degree of legal protection. As will be seen, this supposition is questionable. Moreover, plausible deniability implies a loss of control: the company cannot claim ignorance if it is found to have been closely involved in managing the intermediary's activities. Loss of control in turn has a 'boomerang effect' exposing the company to new costs and risks, in addition to the legal hazards that it is trying to avoid.

First, at the most basic financial level, there will be important cost implications. If agents regard bribe-paying as normal, they will make no attempt to resist demands, or reduce prices. The employer is in no position to monitor the bargaining process because it has deliberately chosen not to be involved. If the intermediary is paid according to a percentage of the contract value, he has an incentive to raise prices – to the financial detriment of the company but, still more, the host government.

Second, the use of an intermediary is meant to provide a short cut to local knowledge and expertise. However, if the foreign company fails to make an initial investment in gathering such knowledge, it is likely to be cheated. Two examples from different jurisdictions illustrate the potential risks:

1   A defence services company operating in the Middle East was approached by a would-be intermediary who claimed to be a close relative of a local ruler. He promised to use his connections to help win a large contract. The company made due diligence enquiries. It established that the would-be agent was indeed a relative of the ruler, but had fallen out with him some years previously. His services would have been useless.
2   A development specialist in the Philippines reports that agents frequently approach contractors hoping to work for his organisation. In some cases they offer to work for a 'success fee', receiving payment only if the client

wins the contract. Then they do nothing. Sometimes the client wins the contract on merit, in which case the agents claim a fat fee. Even if this only happens in a minority of cases, they can still make a good living. At least there are no social costs here. Indeed, the agents arguably perform a useful social function by imposing a gullibility tax on unscrupulous contractors.

Third, the international company may find it difficult to enforce contracts with intermediaries even when – or particularly when – they do have the 'right' contacts. This applies particularly to joint venture partners who are chosen on the basis of their political connections. In the short term, the local partner may use its connections to assist the foreign investor. In the longer term, it may use them to take control over the joint venture altogether and the foreign partner may have little recourse, particularly if it lacks majority ownership. The follow-ing case study from Central Africa provides an example:

> A Western company was looking for a joint venture partner in a project to make and sell office machinery. It selected a prominent local businessman who had no technical expertise but was closely associated with the national president. The project was a commercial success, but the original investors did not benefit. The local partner used his presidential connections to help him gain majority control over the venture. The foreign investors threat-ened to go to court, but this was an empty threat in a country where legal disputes last for years, and underpaid judges are notoriously susceptible to financial inducements from people in power.

Fourth, by breaking the law, the company exposes itself to blackmail, includ-ing by the intermediary himself. In one case there was a dispute over payment between a Western European company and a commercial representative in South-East Asia. The representative threatened to leak details of the company's dealings to the international press unless his claims were paid in full. The head office had not previously known, or wished to know, about the subtleties of local transactions carried out on the company's behalf. The blackmail threat meant that it was forced to confront its own lack of knowledge, and loss of control. Deniability had turned into a liability.

The changing legal environment

Recent reforms

Current legal reforms increase the risks of using intermediaries without proper controls. The most important recent international legal initiative is the OECD Convention on Combating Bribery of Foreign Public Officials in International Business Transactions.[6] The convention was signed in December 1997 by 34 countries, the then 29 OECD member states and five others.[7] Since then a further country, Slovenia, has acceded to the convention. The convention follows the example of the US Foreign Corrupt Practices Act (FCPA) in that signatories have undertaken to introduce laws making it possible to prosecute companies for paying bribes outside their home countries.

Article 1 of the OECD convention states explicitly that companies may not pay bribes 'either directly or through intermediaries', and this principle has been carried through into the national laws introduced by the signatories to the convention.

As with other aspects of anti-corruption legislation, the clearest legal precedents to date come from the US where companies may be liable for prosecution even if they do not have direct knowledge that the intermediary has paid a bribe on their behalf. The FCPA is particularly clear on this point: it states that companies are deemed to have knowledge of corruption if they believe that it is 'substantially certain to occur' in the circumstances. A US lawyer specialising on the FCPA comments as follows:

> Such circumstances would obviously include, for example, the making of payments to an 'agent' who did not perform any apparent service, or whose payment was grossly disproportionate to the value of any services that he or she could legitimately render, or where payments ended up in the hands of a prohibited recipient who rendered or was expected to render, improper services.
>
> (Deming n.d.: 5, citing Cruver 1994)

Case studies

The US authorities have on several occasions taken action against companies that have allowed intermediaries to pay bribes on their behalf, and cases involving intermediaries are also emerging in other jurisdictions. The following examples illustrate some of the issues.

International companies in Singapore

In February 1996 the Singapore government banned five large foreign companies from bidding for new government contracts for a period of five years. The five companies were Marubeni, Tomen (Japan), BICC (UK), Siemens (Germany) and Pirelli (Italy). Earlier the Singapore courts had prosecuted Choy Hon Tim, a former deputy chief executive of the state-owned Public Utilities Board (PUB), on charges of criminal conspiracy and receiving bribes worth a total of US$9.82m since 1979. Choy was accused of passing on privileged information on PUB tenders to a former colleague, Lee Peng Siong, who in turn served as a consultant to foreign companies. Choy was sentenced to 14 years in jail; Lee had already moved to Australia.[8]

A spokesman for Marubeni acknowledged that it had had a consultancy contract with Lee, but it had only paid him consultancy fees: it was not involved in bribery.[9] The Singaporean authorities did not accept ignorance as a defence.

Triton Energy Corporation in Indonesia

In early 1997, the US Securities and Exchange Commission (SEC) filed a civil action against Triton Energy Corporation and Philip Keever and Richard McAdoo, two former senior officers of the subsidiary company Triton Indonesia. They were accused of authorising 'numerous improper payments' to Roland Siouffi, a business agent acting as an intermediary between Triton Indonesia and government agencies.[10]

In 1989 Triton had become the operator of a joint venture oil and gas recovery project on Sumatra, and had to pay Indonesia's national oil company for the use of the pipeline. The payments were allegedly part of an effort to obtain a favourable judgement on tax refunds on these payments.

The SEC charged Triton with 'knowing or recklessly disregarding the high probability that Siouffi either had or would pass such payments along to Indonesian government employees . . .' The phrase 'recklessly disregarding the high probability' underlines the point that the US authorities will not accept ignorance as a legitimate defence. Triton agreed to pay a US$300,000 penalty and Keever a US$50,000 penalty, without admitting or denying the charges.[11]

Saybolt in Panama

Saybolt Inc. was a US company specialising in the inspection of bulk commodities, including gasoline and other petrochemical products. In December 1995, it paid a US$50,000 bribe to a Panamanian official in order to obtain a favourable location for an inspection facility near the Panama Canal. Saybolt paid the bribe through a Dutch-affiliated company in the mistaken belief that it would thereby escape liability under the FCPA.

The bribe came to light during government investigations into a completely separate issue – a violation of the US Clean Air Act through false data submissions to the Environmental Protection Agency (EPA). In January 1999 Saybolt pleaded guilty to making an illegal payment of US$50,000 to Panamanian officials.[12] The company paid a fine of US$1.5m. David Mead, Saybolt's former chief executive, was later sentenced to four months in jail, four months of home detention and three years' probation.

The Lesotho Highlands Water Project

The Lesotho Highlands Water Project (LWHP) cases are the most recent and – arguably – the most important of the examples under review.

In September 2002 Acres International, a Canadian engineering firm, was convicted on two charges of paying some US$260,000 in bribes to Masupha Sole, the chief executive of LHWP. Acres was subsequently ordered to pay a fine of 22m Maloti (US$2.25m). The company appealed, and in August 2003 the appeal court issued its judgment. It upheld the first charge, dismissed the second, and reduced the fine to 15m Maloti.[13]

The LWHP is a major dam project designed to supply water and electricity from Lesotho to South Africa. The project is sponsored by – among others – the World Bank, the European Investment Bank, a number of commercial banks, and the British, French, German and South African export credit agencies. In 1991 Acres was awarded a contract worth US$21m through a sole-source tendering process.

The case revolved around Acres' relationship with its Lesotho representative, Zalisiwonga Bam. Many of the key facts of the case were uncontested. Acres had made a series of payments to Bam and his wife through numbered Swiss bank accounts. Bam in turn had regularly passed on some 60 per cent of the money that he received to Sole. In a separate case, Sole was himself convicted of receiving bribes from a dozen international companies in May 2002: he was subsequently sentenced to 18 years' imprisonment.

The key question in the Acres case was whether the company had known that Bam was passing on the money to Sole. Bam himself died in 1999, and was therefore unable to testify. Sole has maintained silence both in his own court case and in related trials. In a statement issued in September 2002, Acres maintained that it had no knowledge of the payments:

> Acres had no knowledge or suspicion of these payments, could not have anticipated them, had no motive for them, and received no benefit. The unlawful payments were entirely between the now-deceased representative and the project director.[14]

The company added:

> This decision sets a dangerous precedent that, if allowed to stand, will greatly increase the risk to companies (consulting engineers, contractors, suppliers, etc.) who do business in developing countries. The trial court surprisingly ignored Acres' entirely legitimate reasons for retaining a local representative in a particularly unstable country at that time, as well as the fact that Acres' agreement with the representative expressly prohibits illegal activities such as the payment of bribes.

Both the original judgment and the appeal acknowledged that – in the absence of a statement from either Bam or Sole – the court's verdict was based on circumstantial evidence. However, they argued that the evidence was compelling. The arguments brought by the Crown included:

- It was not clear why Acres needed to employ Bam as its representative. The final draft of the representative agreement was concluded in November 1990. Acres had already been working on an earlier contract with the LWHP since 1986, and Acres' executives were already employed on secondment at a senior level in the LHWP. Bam himself was resident not in Lesotho but in Botswana from 1988–91.

- No documents such as invoices were made to justify the payments, and no one in the Lesotho Highlands Development Authority or the Lesotho/ South African Joint Permanent Technical Commission (JPTC), which administer the project, was aware that Bam was Acres' agent. The payments were ostensibly made to an entity known as Associated Consultants and Project Managers (ACPM). The Crown argued that Bam had formed ACPM – which was otherwise unknown in Lesotho – to disguise his identity.
- Bam passed on 60 per cent of the payments to Sole either on the same day that he received them, or shortly afterwards. After January 1997, when Sole finally lost his appeal against dismissal from the LHWP, Acres reduced the payments by 60 per cent. The Crown contended that Acres knew that Bam was passing on part of the money, and made the reduction because Sole was no longer in a position to be of service.

The Appeal Court summarised the Crown's case and confirmed the original judgment as follows:

> The only reasonable inference to be drawn from all these facts is that the appellant [Acres] knew that it was paying Bam to use its money to bribe Sole, and that it used Bam as a conduit to disguise this fact. The Crown contended that the RA [representative agreement] between the appellant and Bam was a device to disguise the true purpose of appellant's payments, being corrupt payments to Sole.[15]

Acres is the first of several companies that may face trial on account of payments made to Sole. In June 2003, the German company Lahmeyer International was convicted of paying some US$150,000 to Sole – again through Bam. Lahmeyer had adopted a similar defence to Acres: it said that the payments had been made by Bam in his capacity as a *Freier Mitarbeiter* ('independent co-worker', consultant) without the company's knowledge.[16] Lahmeyer has been sentenced to a fine of 10.65m Maloti (US$1.4m).

These cases have ramifications that extend well beyond Lesotho itself. First, they illustrate the international reputational damage that can be inflicted on companies operating in regions that might once have been considered obscure. The cases have been widely reported on the BBC World Service as well as in the press in South Africa, Canada, the US, the UK and Germany. NGO activists – notably the US-based International Rivers Network (www.irn.org) and the Canadian based Probe International (www.odiousdebts.org) – have done their best to publicise the issues.

Second, the cases may affect the ability of Acres, Lahmeyer and any other convicted companies to win future contracts elsewhere. The World Bank, which has helped finance the LWHP, debars companies and individuals found to have been involved in corruption in Bank-sponsored projects from bidding for future work. In early 2002 the Bank conducted its own review of the bribery allegations against Acres, and decided that there was insufficient evidence to debar it. The Bank is expected to review its decision after the court verdict and the failure of the appeal.

Third, the cases challenge conventional judgment on the causes of corruption in Africa, and on African countries' capacity to deal with it. The findings of the court point clearly to international companies as sources of corruption, and not simply as victims. Now, an African state is taking the initiative to tackle the problem. However, as Lesotho officials point out, the costs of investigating and prosecuting a case of this complexity were enormous for a country with limited resources. The Lesotho case sets a precedent. Other developing countries may not find it easy to follow.

Finally, Lesotho has clear lessons for international companies. Conventional wisdom on the employment of agents no longer applies.

Company responses and emerging best practice

The Control Risks survey showed that international companies were responding to the new legal environment arising out of the OECD convention and other reforms, but that the pace of change was uneven. Responses in the UK, Germany and the Netherlands – the three countries who have introduced new legislation as a result of the convention – showed significant variations.

Table 7.6 shows that relatively few companies were familiar with the convention itself – less than half in Germany and the Netherlands. However, levels of awareness had risen in the UK since an earlier Control Risks' survey in 1999, when only 36 per cent of respondents were familiar with the convention (Bray 1999). Germany and the Netherlands were not covered in the 1999 survey.

More importantly, a majority of companies in all three countries were familiar with their own new anti-corruption laws. Many of these had reviewed their own business practices as a result. However, Tables 7.6 and 7.7 point to significant variations both by country and between different commercial sectors. British companies were most likely to have reviewed their practices, and Germans least likely.

In response to other survey questions, some 52 per cent of German survey respondents agreed that corruption was 'widespread in international business', but 80 per cent said that it was 'of no real significance'. By contrast, only 36 per

Table 7.6 Impact of the OECD convention

	Companies familiar with the OECD convention (%)	Companies familiar with main points of their own countries' new laws (%)	Companies that have reviewed business practices as a result of the new laws (%)
UK	56	68	52
Germany	38	52	24
Netherlands	30	60	44

cent of British companies agreed that corruption was widespread, and only 20 per cent said that it was of no real significance.

German companies are heavily exposed in Eastern European countries with a high incidence of corruption. However, it is doubtful whether their exposure to particular markets accounts for the difference in attitudes. If anything, the argument goes the other way: 48 per cent of British companies had stayed clear of an otherwise attractive investment on account of concerns about a country's reputation for corruption, compared with only 40 per cent of German companies.

Differences in public and official attitudes may provide a partial explanation. At the time of writing (September 2003) neither government had prosecuted a transnational bribery case. However, foreign bribes were tax-deductible in Germany until recent legal reforms, and this was widely publicised and accepted. German companies may therefore be less sensitive than their British counterparts to the reputational risks of being caught up in foreign corruption scandals.

Table 7.7 shows that – among sectors – oil, gas and mining were the most responsive to the new legislation, and telecommunications the least. Only 23.5 per cent of public works/construction companies had reviewed business practices, even though the risk of bribery appears to be high in that sector.

The desire to avoid prosecution may be an important part of the commercial case for high standards of integrity, but it is not the only one. As discussed, intermediaries who are prone to bribery may well cost more money. Above all, they put the company's reputation at risk. There is now a growing consensus on best practice concerning the management of intermediaries. The outstanding issues concern implementation rather than theory.

Company codes

At a minimum, a company code will need to make clear that its integrity requirements apply equally to company employees and to third parties acting on the company's behalf.

Table 7.7 Companies that reviewed procedures as a result of the new anti-corruption legislation

Sector	Percentage
Oil, gas and mining	63.6
Banking and finance	55.8
Retail	37.5
Pharmaceuticals/medical care	33.3
Power generation/transmission	33.3
Arms and defence	31.3
Public works/construction	23.5
Telecommunications	18.2

The International Chamber of Commerce (ICC) rules of conduct on *Extortion and bribery in business transactions* are more specific. These call on enterprises to take measures reasonably within their power to ensure that 'any payment made to any agent represents no more than an appropriate remuneration for legitimate services rendered by such agent'. The definition of an 'appropriate remuneration' is obviously subject to differing interpretations. One approach is to offer a sliding scale of payments rather than a simple percentage, regardless of the size of the project. Payments should be made by cheque or bank transfer rather than in cash, and they must be properly recorded.

The ICC continues by calling on companies to ensure that 'no part of any such payment is passed on by the agent as a bribe or otherwise in contravention of these Rules of Conduct'. In order to obtain this kind of assurance, US companies now typically conduct extensive, well-documented due diligence enquiries into potential agents and business partners, and the employment of agents is subject to senior management approval.

Pre-employment screening of agents

It is therefore all the more important for companies to ensure that they employ the right agents, and a majority of companies conduct background checks in almost all of the jurisdictions included in the Control Risks' survey. However, Table 7.8 points to significant variations between countries. Examples of warning signs include:

- Agents who want to be paid in cash or by other unusual channels.
- Agents who require large cash payments in advance.
- Would-be intermediaries who – by apparent coincidence – volunteer their services at a time when the company is running into unexpected difficulties in its negotiations.
- An agent recommended by one of the officials with whom the company is negotiating.
- Agents who wish to remain anonymous.

Table 7.8 Companies with procedures to vet agents/representatives

Country	Percentage
UK	80
US	74
Netherlands	68
Hong Kong	52
Germany	50
Singapore	40

Integrity clauses in contracts

It is now best practice to include integrity provisions in companies' engagement contracts with agents, and the Control Risks' survey shows that 72 per cent of US companies and 70 per cent of UK companies had such agreements. By contrast Table 7.9 shows that the practice is significantly less common in the Netherlands and Germany – and still less in Hong Kong and Singapore.

Similarly, Table 7.10 points to wide variations by sector, with companies in the extractive industries nearly twice as likely to have formal agreements compared with retail companies.

The provisions in a typical agent's contract should include:

- an acknowledgement by the agent that he understands the company's anti-corruption policy;
- provision for automatic termination of the contract without compensation if the agent makes any improper payment;
- retention of the company's right to audit the agent's agreement, including expenses and invoices.

The OECD Guidelines for Multinational Enterprises calls on companies to maintain 'a list of agents employed in connection with public bodies and state-owned enterprises' that should be 'made available to competent authorities'. It

Table 7.9 Companies that have formal agreements with agents that they will not pay bribes to obtain business, by country

Country	Percentage
UK	72
US	70
Netherlands	46
Germany	32
Hong Kong	24
Singapore	12

Table 7.10 Companies that have formal agreements with agents, by sector

Sector	Percentage
Oil, gas and mining	65.2
Banking and finance	54.4
Arms and defence	50.0
Pharmaceuticals	50.0
Public works/construction	38.5
Power generation/transmission	37.5
Telecommunications	36.4
Retail	35.7

is certainly good practice for companies to keep accurate records of the agreements they have made, whether or not the authorities require them.

Due diligence in joint venture partnerships

Similar issues arise when choosing joint venture partners. Is the foreign partner looking solely at the locals' connections or do they have a technical and commercial track record? What is known about their past? Might they have links with organised crime? Do they have personal or family links with government officials?

As discussed, the question of management control is crucial. Foreign partners are more likely to be exposed to integrity risks – and, in the worst case, the loss of their investment – if they lack control. As one British executive in China explained in a recent interview with Control Risks, it is necessary to 'put your arms around your partners' to ensure that they do not allow standards to slip. More positively, another foreign executive commented that Chinese companies value their relationships with foreign joint venture partners because these make it easier to resist official demands for bribes. They may say that they simply cannot pay because their agreement with the foreign partner will not permit such practices.

Other 'alternatives' to corruption

The use of intermediaries is one of the most popular means of avoiding the appearance – but not necessarily the reality – of involvement in bribery. However, there are many other means of exercising influence. What these strategies have in common is – depending on the precise circumstances – a degree of legal and moral ambiguity, which means that they are not easily captured by legal regulations. By the same token, it may be difficult for the company to enforce what is at most an implicit bargain rather than a legally sanctioned agreement.

Charity and community relations

Corporate charitable donations are often good in themselves, but are rarely wholly disinterested. In principle, authentic charity is unconditional – the giver

Table 7.11 Companies with procedures to vet joint venture partners

Country	Percentage
UK	84
US	70
Netherlands	70
Singapore	64
Germany	54
Hong Kong	48

expects nothing in return. In practice, companies do expect some kind of return, if only in the form of an improved local reputation. Arguably this is entirely legitimate: if a company engages in wholly disinterested charity it may be betraying its fiduciary responsibilities to its shareholders.

Rose-Ackerman (2002: 91–110) has discussed the similarities, differences and occasional overlaps between gifts and bribes. Donors cannot expect a legally sanctioned *quid pro quo* in return for either gifts or bribes. However, there may be an understanding between giver and receiver that is either explicit but concealed in the case of bribes, or implicit in the case of certain kinds of gifts. Corporate charity can lead to similar ambiguities. The Control Risks' survey points to a widespread belief that companies frequently use charitable donations as a means of gaining business advantage (see Table 7.12).

Charitable donations are unlikely to be confused with bribery if they fulfil the following conditions:

- the donations are public;
- they fulfil a genuine need that has been established through local consultation; and
- they are administered by a well-managed organisation which publishes its accounts.

The company is not necessarily expected to be wholly disinterested – indeed it often helps if there is a tangible local connection. For example, corporate donations to hospitals or schools make particular sense if they are likely to be used by company employees.

Genuine charitable donations constitute an expression of goodwill rather than a formal contract: the company may hope for favourable treatment but cannot guarantee it. Nevertheless, if a company has a good local reputation, it is less likely to receive demands for bribes and may find it easier to negotiate with local officials. To that extent, charitable donations can be seen as a strategy to pre-empt bribery, instead of succumbing to it.

Problems arise when donations are seen to lack transparency, or favour powerful individuals rather than the wider community. A donation to a private charity that is run by the president's wife but which does not keep proper accounts would rightly be seen as a bribe by another name. Three companies'

Table 7.12 In your opinion, how often do companies make donations to charities favoured by decision-makers to gain business advantage?

	Never (%)	Occasionally (%)	Regularly (%)	Nearly always (%)	Don't know (%)
US companies	12.4	48.8	14.8	1.2	22.8
Companies from other OECD countries	12.0	52.4	10.8	4.0	24.4

experiences in Pakistan, Eastern Europe and Colombia illustrate the benefits and potential hazards:

> A Western company was drilling for oil in rural Pakistan. Powerful families of landowners still dominate the social hierarchy in that particular region and tend to expect some form of 'tribute'. They have the capacity to create significant obstacles for any company that does not seek their approval. The company found that the landowners appreciated cash, but they also attached considerable importance to status and prestige. The company appointed selected landowners to the boards of its charitable ventures, such as schools and hospitals, thus responding to their desire for status. It took care to ensure that they were not in a position to exercise financial control over the projects, or to allocate funds to favoured recipients. This approach has helped the company to make friends at different social levels, and to pre-empt demands for bribes or other pressures.

In this case, the company did its research and, by imposing financial and administrative control, helped to ensure that its projects were not open to abuse. The second example is more ambiguous:

> A Western company operating in Eastern Europe discovered that the local mayor was keenly interested in the restoration of ancient churches, despite his long-standing personal record as an atheist *apparatchik*. The company decided to sponsor the restoration of a church opposite its offices. It employed a construction company that turned out to be owned by the mayor's brother. The Western sponsor may have had entirely legitimate reasons for employing the mayor's brother. Perhaps his company was the only one with the right technical skills. However, the sponsor is open to accusations that it has simply found another way to channel funds to the family of a senior official.

The third example – this time from Colombia – is perhaps more readily classified as extortion rather than bribery, but illustrates many of the same points. In this case, the international company was even less successful, either in protecting its own interests or in contributing to the local community:

> Company managers tried to pre-empt extortion demands from rural guerrillas in Colombia by building a school for local villagers. The idea was that the villagers would be pleased with the school, and would use their influence with the guerrillas to dissuade them from attacking the company. The plan backfired because the company found itself dealing with a construction firm that was, in effect, a front for the guerrillas. The construction firm's representatives took the money, and the school still has not been built. No one dares complain.

Whatever its intentions, the company's donation had turned into another extortion payment, and it was likely to face further demands.

'Legitimate expenses'

The US FCPA excludes 'legitimate business expenses' from its definition of bribery. Legitimate expenses could include paying for an official to visit a power station or a mine abroad in order to give him a better idea of how such a facility would function in his own country.

The official may well enjoy a foreign trip, and such visits have a legitimate function. However, the practice is open to abuse when – for example – the official is invited to bring family members with him and they are hosted with extra lavishness. In such cases the trip may be seen as a bribe paid in kind. The company thereby incurs several kinds of risks. First, as with other kinds of bribery, the fact that the company has shown itself willing to bend the rules means that it is likely to face further demands for other favours – licit or illicit. It may also face unwelcome publicity when its generosity comes to the attention of the press. Moreover, at least in the US, the company may face legal action.

The Metcalfe & Eddy case: unacceptable expenses

The Metcalfe & Eddy case was a test case brought by the US Department of Justice in 1999. In December 1999, US company Metcalfe & Eddy agreed to pay a civil penalty of US$400,000 and US$50,000 costs incurred by US government investigators in connection with its activities in Egypt.[17] It also agreed to institute remedial actions, including modifications to its FCPA compliance programme.

Metcalfe & Eddy obtained two contracts, worth a total of US$36m, in connection with the US-funded modernisation of Alexandria's sewage and waste-water facilities between 1994 and 1996. Before the first contract was awarded, the company invited the chairman of the Alexandria General Organisation for Sanitary Drainage (AGOSD) to the US, together with his wife and two children. On the first occasion the chairman was invited to a water conference in Chicago. He also visited Boston, Washington and Orlando, Florida. On the second trip, which was linked to the award of the second contract, the chairman and his family visited Paris (France), Boston and San Diego.

On both occasions the company paid almost all of the family's expenses, and paid to upgrade their air tickets from coach to first class. The Department of Justice argued that these benefits were meant to persuade the chairman to exert his influence on the company's behalf.

By prosecuting this case, the US authorities wanted to make clear that the FCPA's 'legitimate expenses' exclusion was not intended to be used as an alternative to more conventional forms of bribery.

Development aid and diplomatic pressure

Embassies play a valuable role in helping companies to identify openings in new markets. In many cases they can help to make introductions both to officials and business partners. They can also warn of potential obstacles, including high levels of bribery. If a company encounters corruption-related problems, the embassy may be able to intercede with senior officials on its behalf. Again, diplomatic intervention can be a means of resisting corruption rather than succumbing to it.

However, like other kinds of influence, diplomatic intercessions need to be carefully judged. From a political risk point of view, inappropriate diplomatic pressure may lay up problems for the future. If a company or project is seen to be 'imposed' on the host country it will eventually face a backlash. The foreign companies that ostensibly benefit from such intervention may not achieve what they hope.

In Transparency International's Bribe Payer's Index (2002), 835 respondents in 15 emerging markets were asked whether they thought that there were 'other means by which governments gain unfair advantage for companies in their countries'. Some 68 per cent of the sample responded affirmatively. The examples of such 'unfair advantage' included diplomatic and political pressure, financial pressure, commercial pricing issues, tied foreign aid and the threat of reduced foreign aid.

The respondents in the Control Risks' survey gave a similar response in answer to a question as to how far US companies and companies from other OECD countries resorted to political pressure as a means of winning business. Table 7.13 points to a widespread belief that they did so either 'regularly' or 'occasionally'.

Both the Transparency International and the Control Risks' surveys pointed to the issue of 'tied aid' whereby donor governments have specifically designated development funds for companies and experts from their own countries. In recent years, this practice has become more controversial in development circles, and the Japanese and many Western governments have officially de-linked aid from commercial opportunities for their own companies. However, Table 7.14 shows that tied aid is still an issue for many international business people.

As with gifts and charitable donations, the link between development aid and specific commercial contracts is often implicit rather than explicit. Nevertheless, diplomatic intercessions will leave the host government with little room for doubt about what is expected.

Table 7.13 In your opinion, how often do international companies use political pressure from their home governments to gain business advantage?

	Never (%)	Occasionally (%)	Regularly (%)	Nearly always (%)	Don't know (%)
US companies	7.6	48.8	25.2	6.0	12.4
Companies from other OECD countries	9.2	54.8	25.6	2.0	8.4

Table 7.14 In your opinion, how often do international companies use tied aid to gain business advantage?

	Never (%)	Occasionally (%)	Regularly (%)	Nearly always (%)	Don't know (%)
US companies	12.4	48.0	22.8	2.8	14.0
Companies from other OECD countries	8.0	58.4	22.8	1.2	9.6

These intercessions do not always succeed. A Scandinavian businessman recently told Control Risks that there had been several cases where his competitors had won contracts as a result of diplomatic pressure or promises of aid from their home governments. On one occasion, this diplomatic manoeuvring unexpectedly worked in his favour. The host government was caught up in fierce diplomatic and commercial rivalry between two major Western countries, and could not decide between them. It therefore 'compromised' by selecting the neutral Scandinavians.

Conclusion and implications

The task of government policy-makers is to erect 'firewalls' against corruption, typically by using legal instruments. It may not be realistic to expect to deter all kinds of corruption, but the legal firewalls should at least make bribery more difficult, and reduce the chances that bribe-payers will achieve their objectives.

The fact that bribery is illegal in itself imposes significant constraints on corrupt relationships. The bargain at the centre of the relationship has to be kept secret, and it may be hard to enforce. Bribe-givers may try to protect themselves by operating via intermediaries. However, this chapter has shown that deals conducted via intermediaries involve costs and risks that do not apply to legitimate business deals. Finding the 'right' intermediary is a hazardous process. Operating via a middleman increases financial costs. And, if trust breaks down, the employer may be subject to blackmail. These risks apply even if there is a low level of legal enforcement.

The risks obviously increase when there is a higher level of enforcement. The US has taken the lead by making clear that the FCPA applies to intermediaries as well as direct employees, and has prosecuted offending companies accordingly. The OECD anti-bribery convention applies to both direct and indirect bribery. Lesotho has successfully prosecuted two international companies for paying bribes through a representative. The Lesotho court's rejection of the claims by Acres and Lahmeyer that they were not aware, and could not have been aware, of their representative's bribe-paying activities sets a particularly important precedent.

Nevertheless, there may still be gaps in the legal frameworks of other jurisdictions. In mid-2003, a UK Joint Parliamentary Committee, made up of members of the House of Commons and the House of Lords, held an inquiry to examine the government's Draft Corruption Bill which was intended to update existing British legislation (House of Commons/House of Lords 2003). The draft does not explicitly address the problem of indirect bribery, and there was some doubt about the extent to which it would cover the activities of British companies' local representatives and other foreign intermediaries. There should be no room for ambiguity on this point.

A related issue concerns the foreign subsidiaries of UK-based companies. The Joint Committee explicitly rejected suggestions that UK anti-corruption laws should extend to foreign subsidiaries, and other Western governments have taken a similar view. Yet subsidiary companies, along with agents and joint venture companies, are among the most commonly used intermediaries for bribe-paying companies.

In any case, legal sanctions are only part of the answer. For major international companies, fear of reputational damage is as important a deterrent as the law. One UK executive interviewed for the Control Risks' survey emphasised the risks to his company of being associated with corruption in any way: 'We carry a well-known logo and therefore cannot afford to have any reports that might damage the company.' Similarly, a Dutch executive commented: 'I think that the risk of reputational damage is a much more effective tool [than the law] in combating corrupt practices.'

The Acres and Lahmeyer cases in Lesotho have shown how the activities of an intermediary can affect a company's reputation just as much as those of a full-time employee. In the long term the reputational damage to these companies may prove to be much more significant than the financial losses inflicted by government fines.

As this chapter was going to press, in September 2003, three cases concerning companies' use of intermediaries were still unfolding. These involved a US company whose agent had allegedly had used Swiss bank accounts to pass on money to Central Asian politicians; a series of scandals concerning 'commissions' paid by European defence manufacturers in South Africa; and a European company's use of a suspiciously expensive consultancy with local political connections in the Middle East.

The existence of these cases points to the continued use of intermediaries as a means of winning international contracts. The legal outcomes are still unresolved, but the secretive nature of the intermediaries' business arrangements – and suspicion of illicit payments – has prompted wide public controversy. Companies have always faced significant financial, legal and reputational risks when employing middlemen without proper controls. These risks are now higher than ever.

Notes

1 The survey was conducted by IRB Ltd on Control Risks' behalf. IRB conducted a total of 250 telephone interviews with 50 companies each in the UK, the US, Germany and the Netherlands, and 25 companies each in Hong Kong and Singapore. All respondents were senior decision-makers at or near board level. All the companies operate internationally. The respondents represented eight different commercial

sectors: banking and finance (31.6 per cent); public works/construction (20.8 per cent); arms and defence (12 per cent); oil, gas and mining (9.2 per cent); telecommunications (8.8 per cent); power generation and transmission (6.4 per cent); retail (5.6 per cent); and pharmaceuticals/medical (5.6 per cent). They represented a range of different sizes of company: over 1,000 employees (44 per cent); 751–1,000 (11.6 per cent); 501–750 (8.4 per cent); 251–500 (19.2 per cent); 0–250 (16.4 per cent).

2   In these cases, details of names, places and companies are disguised in order to preserve confidentiality.

3   The following comments are based on interviews in Brazil in March 2001.

4   For a discussion of the issues involved in petty corruption, see Bray 2001.

5   'Corruption kills people, not earthquakes', *Financial Times*, 19 August 1999.

6   The text on the convention is published on the OECD website: www.oecd.org

7   In 1997 the 29 OECD member states were: Australia, Austria, Belgium, Canada, Czech Republic, Denmark, Finland, France, Germany, Greece, Hungary, Iceland, Ireland, Italy, Japan, Korea, Luxembourg, Mexico, Netherlands, New Zealand, Norway, Poland, Portugal, Spain, Sweden, Switzerland, Turkey, the United Kingdom and the United States. The additional signatories were: Argentina, Brazil, Bulgaria, Chile and the Slovak Republic. Since then, the Slovak Republic has joined the OECD.

8   'Singapore bars five foreign firms from tenders', *Reuters*, 14 February 1996.

9   Sim Wai Chew and Douglas Wong, 'Firms under graft-linked ban "hit badly"', *Straits Times*, 15 February 1996.

10   Tracy Corrigan, 'SEC lodges bribes charges', *Financial Times*, 28 February 1997.

11   'US Securities Exchange Commission. Accounting and Auditing Enforcement', *Release*, no. 889, 27 February 1997, www.sec.gov/litigation/admin/3438343.txt

12   'Former Saybolt Exec gets 4 months in prison, fine', *Reuters*, 2 March 1999. 'Saybolt to pay fine for illegal foreign payments', *Reuters*, 22 January. 'FCPA-related cases', *Business Laws Inc* (4 Supp. 91) April 2000, pp. 600.032–600.039.

13   Lesotho Court of Appeal. *Acres International Limited* vs. *The Crown*. Judges Jan Steyn, Michael Ramobedi and Chris Plewman, 15 August 2003. The full text of the judgment is published on a website administered by the Canadian NGO Probe International: www.odiousdebts.com

14   Acres' press statement. 'Acres International to Appeal Lesotho Court Decision', Toronto, 17 September 2002. Downloaded from www.acres.com

15   Lesotho Court of Appeal judgment, pp. 12–13.

16   Bettina Stang, 'Bestechungsaffäre wird Staudamm-Firmen zum Verhängnis', *Süddeutsche Zeitung*, 20 June 2003.

17   'USAID contractors agrees to pay US$450,000 to resolve Foreign Corrupt Practices Act Allegations', *PR Newswire*, 21 December 1999; *United States of America* v. *Metcalfe & Eddy Inc*, Massachusetts District Court.

References

Bray, J. (1999) 'Surveying Corruption', *Outlook 2000. Global Risk Forecast*, London: Control Risks Group, pp. 13–15.

Bray, J. (2001) 'Bribery and Petty Corruption. Don't Pay', *The World Today 57*, no. 6, London, pp. 17–19.

Control Risks Group (2002a) *Facing up to Corruption. Survey Results 2002*, London.

Control Risks Group (2002b) *Facing up to Corruption. A Practical Business Guide*, London.

Cruver, D. (1994) 'Complying with the Foreign Corrupt Practices Act: a Guide for US Firms Doing Business in the International Marketplace', *American Bar Association Business Law Section*, Chicago.

Deming, S.H. (n.d.) *The Foreign Corrupt Practices Act and the Emerging International Norms*, Washington.

House of Lords/House of Commons (2003) 'Joint Parliamentary Committee on the Draft Corruption Bill. Report and Evidence', HL Paper 157, HC 705, London: The Stationery Office.

Husted, B.W. (1994) 'Honor Among Thieves: a Transaction-cost Interpretation of Corruption in Third-World Countries', *Business Ethics Quarterly*, vol. 4, no. 1, pp. 17–27.

Lambsdorff, J. Graf (2002) 'Making Corrupt Deals: Contracting in the Shadow of the Law', *Journal of Economic Behaviour & Organisation*, vol. 48, no. 3, pp. 221–41.

Moody-Stuart, G. (1997) *Grand Corruption*, Oxford.

Rose-Ackerman, S. (1999) *Corruption and Government. Causes, Consequences and Reform*, Cambridge.

Schramm, M. and Taube, M. (2004) 'The Institutional Economics of Legal Institutions, Guanxi and Corruption in the PR China'. In this volume.

Scott, J.C. (1972) *Comparative Political Corruption*, Englewood Cliffs, N.J.: Prentice-Hall.

Transparency International Bribe Payers Index (2002). Available on www.transparency.org

8   Corrupt relational contracting

Johann Graf Lambsdorff and Sitki
Utku Teksoz

Introduction

> Why are so many politicians lawyers? – because everyone employs lawyers,
> so the congressman's firm is a suitable avenue of compensation, whereas a
> physician would have to be given bribes rather than patronage.
>
> (G.J. Stigler, 'The Theory of Economic Regulation')

There is no doubt that corruption is regarded as one of the modern evils. It is
carried out by those with a criminal intention and motivated by greed. Yet, if
this simple explanation were valid, why would we have to face in reality some
disturbing counter-examples? Why, in particular, do we face a significant pattern
where corrupt people tend to be involved in a variety of charitable institutions?
Why are many bribers and bribees engaging in an assortment of regular business
transactions and political initiatives where they are regarded as trustworthy and
honest partners? Our viewpoint of them as criminals contradicts their social
engagement. The trust they enjoy in their regular relations sounds rather controversial, given their misuse of entrusted power.

A straightforward argument, certainly, would point out that corrupt actors
must be entrusted with power prior to misusing it. There must be opportunities
for corrupt misbehaviour. These opportunities commonly arise where public
office holders are in a monopoly position, have discretion in interpreting, applying or changing the law and are lacking accountability (Klitgaard 1988: 75).
This often takes place in the area of public procurement or where excessive
government regulation interferes with market forces. Since elected politicians
are entrusted with power, while appointed bureaucrats have informational
advantages over their superiors, they can also misuse their position for corrupt
purposes. A certain level of trust is therefore a basic prerequisite to corruption.
But what motivates corrupt people to misuse this power? One hypothesis would
suggest that these are just hypocrites. They may seek to profit from a reputation
for altruism and commitment while in reality self-seeking is all that guides them.
Social engagement would simply serve to camouflage their true intentions.
Their trustworthiness is based on their capacity to disclose their true corrupt
goals. Indeed, there is some truth to this explanation. Nonetheless, this chapter

provides an alternative one. We suggest that a purely corrupt relationship is a rare thing. Corrupt deals are commonly embedded in more complex relationships between different actors. More often than not these relationships entail also a variety of legal transactions, and even charitable ones.

This study aims to examine the link between completely legal relationships and illegal ones. This link, basically, relates to the fact that corrupt arrangements go along with high transaction costs. Corrupt relationships are unstable, and one's word may be dominated by betrayal and fraud. Corrupt agreements may even end in mutual denunciation. Pre-existing legal relationships can lower these transaction costs and serve as a basis for the enforcement of corrupt arrangements. With a focus on transaction costs, the methodology applied here is that of New Institutional Economics. Investigating corruption with the help of New Institutional Economics is a rather novel approach, which has only been implemented recently (Husted 1994; Rose-Ackerman 1999: 91–110; Della Porta and Vannucci 1999; Vannucci 2000; Schramm and Taube 2002; Lambsdorff 1999, 2002a, 2002b). This study contributes to this avenue of research.

In order to establish the link between corruption and legal exchange we will start with a brief review of the New Institutional Economics framework and apply it to corrupt deals (pp. 135–42). How legal exchange can serve as a basis for sealing and enforcing corrupt deals will be illustrated, based on case studies, on pp. 142–3. A final section concludes and provides policy recommendations.

The contribution of the New Institutional Economics

Transaction cost analysis

Since Coase (1937) it has been standard practice to assume that exchanging goods or services goes along with transaction costs. A crucial cause for the existence of these costs is that information is substantially incomplete. A good deal of time and material resources are therefore spent for searching the right contract partner, gathering enough background information about the market conditions, working out the details of the contracts and seeking measures – legal or informal – to cover the parties against opportunistic behaviour. Due to these costs, people's information to assess market opportunities and to predict the future is necessarily incomplete. Another aspect of the transaction costs is that their level is negatively associated to the level of mutual trust among the contract partners (Furubotn and Richter 1998: 49). That is, the less trust among contractors, the more time, effort and money must be spent to organize an exchange. This explains partly why, in the case of large transaction costs, contractual relationships tend to be sticky in that most transactions are carried out repeatedly with well-acquainted business partners rather than with anonymous market participants.

The limited information available to some business partners can be exploited by others who possess an informational advantage. This type of behaviour is generally termed 'opportunism', defined as self-interest seeking with guile

(Williamson 1985). This includes intended forms of deceit such as lying, stealing, distorting, obfuscating, disguising, etc. Opportunism can only arise when information is distributed asymmetrically. Given the presence of *ex ante* asymmetric information, the problem of adverse selection may arise depending on the contract design. A similar argument is viable for the case of *ex post* asymmetric information and the problem of moral hazard. In order to cope with this situation, *ex ante* screening efforts are made and *ex post* safeguards are created (Williamson 1985: 64).

The problem of informational asymmetry is not only one between the contracting parties but also *vis-à-vis* outsiders. Even if both contracting parties are well informed about each other and efforts are exerted, they may not be able to communicate this to a third party. While an employer may know about the shirking of his employee, he may fail to prove this to a court. The issue of informational asymmetry therefore becomes even stronger, because deviations from contracts must not only be observed by partners but also be proven to outsiders. Some issues become non-contractual – not because partners differ in the extent of their knowledge, but because they differ in their ability to prove an accusation to outsiders (Hart 1987: 753).

Relational contracting

Informational asymmetries and the risk or opportunism suggest that resources should be devoted to gathering as much information as possible. Yet, there are transaction costs involved for this purpose. Gathering information is particularly dear in the case of long-term contracts. Here it becomes difficult to anticipate the various eventualities that may occur during the life of a relationship. There arise costs of deciding and reaching an agreement about how to deal with such eventualities, as well as those of writing the contract in a sufficiently clear and unambiguous way so that the terms of contract can be enforced (Hart 1987: 753). Given these costs, it becomes preferable to live with limited information. Contracts will be incomplete because it might be either impossible or simply uneconomic to anticipate all contingencies in advance. As a matter of fact, the information that parties have on the agreed-upon process tends to increase during the contract execution stage compared to the outset (Nelson and Winter 1982: 96–139). Parties generally set off with an initially incomplete contract, especially in long-term relationships such as labour contracts. When further information is obtained in the process of exchange, contracts can then be further specified. Consequently, leaving certain gaps in the contract design appears to be a perfectly rational approach in order to make the contract flexible enough to fit any contingencies. This suggests a 'relational' type of contract with the duration and the complexity of contracts increasing progressively (Macneil 1978: 890). Based on Macneil's work, Williamson (1985) recognizes that between the neo-classical and relational contracting schemes there is a shift of emphasis from the original agreements in the former to the entire relation as it evolves through time in the latter.

Contracts are relational to the extent that it is impossible to reduce the terms of agreement to well-defined obligations (Goetz and Scott 1981: 1091). Instead of well-defined obligations partners now anticipate trouble as a normal outcome, seeking certain measures – apart from legal ones – for their resolution (Macneil 1974: 738–40). Defined as such, relational contracts are implicit, informal and non-binding transactions that are embedded in a structure of relations and long-term business associations (Furubotn and Richter 1998: 158). Due to their incomplete nature, the contracts make part of a continuous relationship. The negotiation stage assumes a continuous character, since it is the implicitly or explicitly stated intention that settling new arrangements takes place by negotiating over future transactions. The term 'continuous' is employed in the sense that there are no strictly defined and pre-specified beginning and ending terms of the relations. The continuity of enforcement and renegotiations stabilizes the relationship (Macneil 1974: 753).

While a simple neo-classical analysis of exchange assumes anonymity of exchange partners, relational contracting suggests that the identity of the people engaged in transactions matters. Certain transactions are bound to remain within a closed group of associates. Such cost-minimizing transactions require an initial investment in transaction-specific resources. One refers to this as a specialization of identity. Identity matters because engaging in a certain transaction necessitates the negotiation of certain rules, norms or codes of conduct among the related parties. Once the identities of the contracting parties change, the whole process starts over, implying new transaction costs. The identity-specific exchange relationships are themselves deterrent against opportunistic behaviour, as cheating now would spare the parties from future benefits of the ongoing relation (Ben-Porath 1980: 1–6). Individuals tend to conduct their relations within their own group, not only because of the transaction costs of finding new partners but also because effective sanctions can be imposed more efficiently within a small group.[1] Accordingly, reliance on reciprocal business relationships and group enforcement mechanisms are transaction cost-reducing mechanisms (Klein, Crawford and Alchian 1978).

Contract enforcement mechanisms can be purposefully designed with an aim to contain opportunistic behaviour. However, the causality may also run in reverse direction; that is, relationships might be conducted exclusively among people with an already established degree of social embeddedness so as to ensure the honouring of contracts. Presence of social embeddedness, such as being colleagues in a certain institution or network, makes opportunism a less likely outcome. Being embedded in a social relationship facilitates containing opportunism, thanks to the presence of safeguarding mechanisms (Granovetter 1992). Social embeddedness, such as family and kinship ties, is a condition that outlives the duration of contracts. Furthermore, these cannot be changed easily. Therefore, an individual would have an interest in staying loyal to his group, even when the temptation for opportunism is great.

Corrupt contracting

In a variety of respects, an analysis of legal contracts can fruitfully be applied to corrupt contracts. There are apparent parallels: partners may cheat each other; there might be informational asymmetries; safeguards against opportunism must be supplied; trust might be instrumental to design a corrupt transaction; social embeddedness may facilitate corrupt deals. And because all these mechanisms go along with transaction costs, unresolved contractual problems between partners are likely.

However, there are three major differences between corrupt and legal deals concerning transaction costs and enforcement mechanisms (Lambsdorff 2002a). First, courts do not enforce corrupt deals. Therefore, private ordering must be perfected to such an extent that it completely substitutes for the lack of legal sanctions. The associated transaction costs are likely to increase considerably and the remaining loopholes are expected to be numerous. Second, corrupt deals are sealed in secrecy. This implies that transaction costs associated with sealing corrupt deals are substantially higher. Searching partners, negotiating and enforcing contracts has to be carried out away from the eyes of the public. Transparent means, such as advertising, are not available. Alternative forms have to be sought that are likely to be more expensive. Third, the corrupt deals have an aftermath, unlike the legal ones. The parties are mutually dependent on one another because they hold secret information about the other party. Corrupt deals put the partners of such deals at the mercy of one another. Even long after the service in question is rendered, the partners remain in a binding relationship of mutual dependence, which can also serve as a basis for extortion or hush money. Denunciation can be used as a threat when one of the parties has more to lose from a potential exposure of involvement in corrupt activities.

If there are prospects of negotiating further contracts with the same people over time, both the transaction costs and risks associated with the advertising, gaining trust and forming a capital of common knowledge are substantially reduced. The process of seeking partners, negotiating and enforcing contracts displays considerable risks of denunciation in each stage, which forces corrupt relationships to have a closed nature *vis-à-vis* the outsiders. Therefore, the very illegality of corruption makes it imperatively an identity-specific transaction. Trust becomes a crucial element in corrupt deals. In order to cover the parties against *ex post* opportunistic behaviour, corrupt deals are more often than not sealed between parties enjoying a considerable degree of mutual trust.

Linking corruption to legal exchange

Corrupt contracts go along with higher transactional difficulties than legal contracts. There exists a variety of mechanisms to lower these transaction costs. Some of these are discussed in Husted (1994), Lambsdorff (1999, 2002a, 2002b), Della Porta and Vannucci (1999), Vannucci (2000) and Rose-Ackerman (1999: 91–110). Here we focus on one such mechanism: linking a corrupt deal to an established legal relationship. The presence of a perfectly legal relationship between two parties may set a fertile ground for corrupt deals to flourish. Corruption in this case is not a single act between anonymous partners. Rather, it is embedded into a complex relationship. Corruption comprises implicit, informal and non-binding agreements, which are enforced by being rooted in long-term business or hierarchical associations.

In an attempt to carry out legal deals there are commonly a variety of means available to business partners to sanction each other. They can destroy each other's reputation, end profitable future exchange, penalize each other when provided with hierarchical control, or transform their existing friendship into a relationship with mutual accusations. Threatening such sanctions helps the enforcement of legal deals. In the presence of already established legal relationships, the parties might find it tempting to collude for proceeding with a corrupt deal. As their legal relationship provides the possibility to sanction each other, threatening sanctions can also be used to enforce a corrupt side-agreement. Above that, they can economize on search costs because they already know each other and simply expand the range of exchange to also include also corrupt agreements. For anonymous partners it will be difficult to carry out a corrupt transaction. But for those with pre-existing legal ties it will be much easier to link their corrupt transaction to the established legal relationship. Parties may initially start off with a legal relationship, which later deteriorates into one where corrupt deals are also carried out. The presence of trust in this case facilitates the process. The core proposition of this study is therefore that corrupt transactions are often linked to legal ones. Corrupt transactions are often embedded in social relationships where also a variety of legal transactions are carried out. We will discuss some case studies in this section to show how the theory applies to real life.

Three case studies from Germany

Case study 1

A recent corruption scandal in Germany involved Günter R., an ex-social democratic MP from Bielefeld.[2] The news that Günter R. was arrested on charges of corruption fell like a bomb right into the heart of his hometown, Bielefeld. Hadn't he been almost an ideal example of a 'good citizen' for years and years? His social commitment had been exemplary. He was engaged in a series of charity organizations, NGOs and non-profit organizations, with a particular emphasis on education. Nonetheless, he was accused of having abused these positions for self-enrichment, this amounting to six-digit figures of deutschmarks in a period spanning 1995–2000. One of the foundations, whose chair was held by Günter R., operated a non-profit company for lifestyle and education projects co-operation with the German youth hostel association. These projects involved a considerable amount of construction. In the mid-1990s, the acquaintance between Lutz-Peter B., the managing director of a construction enterprise, and Günter R. grew closer. This acquaintance pushed the non-profit targets of the Bielefeld politician to the background. He had a free hand to mediate certain contracts to the former's enterprise. Over-invoicing was used to hide the crimes. Against these invoices, the non-profit organizations led by Günter R. paid exaggerated sums, the kickbacks being divided between himself and the managers of the enterprise. The illegal cash flow was also masked by the fact that Günter R. received wages for his alleged activity as a 'construction supervisor'.

What conclusions should one draw from this case and countless similar ones? One might suggest that these people simply disguised their true nature and used their position to camouflage their corrupt transactions. An alternative proposition is that social engagement, trusted relationships within firms, and a reputation for honesty are not at all in contrast to corrupt dealings. Quite to the contrary, Günter R. needed his reputation so as to be trusted when it came to striking corrupt deals. Had he been regarded as purely self-seeking he might not have been able to establish a trusted relationship with Lutz-Peter B.

Case study 2

As of 1992, Leonard A., director of Bayerische Vereinsbank in Potsdam, was tired of working in hastily erected provisional accommodation – like most of his competitors who had rushed into the former East Germany's banking market after reunification. Instead, he dreamt of a luxurious office in the best area of the city of Potsdam, on a site owned by the city where construction was still blocked by pending restitution claims. There was yet another problem: one of the major competitors of the Bayerische Vereinsbank also showed interest in the property, hence drawing attention to the area. In order to work around these impediments A. sought out his friend and tennis partner Detlef K., city official for construction and housing since 1990. He let their personal relations play a role in the quest for the site. Consequently, A. obtained a construction permit before ordinary procedures had been finalized, and his bank was pre-ferred over its competitor when the city sold the building site. In exchange, the bank gave K. a legally certified option for buying an exquisite mansion for a price considerably below the market price. The contract was formulated such that K. did not participate directly as a buyer; instead he was only given an option to buy the aforementioned dwelling. The winds, however, changed for all participants. First, the city mayor Horst G. rotated the personnel in the city office for construction and housing. In the meantime, higher authorities from the Bayerische Vereinsbank declared the option for K. void. This had an impact on the friendship between the two tennis partners. What other explanation could there be for the fact that years later, two friends of K. accused A. of demanding personal gratification in exchange for giving out bank loans, provid-ing taped evidence? A. fought back by denouncing the former illegal deal with K. While A. was serving a 30-month prison term, K. was expelled from office in 1998.[3]

A regular relationship – in the legal sense – and friendship served as a basis to strike a corrupt deal. In A.'s case, seeking a city official with sufficient criminal capability to deliver him the corrupt service would have been a costly and risky undertaking. Offering bribes in the open might also have backfired. However, he had an established relation with the right official, which happened to be his tennis partner K. Therefore, he did not have to invest resources into seeking a partner or into enquiring about a potential partner's criminal capacities. Resources were spent into organizing a contract for K. to buy a mansion below the market price, a hidden agreement that would pass for the actual payment for the corrupt service under consideration. Here one sees clearly the inevitable need for secrecy, a distinguishing feature of corrupt deals. For whatever reasons, G. decided to rotate his officials and K. ceased to hold this critical position. This ended the legal base that was needed to enforce the corrupt side-agreement. There was no scope for future legal transactions that could have limited opportunism. The Bayerische Vereinsbank was therefore induced to act opportunistically by revoking the option for buying the mansion. The former friendship deteriorated into a relationship with mutual accusations.

Case study 3

A 33-year-old police officer, assigned to the monitoring of the drug scene at the main station of Frankfurt, Germany, initiated a personal relationship with a brothel manager as well as with a prostitute from Colombia. Apparently, there was a divergence of viewpoints between how the parties viewed one another. While the officer naively believed in the sincerity of the relationships, the brothel manager and the prostitute seemed to have valued him basically as a contracting party from the outset, valuable for the information which he could access and deliver. The officer shared the information about the warranted persons in the environment with the brothel manager and passed on certain other tips, such as informing the brothel manager about an impending police raid. The officer first encountered the brothel manager when he searched the brothel for drugs and dealers in 1997, and developed a personal relationship with him from 1998 onwards. Then he started showing up frequently at dinners, and participating at some parties with the women from the brothel. The official got involved in intimate relationships with three women from the environment. Upon the official's arrest on 28 May 2000, the brothel manager is reported to have fled to Spain. As to the financial aspects of the relationship, the official rented three dwellings. These were then sublet at double the rent to prostitutes supplied by the brothel manager. While this contract design should have provided the officer with extra income, in fact, it set him even more at the mercy of the brothel owner. In case the dwellings were not fully occupied, which indeed happened, the officer would even risk making losses. After his arrest, the official regretted his relationship with the woman, declaring that she was nothing more than an ice-cold prostitute who used him.[4]

Police officers can be in a strong bargaining position. The case suggests that if they are in charge of controlling a fixed area, such as the red-light district, they have ample possibilities to demand a bribe. Given the frequent contact with those they control, transaction costs can be lowered considerably. For example, Borner and Schwyzer (1999) argue that policemen can lower the transaction costs of corrupt agreements with criminals by regularly controlling the activities of such people. The idea would be that opportunism among the criminals could be avoided by threatening increased supervision or even harassment. There exists a legal relationship of control that can serve as a base for corrupt deals. While this may have been relevant for our case too, the friendship, as felt by the official, seems to have been a sufficient condition for enforcing the corrupt agreement.

The Philippine jueteng

Another case study comes from the Philippines and is described in detail by Coronel (2000: 26–36). *Jueteng* was an illegal lottery, a variation of an old Chinese numbers game. Illegal as it was, the game was popular throughout the country thanks to various layers of protection. Officials and law enforcers from the village level to the national protected the activities of the *jueteng* operators. Bet collectors (*cobradores*) reported to headmen (*cabos*), who were, in turn, supervised by a *jueteng* operator. It was the operator's task to ensure that influential officials protected the game. Of course, protection always comes at a price. According to estimates in 1995, every year some 2.5 billion pesos (almost US$100m) of *jueteng* money was going to bribes in return for toleration of the game.

Enjoying such protection, the game was hardly ever kept secret. The *jueteng* operators were well known both by the folk in their area and by government officials. In October 2000, Ilocos Sur Governor Luis 'Chavit' Singson charged the president, Joseph Estrada, with having received more than 540 million pesos (US$10.8m) from the illegal gambling payoffs between November 1998 and October 2000. In the Philippines, daily politics and the *jueteng* network were so much intertwined that it is hard to draw a line between the two. It was not uncommon for a *jueteng* operator to be a member of a political clan, or even to hold an official position. Singson himself is no exception to the rule. He and his brother Jose 'Bonito' Singson appeared frequently in police reports as *jueteng* operators. At the same time, *jueteng* money seems to have played some role in campaigns for the top administrative offices.

According to the story of Singson, Estrada invited him, Bong Pineda (another *jueteng* operator), and a close friend of his, Charlie 'Atong' Ang, to his residence in August 1998. There he appointed Pineda with the duty of collecting *jueteng* payoffs and handing them in to Ang. However, Singson was asked to take over the collection of *jueteng* payoffs two months later as a result of a problem between Estrada and Ang. Singson kept a ledger of the collections from 22 provinces and estimated the daily *jueteng* money collection at 50 million pesos (US$1m). Of this amount, 3 per cent was the kickback to the president. Singson confessed that he collected the money and delivered it to Estrada either at his home or at Malacañang Palace.

Up to this point, everything seemed to be in perfect harmony, yet Estrada wanted a higher cut from the *jueteng* network. The means to achieve this end was to legalize *jueteng* under the name Bingo-2 Ball via the Philippine Amusement and Gaming Corporation (Pagcor). It was Atong Ang who was to supervise the operation of replacing the illegal *jueteng* game with the new legal alternative. Ang set out by appointing some of the existing *jueteng* operators as Bingo-2 Ball franchisees. However, he awarded an impressively high 27 per cent share of the total collections to a private firm, headed by himself. In essence, this represents a form of embezzlement. According to Singson, he was merely fronting Estrada in the firm, and the whole scheme was not one of legalizing the business but of grabbing a higher share from gambling. Interesting to note is that Ang proceeded without the permission of the Congress to legalize the game. The backing of the president furnished him with the due flexibility to do so. By legalizing the game, what was formerly given to the police as protection money (*intelihensiya*) would now belong to him. In the meantime, the police were reported to be negotiating with Pagcor to have a legal cut from these proceedings to make up for the *intelihensiya* money that they lost from legalizing the game.

The events then took a turn that rid Chavit Singson of the potential gambling profits from his region. The Bingo-2 Ball franchise was given to Bonito Singson, Chavit Singson's brother, but at the same time his rival as a *jueteng* operator. Chavit Singson was carelessly pushed out of the game. He struck back, exposing the hidden deals of the president. He later admitted that he made the whole story public because Estrada gave a gambling concession to someone else.[5]

The *jueteng* case demonstrates how an existing perfectly legal relationship, that of a local governor and a president, could be used as a means to seal a corrupt deal. Politics and *jueteng* were highly intertwined. Day-to-day political dealings provide affluent opportunities of building trusted relationships, or of sanctioning one another. This provided a robust base for striking illegal deals. Singson, in particular, already depended on the benevolence of the president, because he was a public servant. This would put a check on his potential opportunism. The political positions Singson and Estrada held enabled them to strike a corrupt deal behind closed doors. Therefore, they saved on the transaction costs of seeking a partner and minimized the risk of raising some eyebrows through advertising for their corrupt intents. The deal enabled Estrada to claim his cut from the national collection of gambling proceeds in return for tolerance, or protection, of the illegal game. The end result is a striking case of centralized corruption. It was Estrada's strive for further acquisition that brought the stable relationship to an end. Singson was pushed aside instead of being retained as an insider that could have been handy in future corrupt prospects. As such deals are sealed within a closed group, it was surely a mistake for the corrupt parties to exclude an insider without providing him with an incentive to remain silent.

Such cases of highly organized and centralized corrupt practices are rare because the inevitable publicity commonly calls for counteractive measures. As shown, their organization was only possible because hierarchical government organizations, political parties and clans were highly intertwined with *jueteng*. These legal relationships provided for sufficient mechanisms to sanction opportunism and to guarantee loyalty. Corrupt relationships could then be parasitically linked to these legal relations. While the corrupt relationships have broken up, it will remain an issue whether the Philippine government organizations, political parties and clans will manage to contain this effective base for corruption in the future.

Conclusion and policy recommendations

This study has argued that corrupt deals require particularly high transaction costs because (1) the deals necessitate secrecy; (2) court ordering (i.e. legal enforcement mechanisms) is not available; (3) corrupt partners live at the mercy of one another after contract fulfilment. A variety of institutional mechanisms can be employed to seal and enforce corrupt agreements. Linking corrupt relationships to legal ones is a measure used to economize on transaction costs. Corrupt relationships *per se* are not necessarily secure in and of themselves. What makes them more secure (i.e. less vulnerable to opportunism) is their embeddedness in a legal relationship. In this context, one can no longer talk about a corrupt relationship, but about a relationship which has legal aspects as well as corrupt ones. The presence of existing legal ties, either in a political context or in a context of friendship, between the parties may create ripe opportunities to secure a corrupt deal. The case studies presented also support the hypothesis that sealing corrupt deals in an ongoing context of a legal relationship saves a considerable amount of transaction costs and reduces the related risks.

There is rarely ever a purely corrupt relationship in life; instead corrupt deals are sealed in a framework of existing legal relationships, due to transaction cost considerations. Corrupt partners often need a legal base on which, at a later stage, to build their corrupt side-dealings. The same ambivalence might also arise with people's motivations. There might not be such a thing as a purely corrupt intention. It is not just due to psychological reasons as to why a person's motivations are commonly more complicated and more diverse. Even those who are charged with the most unscrupulous and corrupt self-seeking must pursue some further genuine goals and interests: they must find partners and friends to establish trusted relationships; they must find jobs and seal contracts where they are expected honestly to deliver what was promised. In sum, legal and illegal actions are not substitutes, where one is chosen and the other is omitted. Very often they are complements. Legal relationships can provide the basis for sealing and enforcing corrupt agreements.

This approach suggests various avenues for future research. First, while there is consensus about the negative welfare effects of corruption, it is plausible that some forms of corruption are more disruptive than others. One issue could relate to the legal base that is used for the enforcement. For example, where corruption is linked to otherwise fertile business relations it may be less harmful than where it is embedded in less productive political connections.

Reform commonly focuses on how to avoid corrupt opportunities by limiting bureaucratic discretion and increasing public servants' accountability. This study suggests one further important pillar of an anti-corruption strategy. A public servant's office not only provides the opportunity for exacting a corrupt pay-off but may also supply mechanisms to enforce a corrupt deal and to economize on transaction costs. Reform strategies should therefore focus on aggravating the enforcement of corrupt deals as well as preventing a public office from being used as a means to lower transaction costs.

Alongside official duties, all other legally undertaken relationships of a public servant must equally form part of a reform strategy. In cases where a conflict of interest arises, supervision and regulation are required. Based on our approach, such conflicts of interest arise particularly where such relationships – for example, long-term business relationships – can serve as a basis for the enforcement of corrupt deals. Regulation must in this case limit misusing a public office for the enforcement of corrupt deals. Friendship belongs to the private sphere of a public servant and should not overshadow his or her duties. This is true not only because a public servant might otherwise be tempted to favouritism but also because friendship allows a bribe to be camouflaged as a gift, obfuscation of the *quid pro quo*, and encouraged reciprocity even years after a favour has been given. It thus helps to enforce a corrupt agreement. As this study highlights, investigating the potential of legal relationships to allow for corrupt spin-offs is an indispensable element of a successful reform strategy.

Acknowledgements

This chapter was written while Sitki Utku Teksoz was a visiting researcher at the University of Göttingen. He is grateful to the Konrad-Adenauer-Foundation for providing funding. Both authors are grateful to Professor Fikret Adaman for helpful comments on an earlier version of the chapter, and to Michael Schinke for revising the manuscript.

Notes

1 See Schramm and Taube (2002) for an interesting discussion of the Chinese *guanxi* networks and how the efficiency of the sanctions are jeopardized as the group size increases.
2 See 'Langjähriger Bundestagsabgeordneter in Haft', *Süddeutsche Zeitung*, 11 January 2002.
3 See 'Ex-Bankchef wegen Erpressung verurteilt', *Der Tagesspiegel*, 16 December 1997; 'Staatsanwalt prüft Ermittlung gegen K.', *Der Tagesspiegel*, 29 November 1997; 'Potsdams schillerndster Politiker lässt Stadtoberhaupt wanken', *Main-Echo*, 13 January 1998; and Lambsdorff (1999: 56).

4 See 'Polizist ließ sich vom Rotlicht-Milieu bestechen', *Frankfurter Neue Presse*, 9 August 2000.
5 See Coronel (2000: 26–36), and 'The Philippines turns on its president', *The Economist*, 19 October 2000.

References

Ben-Porath, Y. (1980) 'The F-Connection: Families, Friends and Firms and the Organization of Exchange', *Population and Development Review*, vol. 6, pp. 1–30.
Borner, S. and Schwyzer, C. (1999) 'Bekämpfung der Bestechung im Lichte der Neuen Politischen Ökonomie', in M. Pieth and P. Eigen (eds) *Korruption im internationalen Geschäftsverkehr, Bestandsaufnahme, Bekämpfung, Prävention*, Basel and Frankfurt am Main.
Coase, R.H. (1937) 'The Nature of the Firm', *Economica*, vol. 4, pp. 386–405.
Coronel, S.S. (2000) 'The Jueteng Republic', in Sheila S. Coroner (ed.) *Investigating Estrada: Millions, Mansions and Mistresses*, Manila, pp. 26–36.
della Porta and Vannucci, A. (1999) *Corrupt Exchanges: Actors, Resources and Mechanisms of Political Corruption*, New York.
Furubotn, E.G. and Richter, R. (1998) *Institutions and Economic Theory: The Contribution of New Institutional Economics*, Ann Arbor.
Goetz, C.J. and Scott, R.E. (1981) 'Principles of Relational Contracts', *Virginia Law Review*, vol. 67, pp. 1089–150.
Granovetter, M. (1992) 'Economic Action and Social Structure: The Problem of Embeddedness', in M. Granovetter and R. Swedberg (eds) *The Sociology of Economic Life*, Boulder, pp. 53–81.
Hart, O.D. (1987) 'Incomplete Contracts', in J. Eatwell, M. Milgate and P. Newman (eds) *The New Palgrave-Allocation, Information and Markets*, vol. 2, London, pp. 752–9.
Husted, B.W. (1994) 'Honor Among Thieves: A Transaction-Cost Interpretation of Corruption in Third World Countries', *Business Ethics Quarterly*, vol. 4, no. 1, pp. 17–27.
Klein, B., Crawford, R.G. and Alchian, A.A. (1978) 'Vertical Integration, Appropriable Rents and Competitive Contracting Process', *Journal of Law and Economics*, vol. 21, pp. 297–326.
Klitgaard, R. (1988) *Controlling Corruption*, Berkeley.
Lambsdorff, J. Graf (1999) 'Korruption als mühseliges Geschäft – eine Transaktionskostenanalyse', in M. Pieth and P. Eigen (eds) *Korruption im internationalen Geschäftsverkehr. Bestandsaufnahme, Bekämpfung, Prävention*, Basel and Frankfurt am Main, pp. 56–88.
Lambsdorff, J. Graf (2002a) 'Making Corrupt Deals – Contracting in the Shadow of Law', *Journal of Economic Behavior and Organization*, vol. 48, no. 3, pp. 221–41.
Lambsdorff, J. Graf (2002b) 'How Confidence Facilitates Illegal Transactions – An Empirical Approach', *American Journal of Economics and Sociology*, vol. 61, no. 4, pp. 829–53.
Macneil, I.R. (1974) 'The Many Futures of Contracts', *Southern California Law Review*, vol. 47, pp. 691–816.
Macneil, I.R. (1978) 'Contracts: Adjustment of Long Term Economic Relations under Classical, Neo-classical and Relational Contract Law', *Northwestern University Law Review*, vol. 72, pp. 854–905.
Nelson, W. and Winter, S.G. (1982) *An Evolutionary Theory of Economic Change*, Cambridge.

Rose-Ackerman, S. (1999) *Corruption and Government: Causes, Consequences and Reform*, Cambridge.

Schramm, M. and Taube, M. (2002) 'The Institutional Economics of Legal Institutions, Guanxi, and Corruption in the PR China', in J. Kidd (ed.) *Corruption: Its Realities in Asia*, Basingstoke.

Stigler, G.J. (1971) 'The Theory of Economic Regulation', *Bell Journal of Economics and Management Science*, vol. 2, no. 1, pp. 3–21.

Vannucci, A. (2000) 'Corruption, Political Parties and Political Protection', *European University Institute Economics Department Discussion Paper*, San Domenico, Badia Fiesolana.

Williamson, O.E. (1985) *The Economic Institutions of Capitalism: Firms, Markets, Relational Contracting*, New York.

9 The governance mechanisms of corrupt transactions

Donatella della Porta and Alberto Vannucci

Introduction: a neo-institutional approach to corruption

In the contemporary literature on corruption we can distinguish between two main approaches to the interpretation and analysis of corrupt dealings: a sociological one and a political-economic one (della Porta and Rose-Ackerman 2002).

The first perspective looks at the differences in the cultural traditions, norms and values which inform the activities and choices of individuals belonging to different societies and organizations. The central focus is on the so-called 'moral cost', which reflects internalized beliefs, such as *esprit de corps*, the 'public spiritedness' of officials, political culture and public attitude towards illegality. We can define moral cost as the utility that is lost because of the illegality of an action; it therefore increases with the development of a value system that supports respect for the law.[1] For an individual, 'the moral cost is lower the more ephemeral appear to him those circles of moral recognition that offer positive criteria for the respect of the law' (Pizzorno 1992: 46). Individuals suffer higher costs when, in both their own and their peers' perspectives, corrupt behaviour involves a violation of values – like 'public service' – which are deeply internalized and socially shared. Variations in moral cost can therefore explain the different individual responses to similar opportunities for corruption: 'people in a given society face the same institutions but may have different values' (Elster 1989: 39). Given similar institutional conditions, levels of political corruption will vary with the average moral attitude among citizens and public administrators.

In an *economic* perspective, on the other hand, individuals rationally opt for corruption when, given their preferences, the institutional system of incentives and opportunities makes such activity profitable:

> A person commits an offense if the expected utility to him exceeds the utility he could get by using his time and other resources at other activities. Some persons become 'criminals', therefore, not because their basic motivation differs from that of other persons, but because their benefits and costs differ.
>
> (Becker 1968: 172)

As with other behaviours involving deviation from laws and/or informal norms, individual decisions to participate in corrupt exchanges depend upon the probability of being denounced and punished, the severity of the potential punishment and the expected rewards as compared with available alternatives. Political economists have singled out a number of variables that influence the individual calculation to participate in political corruption (Rose-Ackerman 1978). Institutional opportunities and incentives, in fact, constrain corruption choices. Several institutional variables play a crucial role. Among them are the following: the formal rules determining the costs of political mediation; the ease with which new agents or groups can enter the political system, and the probability of electoral defeat; the overall level of state intervention in economic and social fields; the degree of discretionality involved in public acts; the relative efficiency of the various administrative and political controls; the forms of political competition; the types of markets where corrupt exchanges develop (della Porta and Vannucci 1999).

In what follows, building upon our research on the Italian case, we will elaborate on a third approach, which is a combination of elements from both the 'moral cost' and the rational choice perspectives, focusing on the (bad) social capital necessary in order for corruption networks to develop (della Porta 2000). We believe that, as with any other social relationship or collective enterprise, a corrupt exchange requires mechanisms of institutional governance that allow for coordination and cooperation among agents, overcoming free-rider problems.[2] But those institutional arrangements that lower the transaction costs of corrupt dealings, making them viable for rational agents, tend also to modify the values, identities and preferences of agents, rendering them less adverse to illegal activities.[3] The dynamics of corrupt arrangements often reflect the cumulative effects of the intertemporal linkages between institutional change, subjective perceptions and the beliefs and motivations of public and private agents.

Transaction costs are higher in corruption (as well as in other black markets) than in ordinary markets. The 'natural' environmental conditions for corruption are in fact secrecy, lack of transparency, severely restricted participation, and the high costs of 'exit' (Lambsdorff 2002: 222); corrupt activities must be performed clandestinely and cautiously and cannot be guaranteed by courts. The search for a counterpart, the gathering of information on the services exchanged and the potential partners' trustworthiness, the negotiation of an agreement, the exchange of 'commodities', the verification of the fulfilment and the potential enforcement of the 'bribery contract' are extremely risky and costly in terms of the time and other resources required to fulfil them. More specifically, corrupt agreements – being illegal – cannot be enforced by the public institutions (such as the judiciary and the police) which are usually available in order to punish deviation from legally codified contracts and agreements. In addition, corrupt transactions are often non-simultaneous in nature, and one party must rely upon the word of the other. As a consequence, the property rights of the public agents and the corrupter on their quotes of 'political rents' (the bribe and the public benefit allocated to them) are very uncertain, since the activities required in order to collect them present two specific risks: an *external* one, such as being discovered and punished by control agencies or by social stigma, and an *internal* one – for example, buying a 'lemon' or, more generally, being cheated or denounced by the counterpart.[4]

In spite of transaction cost barriers, more or less complex networks of corrupt exchanges can nevertheless develop with governance mechanisms (that is, a kind of organizational framework) that help to meet the 'demands' for protection of the fragile and uncertain property rights at stake in the corruption domain.[5] Such structures can become self-enforcing, sustaining 'honest' trade relationships among different corrupted agents and generating stable expectations that constrain their actions by imposing the fulfilment of the illegal contracts. Various and interrelated sanctioning systems may sustain the enforcement of corrupt agreements. *First-party control* occurs when the informal norms of corruption have been internalized to such extent that their violation produces a psychic cost, such as feelings of guilt or discomfort (Panther 2000).[6] When all partners (as potential cheaters) share similar internalized norms, corrupt exchanges can be successfully concluded. A potential basis for 'reliable' corrupt transactions is thus the involvement in it of relatively homogeneous agents, who share customs and ideological and cultural values (opposed to or at least autonomous from those embodied in the respect for state's norms), which can produce expectations of reciprocal implementation of corrupt agreements. The corresponding endogenous rule of the game relies on the negative feelings associated with the betrayal of commonly internalized codes of behaviour.[7]

The sharing of illegal norms is, however, rarely so strong as to discourage free-riderism: *second-party enforcement*, with sanctions directly administered or credibly menaced by counterparts in corrupt exchanges (Ellickson 1991), is therefore often necessary. The resources used to enforce agreements are normally related to the relation-specific expected advantages of a reiterated relationship. The establishment of personal trust can be interpreted in this perspective: when there are frequent bilateral opportunities for repeated interaction, being cooperative (i.e. not cheating), can become the more advantageous strategy faced with the menace of termination (or other forms of retaliation) in a dishonest transaction. Moreover, the acquisition of a *reputation* for 'honesty' in illegal dealings, thanks to the circulation of information on previous behaviour within the restricted circles of agents involved in the corrupt game, permits the reduction of the expected risks of interactions in a wider network of exchange.

When the domain of the corruption network widens, increasing the costs of the *ex ante* gathering of information, identification of partners, monitoring of agreement and sanctioning of deceitful partners, a *third party*, distinct from those directly involved in the corrupt deal, may become necessary in order to regulate the illegal exchanges. In this work, we will survey and analyse some of these third-party enforcement mechanisms which can guarantee a 'private-order' regulation of corrupt dealings. As we will show, third-party enforcement mechanisms are generally not neutral to the transacting parties, in the sense that the 'enforcers' do not restrict themselves to prescribing and automatically observe and sanction rules for compliance (as in the idealized operations of the protective state). Actually, there are problems of reliability and incentive-compatibility in the activities of individual agents and organizations when they are involved, as suppliers of protection, in the market for corruption. In order to be credible as guarantors chosen and trusted by corrupt agents, they have to control and exhibit specific resources. Moreover, to guarantee property rights and to enforce agreements has a cost, which tends to increase when such dealings and resources are illegal or illegally acquired. At the same time, protection and regulation activity has 'public good' attributes that makes it to a certain extent exploitable by free-riders, a dilemma that modern states have tried to deal with through recourse to compulsory taxation. But third-party enforcers of corrupt dealings, with the possible exception of mafia organizations, cannot use violent resources in order to be paid for their protection services. They must therefore also police their 'extractive' activities in order to control and incentivize payments from partners in corrupt transactions. On the other hand, since the essence of protection consists of the ability to impose costs, partners in corrupt transactions must also be reassured that guarantors will not use their power in order to seize (instead of protect) their resources.[8]

In this neo-institutional perspective, we single out norms and other mechanisms that can develop to sustain, facilitate and enforce illegal, corrupt deals. In the second section we try to shift from a causal model to a more complex path-dependent equilibrium model, assuming that corrupt institutions themselves are active in reproducing the preconditions for their successful development and that accidental factors can induce the development of a number of possible outcomes under the same set of initial conditions. In the third section we present a typology of mechanisms which can be used to regulate and coordinate corrupt activities. Through the crossing of two variables – enforcement services centred in the public sector or outside it and the use of resources related to the role within a hierarchical organization or to the position occupied within a decentralized network – we identify four models of corrupt governance: *party corruption, gang corruption, clan corruption* and *entrepreneurial* or *middlemen corruption*. Finally, concluding remarks are presented.

We shall address the analysis of governance mechanisms by using empirical data and examples derived from the Italian context, both before and after the 'Clean Hands' investigations, which, in the early 1990s, produced an (apparently significant) turnover in the political class and the party system. In order to describe the dynamics of corrupt exchanges we shall make use of the trial records, including interrogations and documents, for about one hundred cases of political corruption, four hundred requests for judicial action against Members of Parliament (between May 1992 and July 1993), articles from daily and weekly newspapers, and about sixty semi-structured interviews with experts from both the public and the private sector.

Due to a quite rare combination of two factors – the large-scale diffusion of corruption networks and the unprecedented exposure given to the judicial 'Clean Hands' inquiries – the Italian case seems particularly well-suited for the study of third-party governance mechanisms in corrupt exchanges. Although focusing mainly on the Italian case, we believe, nevertheless, that this approach has a more general value and can be fruitful in a comparative perspective as well. As North (1990: 3) observes, institutions are the 'rules of the game in a society or, more formally, are the humanly devised constraints that shape human inter-actions', reducing uncertainty and transaction costs. There are three types of institutions: formal rules (constitutional rules, statutory laws, regulations, con-tracts, etc.), informal constraints (social norms, customs, conventions, etc.) and their enforcement mechanisms. A rule is institutionalized when actions taken by agents based on their subjective beliefs and expectations become mutually con-sistent over a certain period: in this case, the observed reality created by their choices tends to confirm their beliefs, which are then reproduced as a guide for further actions (Aoki 2001: 3). The function of shared beliefs about the nature of interaction and other players' expected choices is crucial for the understand-ing of institutional change: when observed actions do not meet anticipated results, a search for new models can lead (more or less rapidly) to the conjoint adoption of a new (relatively) consistent system of subjective perceptions of others' action-choice rules. From this perspective, an institution exists only when agents mutually believe in the summary representation (tacit or explicit) of rules which coordinates their beliefs:

> For example, even if the government prohibits the importation of some goods by a statutory law, but if people believe it effective to bribe customs officers to circumvent the law and make it a prevailing practice, then it seems appropriate to regard the practice rather than the ineffective statutory law as an institution.
>
> (Aoki 2001: 13)

Since in illegal markets uncertainty and transaction costs are higher, 'private-order' mechanisms and other governance structures play a crucial role in these contexts. The use of comparative institutional analysis seems to be particularly fruitful in this field. Investigating the institutional diversity and the complexity of organizational responses to the common problem of reducing the transaction costs of corrupt activities can shed light on the variables that influence the pro-found differences in the diffusion and characteristics of corrupt networks, which are also recognizable in similar political and administrative environments:

> That is, institutional arrangements can be diverse across economies even if they are exposed to the same technological knowledge and are linked through the same markets. Thus we need to rely on comparative and historical information to understand why particular institutional arrange-ments have evolved in one economy but not in others.
>
> (Aoki 2001: 3)

A path-dependent analysis of the dynamics of corruption

Hidden markets for corrupt exchanges are generally characterized by different structures of informal institutions and their enforcement mechanisms, which include the above-mentioned self-sustaining illegal conventions, moral codes, self-enforcing contracts, reputation and third-party sanctioning, as well as several organizational architectures (limited in their scope or more elaborate and wide-ranging), whose resources are used in order to protect illegal dealings and informal property rights.[9] From this perspective, the significant discrepancies in the levels of (perceived) overall corruption, even among countries with similar institutional arrangements and economic development (Transparency International 2002), may be explained by the path-dependent progressive affirmation of more or less efficient governance mechanisms of illegal agreements. While the economic and the 'moral cost' approaches emphasize, respectively, the relevance of the structure of institutional opportunities and that of internalized values as causal factors that can induce corruptive choices, the neo-institutional perspective stresses the dynamic aspects of institutional interdependencies, which can give rise to multiple, sub-optimal arrangements. Path dependency in political processes is grounded in the presence of increasing returns or positive feedback from specific activities: a step in a particular direction increases the probabilities of further steps along the same path, since the relative benefits of that activity, compared with other possible options, increases over time, together with costs of 'exit' (Pierson 2000: 252). According to Arthur (1994: 112–13), *unpredictability, inflexibility* and *potential inefficiency* are among the characteristics of increasing returns processes. Since early events have significant impacts and are often casual, many unpredictable outcomes are possible from the same set of initial conditions. Moreover, the farther a process has developed, the more costly the shift from one path to another, until it eventually locks in one solution, which in the long run may produce less-efficient results than a possible alternative.

Four features of social interaction and institutional adaptation tend to generate positive feedback effects: (1) large set-up or fixed costs of new institutions, (2) coordination effects, (3) learning processes, and (4) the adaptive expectations they generate (North 1990: 95). Once established, institutions reinforce their own stability and further developments through these mechanisms, not only at the level of individual organizations and institutions but also at the macro level of institutional arrangements, which often show complementarities among a number of connected rules and expectations. Corrupt networks can exhibit similar 'scale economies', both at the level of individual activities and at a macro level; that is, the costs of offering illicit services increase less than proportionally to the overall level of the phenomenon's diffusion.

The set-up costs

An analysis of the dynamics of corruption indicates that this illegal activity may feed itself: 'the critical attitude towards the non-corrupt in a corrupt society is a main mechanism behind this snowball effect' (Elster 1989: 268). An individual's or organization's first involvement in corrupt activities usually entails high set-up costs due to the combination of both expected legal penalties and moral costs, as well as the effect of the expected risk of spoiling one's reputation for integrity and honesty. As a former mayor of Miami explains: 'I took my first bribe in my second term on the city commission. It's a terrible thing, like cheating on your wife for the first time' (quoted in Lambsdorff 2002: 234). There may also be a high fixed cost to setting up a corruption-favourable system of regulation or administrative controls, but subsequent acts of corruption will become more profitable, lowering the possibility of legal sanctions being implemented and presumably also the corresponding sense of guilt. A similar effect may paradoxically accompany the stigma suffered by corrupt agents as an effect of being suspected, denounced or convicted. Once they are labelled as corrupt or easily corruptible, agents have an incentive to continue their 'criminal career' since the opportunity cost of further offences has been reduced while the blemish on their social reputation has already diminished legal prospects (Opp 1989). Furthermore, search costs are very high at the beginning of the corrupt agents' career, when they still do not possess information on the characteristics of the corruption environment and potential partners' reliability. Once such fixed costs have already been borne, individuals and organizations have an incentive to pursue illegal activities over time in order to reduce the 'unit costs' of corruption.

Coordination effects

Coordination effects are also very important in the market for corruption. The relative benefits that corrupt agents receive from their activities often increase as others adopt the same strategy. In general, the more widespread the corruption, the lower the search costs and the risk of being denounced for those who decide to engage in illegal practices and the higher the costs for those who try to remain honest and are therefore excluded. The diffusion of corruption reduces both the sense of guilt and the risk of losing face while increasing, on the other hand, the possibility of finding dependable partners for corrupt transactions (Andvig 1991). Where corruption is generalized, the risk of being accused appears to be extremely low, given that the control agencies must distribute their resources over a far wider area: 'If only a few people steal or loot, they will be caught; but if many do, the probability of any one of them getting caught is much lower, and hence the returns to stealing or looting are higher' (Murphy, Shleifer and Vishny 1993: 409). Moreover, they meet increasing difficulties, due to the conspiracy of silence between corrupt agents or the greater ease of concealing evidence. In fact, since corrupt practices are usually closely bound together, the number of people willing to testify or provide information becomes increasingly limited. Even the non-corrupt are then led to collude with corruption or at least to accept it in order to obtain political advantages. The involvement and interests of leading politicians further discourages or obstructs controls and allegations. Given the scarcity of honest administrators and reliable control organs to turn to, the incentives for entrepreneurs to pay bribes increase (Rose-Ackerman 1978).

If corrupt agents sometimes tend deliberately to introduce conditions of arbitrariness in public affairs in order to facilitate corruption, these conditions are spontaneously reproduced because those initially hostile to such practices are increasingly included or forced to exit from the system. The very diffusion of corruption reduces its moral costs as the 'culture of corruption' spreads a particular value system and becomes a mechanism for selecting agents in public and private organizations.[10] As illegality becomes common practice, the codes of behaviour condemning corruption may be weakened by the adoption of a 'situational morality' (Chibnall and Saunders 1977: 151). Its logic has been exemplified by Myrdal (1968: 409): 'Well, if everybody seems corrupt, why shouldn't I be corrupt?'.[11] Pizzarotti explained the payment of bribes to the national administrative secretaries of the PSI and DC in similar terms:

> It was a sort of custom. There wasn't any precise reason. Having heard that someone else did it, I decided to follow the same procedure because I would get an advantage in terms of the financing of the works and more generally ... Since that was the system, more or less, I preferred to be part of the system.
>
> (*Panorama*, 14 February 1993: 61)

Learning effects

The skills, knowledge and information concerning the most effective methods for creating, managing and enforcing corrupt relations are acquired and accumulated with time.[12] When the 'rules' of corruption become an invisible guide to behaviour, the relations between the agents in hidden exchange appear to follow a prepared script, reducing to a minimum uncertainty and tension. Chiesa, the first politicians arrested during the 'Clean Hands' investigations, described the tranquil and unembarrassed atmosphere in which bribes circulated, even on the first occasion he consigned money to Tognoli, his political patron:

> I handed him the envelope of money, casually, like offering a friend a coffee. He thanked me without asking anything. He knew there was money in the envelope but did not ask where it came from, which tender produced it or the percentage of the payoff. Bribery has its etiquette. You accept and say thank you without displaying curiosity.
>
> (Andreoli 1993: 61–2)

There are no negotiations or demands; no suspicions or worries arise. To conclude the transaction successfully with the minimum of risk, it is sufficient to follow the etiquette of corruption.

Since the choice between corruption and non-corruption depends upon not only individual preferences and the institutional context but also strategic interactions with other individuals, increased recourse to corrupt practices encourages further investments in the acquisition of such 'illegality skills' (Pizzorno 1992), attracting more agents in the corruption networks. Corrupt agents (as well as organizations) enjoy, with time, significant learning effects. Interacting repeatedly, they discover through learn-by-doing processes how to act more effectively, reducing the risks and transaction costs of corruption. Their experiences introduce further improvements in the smooth functioning of corrupt agreements, which spread through further learning and imitation within corrupt institutional environments. The 'cashier' of the Milanese PLI (the Italian Liberal Party), Properzj, described such a process:

> I became President of the AEM in May 1987 and remained so until autumn 1990. As soon as I took on the position I was approached by Fiorentino Enrico, who told me that there was a group of firms ... who normally contributed sums of money for the party system. I say this to make clear that the system of cash payments preceded my taking the post and I confined myself to the acceptance of what, according to Fiorentino, was an established practice.
>
> (CD, no. 231, 22 March 1993: 5)

In Italy, business politicians have introduced innovative expertise and capabilities within corrupt arrangements as they become specialized – in fact, precisely in 'operating in the shadows', dedicating a great part of their time and effort to the organization of illegal activities and the elaboration of the specific techniques necessary to minimize the risks of denunciation.[13] As a consequence, they also promote the spread of the informal norms which regulate corruption and the involvement of their political parties as enforcement agencies that reward rather than discourage unlawful behaviour. Moreover, mechanisms exist inside organizations for progressive and painless inclusion in the rituals and informal conventions of corruption. PAPI recalled that when he was nominated manager of the Cogefar, a company controlled by Fiat, he was given 'a notebook recording the various "obligations" and the dates they should be paid. A list of names and sums; an inheritance which had to be respected to the letter. Illegality was so regularized that I didn't feel I was committing a criminal act' (*Panorama*, 16 April 1994: 86). Another more generic form of increasing returns on corruption activities is related to their interaction with productive activities. As in other rent-seeking activities:

> Over some range, as more resources move into rent-seeking, returns to production may fall faster than [returns] to rent-seeking do, and so the attractiveness of production *relative* to rent-seeking will fall as well ...

When this happens, rent-seeking exhibits general equilibrium increasing returns in the sense that an increase in rent-seeking lowers the cost of further rent-seeking.

(Murphy, Shleifer and Vishny 1993: 409)

Adaptive expectations

Finally, adaptive expectations have a critical role in the dynamics of corruption governance. What comes into play here is the self-fulfilling nature of such beliefs. The simple expectation that corruption is (or is going to be) widely practised can induce a growing number of individuals to become involved in the system in order not to be excluded from the anticipated benefits of corrupt deals, the costs of which are proportionally lowered. Marinelli, an entrepreneur, described his involvement in corruption as follows:

> I've been paying and paying bribes since I began to work. For 13 or 14 years now if I want a contract from the Province . . . I have to come up with millions and millions . . . My colleagues also told me that that was the way things worked, that everyone did it and at bottom there was nothing strange about it.
>
> (*L'Espresso*, 18 November 1984: 41)

The perceptions of a generalization of such practices and the very attempt to combat them through denunciations of the 'climate of corruption' thus strengthen the idea that, since so many others are doing it, it must be profitable (as well as 'correct') to engage in corruption. The payment of bribes is thus facilitated by the widespread conviction (emphasized by those seeking contributions) that it is inevitable. The manager of a small enterprise was contacted by a Democrat councillor after being awarded a 250 million lire order for the Fatebenefratelli Hospital of Milan: 'He approached me in a perfectly normal way and asked for a "contribution for the organization", giving me the impression that it was an obligation and the usual practice. I considered it and decided to comply' (TM, 83). Vice-versa, when corruption is perceived as marginal, agents will adapt their actions so as to respect those beliefs, increasing the expected information and protection costs of illegal exchanges.

In the absence of sufficient negative feedback – coming from a state's enforcement agencies or from spontaneous observance of legal rules due to informal codes and values diffused in the population – to counterbalance it, the combination of the above-described mechanisms can cause a path-dependent process of diffusion of corrupt practices. Relying on similar assumptions, some authors have indicated the possibility of multiple equilibria characterized by differing 'market conditions' in the corruption system.[14] Therefore, 'people may have similar values, within and across societies, and similar institutional structures and yet, for accidental reasons, end up in different equilibria' (Elster 1989: 40); that is, in different combinations of overall institutional arrangements and specific governance mechanisms of corruption. Even differences in moral costs between similar countries may be explained by the evolution of different social norms, just as virtuous or vicious circles tend to reinforce reciprocal (mis)trust, cooperation (or defection), (un)civicness, reciprocity and the like – that is, value systems which are more or less favourable to corrupt practices.[15]

When the institutionalization of 'private-order' mechanisms for the regulation of corruption is achieved, a system of shared and mutually consistent beliefs become the invisible guide to strategic choices, which in turn confirm and reinforce such expectations. This perspective is not incompatible with the illegal nature of these activities, since 'the rules implied by particular market governance institutions, organizational conventions, and community norms may be explicitly or tacitly well understood only by agents in the relevant domain' (Aoki 2001: 233). Once established, overall corruption enforcement mechanisms (as well as other institutional arrangements) are basically enduring and resistant to change even if they produce socially inefficient conditions.

One reason of institutional stability is the feedback mechanisms between institutionalization and competence development of individuals and organizations. Since agents are rewarded for their efforts according to the incentives and constraints of the institutional matrix, they will try to develop competence and get assets which enhance their opportunities within that system. When corruption appears to be the most gainful alternative for politicians, businessmen or party leaders, they will have a precise incentive to invest in the acquisition of illegality skills, most rewarding in that environment, thus supporting the extended reproduction of governance mechanisms favourable to corruption. Where better gain opportunities depend upon influencing on the public power, it is expected that the energy, creativity and inventiveness of economic and political agents will concentrate on the field of corrupt practices (Baumol 1990: 893; della Porta and Vannucci 2002).[16] Moreover, it will be in the interest of corrupt politicians and bureaucrats to exercise public authority precisely in order to maintain an institutional status quo favourable to corruption, or to expand corrupt opportunities through selective recruitment of private counterparts and other public agents, *ad hoc* new (de)regulation, etc.

A typology of corrupt networks

Corruption develops with, and helps the development of, some mechanisms that reduce transaction costs, acting on the side of the information and/or the enforcement of corrupt transactions. In order to understand corrupt exchanges we have to look not only at the institutional and cultural constraints against the violation of the contract between the public administrator (the agent) and the state (the principal) but also at the production and reproduction of certain additional resources necessary for the development of corrupt exchanges: trust, illegal skills, political protection, informal norms and consensus are among them. These resources lower the cost of illegal exchanges by reducing their material risks as well as their moral costs.

The development of governance mechanisms accompanies the growth of the network of corrupt exchanges. Where corruption becomes widespread, it often involves groups of administrators and businessmen, who negotiate not only the size of the bribe but also the nature of public decisions. Additional players cannot be easily excluded from the expected benefits of the 'corruption game', since their involvement in public decision-making or their access to confidential information on illegal deals provides them with blackmailing power (della Porta 1992). In this case there are also illegal exchanges internal to each group of corrupt agents, who have to share the expected bribe benefits. Obviously, the enlargement of the network of agents involved in corrupt activities increases their transaction costs, since bargaining turns out to be more complicated and time-consuming, while the complexity of the exchanges makes controls and enforcement more difficult to perform, and consequently the risks of defection increase.

Associations of public agents include various figures with different roles, whose coordination in reaching administrative decisions that can be exchanged for bribes is indispensable, particularly public administrators (both those in elected positions and those with party appointments), career administrators and party functionaries. On the other hand, cartels of businessmen may reach agreements on series of public decisions which they must demand from politicians: they collect money and hand it over to political cartels, and these in turn offer privileged access to the decisions and distribute the money between politicians. Sometimes middlemen intervene to establish contacts within and between the groups of agents, to conduct negotiations and to transfer bribe money. However, corrupt exchanges do not only involve the public administrators and private entrepreneurs who participate directly in them but also other agents, who, although not necessarily taking a direct part in sharing the political rent, nevertheless obtain favours in exchange for resources they control: the need for *consensus* among corrupt politicians can be fulfilled via clientelistic exchanges with voters; the required 'cover-ups' of their illicit activities can be gained through an implicit or explicit agreement with bureaucratic agents or control agencies (Vannucci and della Porta 2003); when coercion is considered necessary to enforce an illegal agreement and avoid individual exit from the occult exchanges, organized crime can supply the resources of physical violence corrupt politicians need in order to punish 'lemons', free-riders, or potential 'whistle-blowers'. In this more complex web of relationships, a combination of first-party internalized mechanisms of self-sanctioning, reciprocal second-party bonds of trust and other forms of third-party guarantees is needed to enable the exchange of precarious property rights on political rents to be brought to a conclusion.

Although some characteristics (spontaneous development of alternative self-enforcing rules of the game and hidden norms, special linguistic conventions, some involvement of political parties or politicians) are almost always present in the evolution of a more complex web of corrupt exchanges, we shall distinguish (see Table 9.1) four different types of governance networks according to the

Table 9.1 Types of third-party enforcement mechanisms of corrupt exchanges

	Public sector-centred	Private-sector centred
Resources of power derived from position within a hierarchical organisation	Party and bureaucratic corruption: party cashiers, party leaders, top public bureaucrats	Gang corruption: Mafia bosses
Resources of power derived from position within a diffused network	Clan corruption: bosses of public bodies	Entrepreneurial or middleman corruption: entrepreneurs with strong connections in the public sphere, brokers

source of protective services (mainly internal or external to public administration) and the nature of the resources which are used to enforce agreements (deriving mainly from their roles within a hierarchical organization or from their strategic positions within a wider network of relationships). In each cell we indicate the corresponding type(s) and the main agent(s) around which the corruption network(s) are formed.

In our analysis, we shall look at the resources available for the main agents in each type of network, the network's specific dynamics and the conditions for its development. Although in the empirical reality of corruption various types of governance mechanisms are often interrelated, we can single out historical circumstances that have facilitated the development of one or the other. From this perspective, the definition and protection of property rights over political rents – that is, the sanctioning of corrupt agreements and the resolution of potential disputes – require the ability of the various parties to impose costs in case of defection or non-fulfilment: 'The essence of enforcement power is in the enforcer's ability to punish (i.e. to impose costs). These costs can be imposed both by the use of violence or by other means . . . Different third parties impose costs by different means' (Barzel 2002: 38–9).

Various means may be used by individuals and organizations in order to enforce corrupt agreements. Third-party sanctioning power may be based on violence, the capacity to impose direct physical costs to induce parties to perform corrupt agreements. Criminal organizations, when available as suppliers of protection, can enforce such illegal exchanges using force (as well as their reputation as violent guarantors) to adjudicate disputes. Another crucial sanctioning resource is control on long-term relationships (Barzel 2002: 42). The enforcers – which in our cases are brokers, entrepreneurs, political bosses, party leaders and high-ranking bureaucrats – can threaten to deprive the partners of the expected benefits of future corrupt interactions. More specifically, some of them can make strategic use of their position within a web of relationships to credibly exclude the agents involved from future opportunities of exchange. The influence of political leaders and cashiers, as well as top bureaucrats, over the allocative power of party machines and public organizations adds a further resource to their enforcement power. They can, in fact, use as an enforcing mechanism their ability to rule out realistically parties in corrupt contracts from other benefits deriving from repeated legal interactions with public bodies or the party structure: the prospectives of carriers for lower-level bureaucrats, support for nomination to publicly appointed positions or candidatures, awards of public contracts or licences to entrepreneurs, etc. Within a party organization leaders may also appeal to common ideological values to obtain the compliance of corrupt members to their pronouncements.

Party corruption

In *party corruption* the corrupt parties play a pivotal role in the governance of corrupt exchanges. They educate their administrators in the rules of corruption, organize corrupt exchanges and enforce their rule by ostracizing outsiders. The basic resource is the control of the party's organization.

In systems of party corruption, the parties not only cultivate illicit practices, reducing the moral costs of corruption; they also secure a kind of continuity for the game of corruption through its diffusion in every geographical area, various public bodies and different sectors of public administration. In this way, whoever respects the unlawful agreements can continue to do business with public administration, while anyone who opts out on a given occasion will be permanently excluded from the market for public works. Controlling the nominations to public bodies and the career of political agents, the parties can generalize the kickback, transforming corruption from an exception into an established practice with accepted norms, at the same time guaranteeing the continuity of the system over time despite changes in the political personnel of public administration. The parties assume, that is to say, the function of guarantors of the illegal bargain, participating in those operations demanding a 'certification of trust: in other words, the promises of others, requiring to be guaranteed in some way, are used to obtain a benefit' (Pizzorno 1992: 31). Moreover, reaching an agreement between them, majority and opposition reduce the material risks connected with identifying suitable parties and negotiating bribes. In this case, transaction costs are reduced by the power (in terms of both potential rewards and potential punishment) related to party control of public tenders and decisions. As Carnevale, councillor of the PDS (Partito Democratico della Sinistra) for the Metropolitane Milanesi (MM), relates: 'On entering the *Metropolitana* I found *an already tried and tested system* according to which, as a rule, virtually all contract winners paid a bribe of three per cent ... The proceeds of these bribes were divided among the parties according to pre-existent agreements' (MPM, 147; emphasis added). In fact, 'In practice and beyond the bureaucratic procedures that were legally established, the names listed [for nomination to the administrative body of the MM] were those chosen by the party secretaries, that is by those who are the final receivers of the bribes' (TM, 36). In this context cooperation is favoured by the prospect that the same political agents will stay in power over a prolonged period of time (Axelrod 1984).

Historically, Italian corruption had similar characteristics in the early days of the Republic, when bribes came especially from public enterprises. A movement in this direction was also seen in the 1980s in the Italian Socialist Party and Christian-Democratic Party, especially in the Northern Regions. According to an entrepreneur, a PSI leader told him:

> Craxi had identified about 20 major Italian firms who, if they wanted to survive in business, would have to commit themselves to making regular cash payments to the PSI, in the order of about two billion a year ... In other words, Craxi realized the penal dangers of associating levies of money with individual tenders and intended to forfeit them against annual contributions.
>
> (TNM, 83)

Party cashiers in the main parties worked together in order to coordinate their efforts to impose a corrupt system. Corruption resembling this type of illegal transaction also emerged around the PS in France in the 1980s and in the CDU in Germany in the 1990s, in which the party is the main provider of information and enforcement of corrupt exchange as well as the main beneficiary of bribes (Becquart-Leclercq 1989; Mény 1992; Blankenburg, Staudhammer and Steinert 1989: 924).

The condition for this type of corruption is a certain degree of centralization in the political party, with a (more or less) recognized leadership. In Germany, resilience to scandals was in fact connected to 'the organizational oligopoly on which parties could build' (Blankenburg, Staudhammer and Steinert 1989: 922). However, in Italy, especially in the 1980s, the centrifugal tendency became too strong for this system to prevail.[17]

Clan corruption

In (political) clan corruption, corruption is mainly organized around a series of bosses of the public body (mainly party-appointed general managers) in a perennial struggle with each other. In this case, the public bosses reduce transaction costs by inculcating corruption among both appointed politicians and career managers, imposing a fixed percentage of bribes on all entrepreneurs who want to do business with the public body. An illustration is provided by Teardo, former president of the regional council in Liguria and leader of the Socialist Party in Savona. Several local entrepreneurs admitted to having paid bribes at a fixed percentage amounting to 10 per cent of the total sum for all the public contracting procedures managed by the public bodies which were under the 'control' of Teardo's clan – 'We all were resigned and paid. Without a bribe you could obtain absolutely nothing' (UIS, 360–1). Fear of retaliation in the form of exclusion from profitable public contracts pushed entrepreneurs spontaneously to conform to prevailing 'codes' of behaviour. An informal but solid organizational structure emerged within the clan of corrupt administrators.

The hierarchical distribution of power was determined partly by the institutional positions held by members of the public administration and the political parties and partly by the possession of power resources connected with illegal activities (blackmail power or illegal skills). As observed by the judges, members were connected to each other by 'a set of ties due to common political memberships, friendship, Masonic brotherhood or simple interested cooperation, which constituted the foundation on which their illegal activity was built' (UIS, 122). In his clan, Teardo is described as a boss: 'he took all main decisions and informed his "lieutenants" with "memos" specifying for each public contract or illicit dealing what amount of money should be required [of] the entrepreneurs, the conditions of payment, the identity of those who should collect bribes, and the shares of subdivision among associates to the clan' (UIS, 433). Other public administrators, who head certain public bodies, are appointed as direct representatives of the boss: with limited autonomous power, they signal and realize occasions of corruption, assuming the corresponding political deliberations. At a lower level a number of gregarious followers operate who have been selected by Teardo on the basis of trust: in fact, they have the delicate task of establishing and maintaining contacts with entrepreneurs, collecting and distributing bribes.

Teardo's public image was that of a dynamic and resolute decision-maker. A pragmatic attitude in political alliances and coalitions in local administrations, with both internal PSI factions and other parties, could guarantee Teardo and his followers a wide occupation of power positions: '*In this* – is the opinion of a Communist local politician – *he was very dependable. He always kept his word*, both with the PCI and with the DC. Thus, he became a firm point of reference. Giving these guarantees to the parties, he obtained the possibility of doing what he wanted in exchange' (SV3). A wide circle of connivance and collusion with public administrators not personally involved in corruption was then increasingly expanded, allowing Teardo and his followers to minimize the risk of being denounced. In several cases they used this 'blackmail power' to tie politicians of different parties who occupied strategic roles in public decision procedures into the network of corrupt transactions. Clientelistic management of their power was decisive in expanding the electoral support of the boss and of the whole Socialist Party on a local level. For instance, Teardo distributed benefits to supporters of the local football team, gifts to small communities of immigrants and specific privileges in public housing assignation (TRIS, 332).

Although the party still decides public administration appointments, corruption revenues facilitate centrifugal tendencies, with each boss forming personal cliques of clients and bribers. This image is well-illustrated in the declaration of Zaffra, regional secretary of the PSI in Lombardy:

There was terrible confusion, with a plurality of referents each directing their own area . . . This parcellized administrative structure corresponded to an analogous structure in the field of political decisions, in the sense that it was not so much the party which counted in decision-making as the single possessors of power, including economic power ... The running of the administration had nothing to do with formal positions because reference was to the person and not the position. So the economic referent could move from one office to another according to the movement of the people who counted most. Also, there was little substantial coincidence between real and formal functions: for example, local functionaries were not paid by the federation but by their political referent through informal, but substantial, payments which did not appear in the party's public financial statements.

(L'Espresso, 17 January 1993: 43)

Rules about the amount (usually calculated as a percentage of the amount of the public contract) and sharing of bribes develop inside the administrative committees of each public body, with bosses and sub-bosses often collecting bribes directly from the entrepreneurs. This type of corruption was very widespread in Italy in the 1980s in the myriads of public bodies, especially, but not only, at the local level (public hospitals, asylums, airports, etc.).

Clan corruption develops with the control of party-appointed managers over administrative bodies and weak political parties. If its centrifugal nature explains frequent crises, clan corruption can, however, easily re-emerge within public bodies where new bosses often substitute for older ones, finding networks of bureaucrats as well as entrepreneurs already acculturated to political corruption. In the recent scandal at the Molinette Hospital in Turin, the manager and Forza Italia's leader Odasso – son of a Christian-Democratic politician – displays all the characteristics of a boss of a public body. First of all, a patrimonialistic use of the hospital allows him to increase his personal clique of supporters who can then be installed in the party organization – and Odasso was indeed described as 'very friendly', 'kind, discreet, and particularly able to meet any demand: a bed in the hospital, a surgical operation, a hiring, a recommendation for your daughter's exam' (*La Repubblica*, 25 January 2001). The importance of dynamic management is also stressed: 'At Le Molinette, he became the Big [Man], since his desire for grandeur emerged at any occasion' (*La Repubblica*, 25 January 2002). At the same time, the boss is also able to arrogantly assess his power upon entrepreneurs looking for a public contract. One of them, Dominelli, confessed to a feeling of 'psychological subornation' *vis-à-vis* Odasso who, besides collecting bribes, also asked for 340 million lira worth of unrecompensed work in the 15,000 square metre park at his villa in Nizza Monferrato (ibid.). Also, Odasso used part of the cash bribes in party activities, buying, among other things, 1,600 membership cards for his party (for a total amount of 160 million lira), financing electoral campaigns for his and allied parties (*La Repubblica*, 17 January 2002) and distributing generous gifts (70 million lira for 'Christmas' presents, including watches worth up to 14 million apiece) to various fellow politicians. As he himself declared, 'I paid [for electoral] dinners, gifts and membership cards in part from my salary and in part from bribes' (*La Repubblica*, 25 January 2002). Moving the membership cards, like shares, from one party candidate to the other, Odasso could then obtain and consolidate his position as general director of the Molinette. Transaction costs were reduced by the development of a system of 'fixed bribes'; according to an entrepreneur, Odasso told him: 'Listen, I don't know how it works at the CTO, but here it is 10 per cent' (*La Repubblica*, 22 December 2002).

This type of corruption develops when there is a widespread party occupation of public and semi-public bodies (a 'power of occupation'), but political parties are organizationally weak. Similar forms of corruption developed also in Japan, where the liberal party's electoral clientele has been organized in *Koenkai*, or support organizations. Because of internal competition, in order to avoid losing his *Koenkai* to a rival, each candidate has to employ ten to fifteen secretaries, whose task it is to organize specific groups, distributing gifts (in particular at marriages or funerals) or invitations to parties or journeys (Bouissou 1997: 136–8; Rothacher 1996: 3).

In clan corruption, a single boss's enforcement services can reduce transaction costs, until illegal activities remain limited to single units or sectors under the clan's sphere of influence. Nevertheless, when bosses start to compete with each other in order to increase their share of bribes, centrifugal tendencies may prevail, causing friction and coordination problems.

Gang corruption

Gang networks normally coalesce around Mafia bosses, who rely upon the resources they control within their hierarchical organizations. Violence is the main resource that can be used to settle or override controversies in those markets in which transactions are dominated by mutual distrust and uncertainty – and especially in those contexts in which the protection supplied elsewhere by the state as a public good is either unavailable or ineffective. Mafiosi operate typically in markets and social relations in which trust between individuals is fragile or less than that required by a society regulated by normal negotiation strategies: illegal markets (and corrupt transactions) are a common case (Gambetta 1993). As it is a factor in a costly productive process, they use violence 'economically' and only to the extent necessary, wherever possible substituting reputation alone. As Judge Falcone observed:

> In these organizations violence and cruelty are never gratuitous but instead represent the last resort, to be used when all other methods of intimidation have failed or when the gravity of the behaviour requiring Mafia 'correction' is such that it must be punished by death.
>
> (Falcone 1991: 28)

Violence and its reputation are also used within corrupt exchanges in order to discourage potential free-riders. The protection of Mafia bosses serves to restore the stability of political exchanges behind the managing boards of municipal agencies. Frightening their enemies and avoiding political crises,

Mafiosi ensure a (more or less) peaceful and continuing division of public funds. One example of a Mafia guarantee of a municipal coalition was described during the investigations into the murder of Ligato, a powerful DC boss in Reggio Calabria. According to a state's witness from the local Mafia, 'The two parties, DC and PSI, competed against each other to divide up between them all the positions of power and all the economic interests in the city of Reggio' (*Panorama*, 13 December 1993: 52), and '[t]he problem became most dramatic once several thousand billion lire were about to arrive in Reggio (through the so-called Reggio decree), because it was clear that whoever held political power in the city would also control these funds' (Galasso 1993: 198). The murder had the effect of consolidating the nascent political coalition in Reggio: 'After the assassination, or, better, because of it, the game was made and the new agreements were implemented thanks to a series of very important decisions, that [previously] would have been discussed for months in the city council' (ibid.). Thanks to this forced 'pacification', the market for corruption could expand undisturbed (CD, no. 256, 1993: 2).

Gang corruption develops when political parties are internally divided and intimidation resources are on supply in the territory because of a tradition of organized crime (often with links to the political parties). This type of corruption was (and apparently still is) particularly widespread in Southern Italy. In the description of the repentant Calderone:

> We [must not] forget that the *mafioso* is a sort of authority, a person everybody addresses to ask for a favour, solve problems ... When we, the Calderones, enjoyed great favour there was a procession in my office, people who asked for the most disparate things ... One looked for a job, another had participated in a selection for a position and wanted to win it, another offered products for an enterprise.
>
> (Arlacchi 1992: 149–50)

The degree of stratification of corrupt transactions in Sicily seems to confirm the 'efficiency' of the services of the Mafia. The system required strong trust: complex exchanges between local and regional politicians, mediators, bureaucrats and firms were based on the delegation of decisions (from regional councillors to intermediaries) and the anticipation of payments (the companies selected to win the bidding paid a bribe equal to 25 per cent of the cost even before the contracting procedure began) (PRP, 10–12).

The Yakuza functions similarly in Japan (Iwai 1986), where the role of organized crime in the protection of corrupt business also emerged during the Lockheed scandal in the figure of Kodama Yoshio, a suspected perpetrator of war crimes and broker between politicians, gangsters and right-wing extremists who had received an annual salary as a consultant for the Lockheed Aircraft Corporation.

In gang corruption, the tendency is for the balance of power to favour organized crime over politicians, which extends not only its control of relevant information but also (and especially) its enforcement capacity via the use or the threat of violence (Vannucci 1997: 57). In cases of conflict, '[t]he relationship between Cosa Nostra and politicians is [one] of dominance of the first over the second; the availability of coercive methods gives Cosa Nostra infinite possibility of demand and persuasion' (CPMF, 16). This is evident, for example, in the distribution of payments for protection (that is, bribes). The Palermo judges write:

> Until the early 1980s, the politicians decided to whom they would assign a contract and pocketed as much as 50 per cent of the kickbacks ... In recent years, the largest share [has] ended up with the heads of the Cupola [the Mafia's multi-family committee, the apex of the organization], then came the local 'family' directly involved in the contract, and the politicians were last.
>
> (*La Repubblica*, 27 May 1993: 8)

This type of network, however, also reflects the difficulties of long-term cooperation in organized crime. So, although the control of organized crime on public tenders in Southern Italy again seems quite widespread, there are frequent periods of turbulence. As happened in the past (in Naples and Palermo but also in Prohibitionist America), internecine wars between the different clans might disrupt corruption transactions as well.

Entrepreneurial corruption

In entrepreneurial corruption, cartels of firms develop with very strong interest in the public market, although often also with public and semi-public careers. Cartels facilitate collusion, acculturating entrepreneurs to the rule of corrupt transaction and providing governance mechanisms for the sharing of the political rents derived from the restricted competition for public contracts. They also enforce compliance via the threat of excluding recalcitrant partners from future transactions. A Milanese entrepreneur described the functioning of the market there in the following terms:

> When tenders for contracts are issued, the interested firms meet on the recommendation of those of us who are most directly interested in the problem in order to find an agreement for a fair distribution of the contracts ... I was contacted and the contract which I could hope to get decided. In consequence, the other firms would not undercut me by presenting a lower bid. At the same time, in relation to the contracts which other firms were supposed to win, I was pledged not to get in their way.
>
> (TM, 45)

Different criteria existed for the division of contracts between the cartel firms: by turn, territory, demanding institution and market sector. Zamorani, a public-sector manager, described the 'scientific' precision with which work for the National Road Authority was distributed:

> For many years a cartel of about 200 firms has existed. They meet period-ically, look at the list of works which have or will be presented to the Board of Directors and decide on the order of (winners). The choice is made by (lottery). The names of the firms are written on pieces of paper and then extracted at random. The first group of firms extracted gets the first con-tract and so on.
>
> (MPM, 172–3; see also TNM, 27)

The repetition of the game created an available sanction to be imposed against violators. Any cheating behaviour could then be punished by exclusion from the long-term gains of collusion: the higher profits deriving from the elimination of competition. Indeed, corruption may become superfluous since the cartel acquires the power to decide autonomously on the attribution to its firms of property rights to political rents. It is possible, however, that purchasing certain services from politicians and bureaucrats will augment cohesion of the cartel. Corruption again becomes indispensable if one wishes to avoid procedural hold ups, acquire restricted information that facilitates collusion, limit the number of firms invited to tender or ensure that the flow of money is not interrupted. For example, according to one entrepreneur in public tenders in Milan:

> after each of us had won the contract they wanted, we were contacted and informed that the 'system' required money in return. Each of us made a one-off payment proportional to the contract ... destined to thank those exponents of the political-institutional system who guaranteed the awarding of contracts independently of the pre-existing cartels of 'non-belligerence' we formed.
>
> (TM, 46; see also CD, no. 417, 11 June 1993: 4)

Cartels are particularly strong in situations of semi-monopoly; that is, when the number of potential suppliers is limited by the technical nature of the product. In fact, cartels develop especially in the construction of big infrastruc-tures – such as high-speed railways or airports – or when semi-monopolies are artificially created by the state via public licences (for instance in television broadcasting). In the latter case especially, entrepreneurs – such as media tycoons – might directly occupy elective or semi-elective positions from which they favour their own businesses. Bribes in this case virtually disappear – at least when public monies are directly attributed to family firms. In order to develop, entrepreneurial corruption needs patrimonialistic control upon parties and weak institutional control on conflicts of interest. Differently than in clan corruption, when entrepreneurial forms of corruption become dominant, politicians involved in them have their own business, not in the public sector but in the private one. Recently, serious concerns for the quality of Italian democracy have arisen because of the development of a political class of powerful businessmen, such as Berlusconi and his entourage of managers of his firms. Unchecked conflicts of interest allow for the type of corruption with the lowest level of transaction costs, with corrupter and corruptee often being the same person.[18]

Concluding remarks

In this chapter we have proposed an interpretation of corruption that goes beyond both sociological analysis of the (culturally determined) moral costs and political-economic analysis of structural conditions that influence the individual costs and benefits of corruption. Borrowing from the literature on transactions costs, we listed several mechanisms that tend to reduce the costs of collecting information on, being involved in and enforcing corrupt deals.

We argued that these mechanisms have a self-sustaining nature, at the same time facilitating the spread of corruption and becoming smoother the more corruption spreads. The governance mechanisms of corruption may be distinguished in first-, second- and third-party types. Path dependency facilitates the spread of corruption because of the fixed costs of new institutions, co-ordination, learning and adaptive expectations. Vicious circles bring about perverse equilibria that facilitate the survival and development of corruption by reducing its transaction costs since mechanisms that lower the transaction costs of corruption tend to affect individual preferences, lowering moral barriers.

Different forms of corruption – party corruption, clan corruption, gang corruption and entrepreneurial corruption – can be distinguished according to the agents that fulfil the main role in the coordination of corruption deals. In party corruption, the main resources used to reduce transaction costs are party-controlled allocations of careers, candidateship and nominations; in gang corruption, resources of (reputation for) violence, deriving from organized crime, are particularly useful as means of coercion; personal clientelistic networks allow the bosses of public bodies to construct their corrupt machines; monopolistic control of relevant markets is a main resource for the development of entrepreneurs able to control public decisions. Although these forms of corruption are not mutually exclusive, they are favoured by differing conditions: strong, centralized parties for party corruption; territorial control by organized crime for gang corruption; dispersed control by party-appointed politicians for clan corruption; and lack of legal checks on monopoly and conflict of interest for entrepreneurial corruption. As we suggested, these different forms of corruption have different combinations of 'strong' and 'weak' points that can sometimes disrupt, more or less seriously, the corrupt equilibrium.

The various mechanisms type of networks can coexist in the same countries, in different regions, times and policy areas. The segmentation of the overall corruption market into several sub-domains, each corresponding to relevant areas of public intervention and to the agents or organizations involved in them, is often a consequence of the demand for secrecy and the restricted nature of illegal dealings, which increases their transaction costs (Lambsdorff 2002).

In each of them different institutional equilibria may prevail with different constraining influences on the action choices and expectations of the agents involved. However, such sub-division is never perfect, especially when the scale of corrupt activities increases. Information flows from one domain to others, while organizations and corrupt agents with specific skills contact one another and negotiate agreements through various structures. The combination of diverse governance mechanisms prevailing in distinct areas of exchange further increases the complexity of overall arrangements for the regulation of corrupt activities. Personal trust between corrupt partners in repeated interactions, for instance, may be reinforced by the sharing of common ideological values and supplemented by the enforcing power of the party organization of which both are members. The mechanisms of corruption governance can be interchangeable rather than complementary with respect to particular contexts of exchange. Middlemen in corrupt dealings, for instance, can be replaced by personal trust developed independently between agents or internalized within the hierarchical apparatus of a private or political organization (i.e. a firm or a party).

Finally, the existence of various complementary interlinkages between governance mechanisms makes them particularly resistant to changes of external conditions, as well as to any attempt to deliberately interfere with the overall 'corruption equilibrium'. Strategies of reform aimed at restricting the smooth operation of institutional arrangements utilized to facilitate corruption, thus increasing its transaction costs, can therefore be countervailed by the reciprocal support which complementary governance mechanisms give to illegal norms and to diffused expectations in the pervasiveness of corruption. The Italian case seems to demonstrate that, ten years after the 'Clean Hands' judicial inquiries guaranteed huge public exposure and promoted legal sanctioning, corruption networks and regulation mechanisms can be formed again and newly created, following the path of previous experiences and accumulated expertise (Vannucci 2003).[19] From this perspective, the action of judges (akin to predators in the natural environment) seems merely to have produced the equivalent of 'natural selection' of the fittest in the bribery market, determining the survival and expanded reproduction of the cleverer corrupt agents (Davigo 1996).

Notes

1 Rose-Ackerman (1978) considers moral cost a kind of fixed cost that derives from the breaking of the law, while Johnson (1975) and Alam (1990) employ the similar concept of 'aversion to corruption'. Economists assume the moral cost as given, and consider economic incentives and opportunities for corruption; we think instead that it can be seen as the expression of an agent's preference for legality and that it may vary over time and for different groups.

2 A neo-institutional analysis of corruption has been developed, among others, by Husted (1994), della Porta and Vannucci (1999) and Lambsdorff (2002).

3 Transaction costs can be defined as the costs of the resources used to establish and maintain property rights (Allen 1991). Such rights are not necessarily legally enforceable, since they simply reflect the individual's expected ability to consume or exchange the services of an asset. From this perspective, transaction costs are 'associ-

ated with the transfer, capture, and protecting of rights ... The transfer of assets entails costs resulting from both parties' attempts to determine what the valued attributes of these assets are and from attempts by each to capture those attributes that, because of the prohibitive costs, remain poorly delineated' (Barzel 1989: 2–3).

4 Corruption is connected with the exchange of property rights to rents created through the political process, being 'actually just a black market for the property rights over which politicians and bureaucrats have allocative power. Rather than assigning rights according to political power, rights are sold to the highest bidder' (Benson 1990: 159). State activity, like market exchanges, can modify the existing structure of property rights. By means of a hidden transaction, corrupter and corrupted share property rights to the political rent thus created. The corrupted official in fact obtains a part of that rent in return for his services (decisions, confidential information, protection), which aim to guarantee or, at least, increase the chances of those property rights being granted, usually in the form of a bribe (della Porta and Vannucci 1999: 35–7).

5 As Turvani notices: 'Prohibition cancels the possibility of referring to a higher, more formal level of institutional orders and sanctions (no court will defend property rights and enforce a contract); it does not cancel transactions. Transactions will take place, but they are now pushed back to another, more primitive institutional environment. A prohibited market is a black market: but the black market is not simply an illegal market, it is a market with a lower degree of institutionalization protecting agents and their transactions' (Turvani 1997: 143).

6 As an example, we can consider the role of Italian party cashiers, who were chosen precisely for their reputation of reliability in illegal transactions. They managed the flux of bribes and could easily conceal part of the illegal revenues going to their party colleagues, being the only ones who possessed a detailed knowledge of the mechanisms governing its allocation (della Porta and Vannucci 1999: 97–9). Party cashiers acquired a favourable reputation in the market of corruption thanks to their observance of a peculiar norm of honesty, implying a complete respect for the obligations assumed in illegal transactions. The importance of this sense of 'honesty' emerges, for instance, in the following description of the national administrative secretary of the PSI: 'a man of honour who personally saw to his obligations and therefore, for reasons of uprightness and personal prestige, consigned in person the [bribe] money due to the local branches' (CD, no. 202-bis, 23 February 1993, p. 12).

7 Any kind of exchange can be facilitated when counterparts are embedded in a social structure (for instance, kinship, ethnic, cultural, ideological or religious links) which reduces its transaction costs (Granovetter 1992; Aoki 2002: 208–9). As Lambsdorff observes, corruption is no exception: 'corrupt relationships can be set up with partners with whom some kind of organizational link already exists ... Pre-existing relationships can lay the foundation for economic exchange by providing the required safeguard against opportunism' (2002: 233).

8 As Barzel observes: 'A third party must be able to impose costs in order to induce each of the principals to an agreement to make one-way transfers to the other. The enforcer induces the parties to an agreement to perform in situations in which they would not be inclined to perform on their own. He do(es) so by threatening to impose costs on them. The amount of cost-imposing power that a third party possesses sets a limit on what he can enforce. Parties making an agreement subject to a third party enforcement will comply only if they think that (the enforcer) is able and willing to impose a cost at least as large as the required transfer' (Barzel 2002: 42).

9 In some circumstances, however, courts can be indirectly used to prevent or resolve conflicts also in corrupt agreements – for instance, when there are brokers officially paid as consultants (Lambsdorff 2002: 228). In this case formal laws and public agencies for enforcement ironically become part of the governance structure of illegal deals.

10 Moral costs may be considered the institutional expression of 'moral conventions': beliefs in a certain rule or principle (such as trust in others or respect for pacts) accompanied by the expectation that they are recognized and shared by others (in large part, at least). These conventions will be stable, forming an equilibrium, only where their social consequences – the sum of the resulting actions – are compatible with the expectations which shape them. If the (more or less corrupt) behaviour of others influences moral aversion to corruption, the expectation that corruption is widely practised becomes self-fulfilling – not simply as a result of rational calculation but also because the moral barriers to that activity are lowered as processes of self-legitimization of corrupt practices come into operation (Hirschman 1982).

11 Moreover, a 'bad' collective reputation of public administrators creates 'more incentives to engage in corrupt activities than if they had always behaved honestly', determining even for newcomers a vicious circle 'where the new generations suffer from the original sin of their elders' (Tirole 1996: 3).

12 As Pizzorno notices: 'Since corruption is punishable by law and the relative transactions must of necessity remain secret, this kind of intermediary must possess certain abilities, which can be generically termed *skills in illegality*. They must be able to act under the threat of sanction, find those paths least open to scrutiny, cover and protect themselves and, even more importantly, have as wide and direct a knowledge as possible of both the individuals willing to participate in illegal transactions and those who, while not wishing to be involved, occupy positions of authority in the areas where such opportunities are most frequent' (Pizzorno 1992: 23).

13 For a detailed empirical analysis of these specialized activities see della Porta and Vannucci (1999: 69–84).

14 Multiple equilibria refer to the amount of the bribes (Cadot 1987), the number of corrupt exchanges (Lui 1986), or both (Andvig and Moene 1990). Murphy, Shleifer and Vishny (1993) single out a model of multiple equilibria in levels of corruption and income.

15 The same applies to similar regions within the same country, such as Northern and Southern Italy, according to Putnam's (1993) analysis of comparative civicness.

16 In addition, opportunities for gain in redistributive activities, such as rent-seeking in corrupt exchanges, will favour the competitive convergence of public and private agents in those areas where the structure of remuneration is most favourable (Baumol 1990: 894). The allocation of talent will then support parasitic activities: the more talented and highly educated (with more valuable human capital) will be more inclined to engage in corruption activities than in productive works, with adverse effects on the country's opportunities for economic growth (Murphy, Shleifer and Vishny 1991).

17 Corruption can also become systemic within specific public bodies relatively sheltered from political interference and controls. In this case top bureaucrats may assume the role of enforcers of access to and the smooth functioning of the 'system' of corrupt deals, as well as to the informal mechanisms of internal bribe sharing. The resource used to impose costs on low-level bureaucrats and their private counterparts is the bureaucrats' official power within the public body. One example is the refined system of calculation for kickbacks developed in the 1980s and 1990s among the revenue police in Milan. According to a Fininvest private manager: 'It was well known, as I learned from friends who were entrepreneurs, ... talking with people of Falck, Fiat, Gemina and so on, that when the revenue police came, you had to pay ... [An official] at the beginning of the control operation told me that he had received the file with a pencil-written number on it, and that that was the amount he had to bring, in any case and independently from any notification of a fiscal nature' (MF, 69). Top officials within the corrupt structures co-ordinated the legal as well as the illegal activities of enforcement agents, guaranteeing the fulfilment of agreements. Hierarchical, centralized public structures appear as favourable conditions for the development of

articulated networks of corrupt exchange within public structures (Vannucci and della Porta 2003).

18 Entrepreneurs who often play a governance role in corrupt markets are specialized brokers. Brokers play a crucial role: they reduce identification and information costs by building contacts (that is, a system of friendship and trust ties); they collect and transmit reserved information, necessary to win the confidence of those who want to participate in the illegal exchange; they assume some of the risks of illegal transactions; they also help solve problems of coordination that arise between the central authorities allocating resources and those at the local level who must manage them. When their network of links with politicians, parties and enterprises is wide and stabilized, brokers can also enforce the illegal dealings they have promoted, thanks to their ability to threaten exclusion from future agreements and to their possession of blackmailing information. An emblematical figure of the enforcing broker is Gelli, Grand Master of the secret P2 Masonic lodge discovered by public prosecutors in 1981. Among its 962 affiliates were three government ministers, thirty MPs, more than fifty generals (including the highest ranks of the secret services), high-level functionaries, diplomats, journalists, financiers and entrepreneurs, as well as the current Italian Premier Berlusconi and two Ministers of his Cabinet. The P2 offered a confidential arena in which powerful agents could negotiate and work out agreements. The lodge operated in a plurality of – at times illegal – markets: national and international finance, publishing, corruption, and arms trafficking. In this context, the P2's Grand Master offered 'an extra-legal system of handling rather murky dealings' (CP2-bis/1, p. 43). As a result of the resources at his disposition, Gelli frequently appeared as guarantor of deals he helped arrange, operating on a scale that even transcended Italy's borders.

19 According to a recent opinion poll, corruption is perceived to be as widespread as in the 'First Republic' by 52 per cent of Italian citizens, more widespread by 26 per cent, and less widespread by 17 per cent (Ipsos-Explorer 2003).

References

Alam, M.S. (1990) 'Some Economic Costs of Corruption in LDCs', *The Journal of Development Studies*, vol. 27, no. 1, pp. 85–97.

Allen, D.W. (1991) 'What Are Transaction Costs?', *Research in Law and Economics*, vol. 14, pp. 1–18.

Andreoli, M. (1993) *Andavamo in Piazza Duomo*, Milano.

Andvig, J.C. (1991) 'The Economics of Corruption', *Studi economici*, vol. 46, pp. 57–94.

Andvig, J.C. and Moene, K.O. (1990) 'How Corruption May Corrupt', *Journal of Economic Behaviour and Organization*, vol. 13, no. 1, pp. 63–76.

Aoki, M. (2001) *Toward a Comparative Institutional Analysis*, Cambridge.

Arlacchi, P. (1992) *Gli uomini del disonore*, Milano.

Arthur, W.B. (1994) *Increasing Returns and Path Dependence in the Economy*, Ann Arbor.

Axelrod, R. (1984) *The Evolution of Cooperation*, New York.

Barzel, Y. (1989) *Economic Analysis of Property Rights*, Cambridge.

Barzel, Y. (2002) *A Theory of the State. Economic Rights, Legal Rights, and the Scope of the State*, Cambridge.

Baumol, W.J. (1990) 'Entrepreneurship: Productive, Unproductive and Destructive', *Journal of Political Economy*, vol. 98, no. 5, pp. 893–921.

Becker, G.S. (1968) 'Crime and Punishment. An Economic Approach', *Journal of Political Economy*, vol. 76, no. 2, pp. 169–217.

Becquart-Leclercq, J. (1989) 'Paradoxes of Political Corruption: A French View', in A.J. Heidenheimer, M. Johnston and V.T. LeVine (eds) *Political Corruption*, New Brunswick and Oxford, pp. 191–210.

Benson, B.L. (1990) *The Enterprise of Law. Justice Without the State*, San Francisco.

Blankenburg, E., Staudhammer, R. and Steinert, H. (1989) 'Political Scandals and Corruption Issues in West Germany', in A.J. Heidenheimer, M. Johnston and V.T. Le Vine (eds) *Political Corruption*, New Brunswick and Oxford, pp. 913–31.

Bouissou, J.M. (1997) 'Gifts, Networks and Clienteles: Corruption in Japan as a Redistributive System', in D. della Porta and Y. Mény (eds) *Democracy and Corruption in Europe*, London, pp. 132–47.

Cadot, O. (1987) 'Corruption as a Gamble', *Journal of Public Economics*, vol. 33, no. 2, pp. 223–44.

Chibnall, S. and Saunders, P. (1977) 'Worlds Apart: Notes on the Social Reality of Corruption', *British Journal of Sociology*, vol. 28, no. 2, pp. 138–54.

Davigo, P. (1996) *La giubba del re. Intervista sulla corruzione*, Roma-Bari.

della Porta, D. (1992) *Lo scambio occulto. Casi di corruzione politica in Italia*, Bologna.

della Porta, D. (2000) 'Social Capital, Beliefs in Government and Political Corruption', in S.J. Pharr and R.D. Putnam (eds) *Disaffected Democracies. What's Troubling the Trilateral Countries*, Princeton, pp. 202–29.

della Porta, D. and Vannucci, A. (1999) *Corrupt Exchanges*, New York.

della Porta, D. and Vannucci. S. (2002) 'Corruption and Public Contracts: Some Lessons from the Italian Case', in D. della Porta and S. Rose-Ackerman (eds) *Corrupt Exchanges*, Baden-Baden.

Ellickson, R.C. (1991) *Order Without Law: How Neighbors Settle Disputes*, Cambridge, Mass.

Elster, J. (1989) *Nuts and Bolts for the Social Sciences*, Cambridge.

Falcone, G. (with M. Padovani) (1991) *Cose di Cosa Nostra*, Milano.

Galasso, A. (1993) *La Mafia Politica*, Milano.

Gambetta D. (1993) *The Sicilian Mafia*, Cambridge, Mass./London.

Granovetter, M. (1992) 'Economic Action and Social Structure: The Problem of Embeddedness', in M. Granovetter and R. Swedberg (eds) *The Sociology of Economic Life*, Boulder, pp. 53–81.

Hirschman, A. (1982) *Shifting Involvements*, Princeton.

Husted, B.W. (1994) 'Honor Among Thieves: A Transaction Costs Interpretation of Corruption in Third World Countries', *Business Ethics Quarterly*, vol. 4, no. 1, pp. 17–27.

Ipsos-Explorer (2003) 'Political Corruption Today, Opinion Poll', May, in <http://www.agcom.it>.

Iwai, H. (1986) 'Organized Crime in Japan', in R.J. Kelly (ed.) *Organized Crime: A Global Perspective*, Totowa and New York.

Johnson, O.E.G. (1975) 'An Economic Analysis of Corrupt Government with Special Application to LDCs', *Kyklos*, vol. 28, no. 1, pp. 47–61.

Lambsdorff, J. Graf (2002) 'Making Corrupt Deals: Contracting in the Shadow of the Law', *Journal of Economic Behaviour and Organization*, vol. 48, no. 3, pp. 221–41.

Lui, F.T. (1986) 'A Dynamic Model of Corruption Deterrence', *Journal of Public Economics*, vol. 31, pp. 215–36.

Mény, Y. (1992) *La Corruption de la République*, Paris.

Murphy, K.M., Shleifer, A. and Vishny, R.W. (1991) 'The Allocation of Talent: Implications for Growth', *The Quarterly Journal of Economics*, vol. 105, pp. 503–30.

Murphy, K.M., Shleifer, A. and Vishny, R.W. (1993) 'Why is Rent-Seeking so Costly to Growth?', *American Economic Review Papers and Proceedings*, vol. 83, no. 2, pp. 409–14.

Myrdal, G. (1968) *Asian Drama: An Enquiry into the Poverty of Nations*, New York.

North, D.C. (1990) *Institutions, Institutional Change and Economic Performance*, Cambridge.

Opp, K.D. (1989) 'The Economics of Crime and the Sociology of Deviant Behaviour: A Theoretical Confrontation of Basic Propositions', *Kyklos*, vol. 42, no. 3, pp. 405–30.

Panther, S. (2000) 'Non-legal Sanctions', in B. Bouckaert and D. De Geest (eds) *Encyclopedia of Laws and Economics*, vol. 1, Cheltenham.

Pierson, P. (2000) 'Increasing Returns, Path Dependence, and the Study of Politics', *American Political Science Review*, vol. 94, no. 2, pp. 251–67.

Pizzorno, A. (1992) 'La corruzione nel sistema politico', in D. della Porta (1992) *Lo scambio occulto*, Bologna.

Putnam, R.D. (1993) *Making Democracy Work: Civic Traditions in Modern Italy*, Princeton.

Rose-Ackerman, S. (1978) *Corruption. A Study in Political Economy*, New York.

Rothacher, A. (1996) 'Structural Corruption in a Gift Culture', Paper presented at the International Conference on Corruption in Contemporary Politics, University of Salford, November.

Tirole, J. (1996) 'A Theory of Collective Reputation' (with Applications to the Persistence of Corruption and to Firm Quality), *Review of Economic Studies*, vol. 63, pp. 1–22.

Transparency International (2002) *Corruption Perception Index*, in <http://www.transparency.de>.

Turvani, M. (1997) 'Illegal Markets and the New Institutional Economics', in C. Menard (ed.) *Transaction Costs Economics*, Cheltenham, pp. 127–48.

Vannucci, A. (1997) 'Politicians and Godfathers: Mafia and Political Corruption in Italy', in D. della Porta and Y. Mény (eds) *Democracy and Corruption in Europe*, London, pp. 50–64.

Vannucci, A. (2003) 'La corruzione nel sistema politico italiano a dieci anni da "mani pulite"', in G. Forti (ed.) *Il prezzo della tangente*, Milano, pp. 3–70.

Vannucci, A. and della Porta, D. (2003) 'Corruption in Policing and Law Enforcement: A Theoretical Scheme for the Analysis of the Italian Case', in M. Amir and S. Einstein (eds) *Corruption, Dealing, Security and Corruption* (forthcoming).

Sources

CD Chamber of Deputees, 'Domanda di autorizzazione a procedere in giudizio', doc. IV.

CP2 bis/1 Parliamentary Committee of Inquiry on the P2: relazioni finali ed allegati, doc. XXIII, no. 2.

CPMF Parliamentary Committee of Inquiry on the Mafia, Final Report on Mafia and Politics, approved on 6 April 1993 (supplement to *La Repubblica*, 10 April 1993).

PRP Public Prosecutor at the Court of Palermo, Request for application of precautionary measures, no. 2789/90N.C.

SV3 Interview in Savona.

TRIS Court of Savona, SC no. 145/85, 8 August 1985.

UIS Court of Savona, IM BI in JP no. 1019/81 R.G.P.M., 24 August 1984.

MF   Tribunal of Milan, Report of evidence of the interrogation with Leonardo Scias-
        cia, 22 December 1994 (in *Le mazzette della Fininvest*, Milano, Kaos edizioni,
        1996).
MPM   E. Nascimbeni, A. Pamparana, *Le mani pulite*, A. Mondadori, 1992.
TM   A. Carlucci, *Tangentomani*, Baldini & Castoldi, 1992 (the book published
        reports of evidence of interrogations).
TNM   Tangentopoli. Le carte che scottano (pp. 65–86 excerpt from the 'Richiesta di
        autorizzazione a procedere nei confronti dell'on. Bettino Craxi', 12 January
        1993), supplement to *Panorama*, February 1993.

10 Private ordering of corrupt transactions

The case of the Chinese *guanxi* networks and their challenge by a formal legal system

Matthias Schramm and Markus Taube

Introduction

In recent years reports of corrupt behaviour by officials have become a regular feature of the Chinese media, revealing a substantial permeation of Chinese society by corruption. Indicating the true dimensions of the phenomenon of corruption in today's China Jiang Zemin, President of State and General Secretary of the Communist Party of China, has been quoted as evaluating the struggle against corruption in the party and government as 'a matter of life and death of the party' (AFP 2000).

Corruption is neither a new phenomenon in China (Heberer 2001), nor is the degree of corruption really outstanding in comparison to other world regions.[1] The organization of many corrupt transactions in China, however, provides a perfect example of the suitability of social networks and economic clubs to provide a full infrastructure for conducting and safeguarding corrupt deals. Two examples indicate the importance of the traditional Chinese *guanxi* networks for the facilitation of corruption in China:

1   The former mayor and party secretary of Beijing, politburo member Chen Xitong, was arrested and convicted of charges of corruption in 1995. In the following months it became obvious that for years a network of cadres, whose formal power was supplemented by informal connections among them, had not only been controlling some of the most lucrative industries in the city but had also employed this power for illicit personal gain. Chen Xitong alone was said to have accepted bribes amounting to US$2.2 billion for awarding permissions for construction projects. The *guanxi* network stabilizing this 'Chen system', and ordering the transactions within the core group, had been strengthened from the outside by strong personal connections to the very top of the central leadership and their children – who were also participating in the economic rents created in the run of Beijing's system reforms and opening up to the outside world. Protected by such a densely knit network of personal connections, Chen Xitong and his colleagues believed themselves to be protected against internal disruptions as

well as attacks from the outside. Rightly so. Eventually, it took nothing less than a power struggle at the very top of the Chinese party echelon, to bring the 'Chen system' down (Bo 2000; Gilley 1998; Tsang 1998).

2   Another widely publicized case of *guanxi*-based corruption concerns the Yuanhua smuggling scandal. During the latter half of the 1990s the Yuanhua Group of Xiamen in Southern China made use of a wide network of personal relationships, with officials occupying leading positions in virtually all areas of the political and economic system. They smuggled oil, cars and other goods worth up to US$10 billion into the PR China. This *guanxi* network that Yuanhua not only employed but at the same time meticulously cultivated and proactively extended, provided a perfect framework for the payment of bribes and facilitated behaviour by officials that made it possible to give all smuggling activities the appearance of officially promoted, legal transactions. Yuanhua's transactions enjoyed the support of the party secretary as well as of the vice-mayor of Xiamen, the director of the local customs office, a bank president, public security officials, managers of trading corporations, etc. The person occupying the highest rank of those having been publicly accused (and convicted) of being a member of the smuggling network is Li Jizhou, then the PR China's vice-minister of public security. The smuggling activities were so well embedded in the social networks permeating Chinese society that serious actions to unveil and stop the smuggling activities were started only after influential state-owned enterprises had employed their own *guanxi* networks to complain in Beijing about the flood of cheap imports which were further eroding their already poor business performances – and therefore endangered Prime Minister Zhu Rongji's plans to reform the state-owned enterprise sector.[2]

The integration of corrupt transactions in the social interaction patterns of *guanxi* networks, which had been the organizational backbone of the Chen and Yuanhua corruption schemes, lies at the centre of interest in this chapter. The study sets out with an analysis of the order-creating function of the Chinese *guanxi* networks (pp. 183–5). Against this background we discuss the relativity of the concept of 'corruption' in the context of *guanxi* networks and analyse their particular suitability to solve the problem of order inherent in corrupt transactions (see pp. 185–7). The topic of China's fight against corruption is discussed on pp. 187–92: is it possible to break up the 'symbiotic' – or shall we say 'parasitic'? – relationship between *guanxi* networks and corruption by establishing a new formal legal system styled on Western models? Building on an analysis of the complementary and substitutive relationship between *guanxi* and a formal legal system we conclude with an assessment of the tasks ahead for the fight against corruption in the PR China (see pp. 192–3).

Private ordering in the confines of the Chinese *guanxi* networks

The Chinese *guanxi* networks can be understood as institutions that arose many centuries ago as a means to stabilize social relations. They were used to secure trade relations in an environment that became increasingly complex but was only insufficiently covered by an overarching system of order (Carr and Landa 1983; Posner 1980). The environment economic actors were facing was characterized by either a complete lack of formal systems of order, or the existence of the legal system was coming along with certain elements of arbitrariness that compromised this institution's power to put order into economic interaction.[3]

Fulfilling its function of providing microcosms of personalistic order in an environment characterized by intransparent formal rule setting and rule execution, the institution of *guanxi* networks has survived through the centuries and become an integral part of the Chinese social system. Especially since the beginning of the reform period in 1979, the organization of economic activities by means of *guanxi* networks has regained importance. The Chinese reform model of gradual transition which has been advancing the restructuring of institutional conditions in the form of a hardly foreseeable trial-and-error procedure (Rawski 1999: 142) has been a cause of great institutional uncertainty in economic interaction (Wank 1999: 251). The reform period has been characterized by the dissolution of established, central-administrative ordering mechanisms and a not-always simultaneous creation of new, more strongly market-oriented elements (Tao and Zhu 2001: 3; Wank 1999: 264, 266). This has led to institutional vacua which have been often filled by economic actors spontaneously reverting to traditional, institutional arrangements and behaviour patterns, and thus to a new heyday of a personally oriented, relational assurance of transactions in *guanxi* networks (Nee 2000: 68; Chan 1999: 317; Hu 1998: 199–220; Yan 1996: 19).[4]

Within the Chinese language the term '*guanxi*' has multiple meanings and is used in various contexts. It can refer to (a) the existence of a relationship between people who share a common element, (b) actual connections with frequent contact between and within groups of people, and (c) a contact person with little direct interaction (Fan 2002a: 371f; Bian 1994). As vague and multifaceted as the usage of the term '*guanxi*' is, so is the interpretation and description of its functional principles in the literature, reaching from 'friendship' (Pye 1982), 'particularistic ties' (Jacobs 1979), 'reciprocal exchange' (Hwang 1987) to 'social capital' (Butterfield 1982). Commonly, *guanxi* is defined as some kind of 'special relationship between a person who needs something and a person who has the ability to give something' (Osland 1990: 4–5); in a wider sense this means 'relationships or social connections based on mutual interest and benefits' (Yang 1994: 64f). All in all even these broad and general definitions fall short on a very important element: of course, *guanxi* networks are based on personal relations, but they are marked by certain common elements such as its members coming from the same village or region, having served in the same military unit, sharing attributes like staying in the same party units, schools, associations, etc.[5] However, membership in a *guanxi* network is not limited to such common experience but can also be arranged by a person in a position of trust whose reputation is the guarantee for the proper behaviour of the person introduced. In this way individual people are able to expand their radius of economic relations, backed up by *guanxi* networks (Krug and Polos 2000). By accepting a gift or service, the involved person obligates himself to perform an undefined reciprocal service at an unspecified time in the future (Fan 2002b; Yang 1994). Thus, an implicit contract is concluded, the fulfilment of which is linked to the particular network (Hsing 1998: 134ff.). Lastly, the acceptance of these contracts establishes obligations that constitute a mutual dependency within the network.

Therefore, the ordering problem lying at the centre of the institution of *guanxi* networks is that individuals are faced with the problem of conducting transactions in an unstable institutional and therefore high-risk environment which – at least to some degree – requires transaction-specific investments without the chance of referring to an independent formal legal system. In this context, the Chinese *guanxi* networks provide a practicable and, under the given conditions, transaction-cost minimizing (best practice) solution: the mutual exchange of services and the acceptance of abstract debt obligations is the main integrating force within a *guanxi* network. It can be understood as a mutual investment in social capital (Dasgupta and Serageldin 1999), which constitutes the framework of a system of order that coordinates the interaction between the network members (Butterfield 1982; Bourdieu 1986). The *guanxi* networks themselves may be understood as clubs that guarantee their members the enforceability of available property rights in an environment of institutional disorder, and thus are lowering transaction costs (Lee, Pae and Wong 2001; Luo 1997). The expenses necessary for club membership (gift-giving, mutual exchange of favours, etc.) have to be understood as investments in social capital which upon joining take the characteristic of sunk costs. Once having joined, the club assures the disposal of property rights to a certain degree: as long as the individual performs economic transactions within the club – i.e. among and with other club members – contract fulfilment is assured in that information regarding the honouring or breaching of contracts spreads rapidly among the club members. Cooperative, contract-honouring behaviour thus becomes the dominant strategy even in one-shot games (unique transactions between club members), since these unique games are bound up in an iterative system of multiple games (transactions) with other club members (Axelrod 1983). As Davis puts it, *guanxi* network transactions are 'the equivalent of an infinitely repeated game with a set of people they know' (Davis 1995). Honouring contracts and cooperative behaviour is positively sanctioned by the possibility of engaging in further, low-cost transactions with club members. In contrast, the response to opportunistic behaviour is a withdrawal of goodwill or even exclusion from the club (Wank 1999), which, for the club member affected, not only means the loss of investment but also a massive cost increase for future transactions (Carr and Landa 1983; Krug and Polos 2000). Thus 'performance is implicitly enforced by the threat of termination of the transactional relationship and communication of the contractual failure' (Klein 1985). The increase in utility that can be gained by maintaining long-term business relations thus clearly exceeds the short-term gains from an opportunistic breach of contract (Hwang 1987; Lin 2002). In addition, it must be assumed that reciprocity as a moral standard and socially embedded norm is positively influencing the honouring of implicit contracts concluded with members of one's own network. There is evidence that 'reciprocity . . . is a universal moral standard in most, if not all cultures, and is of particular importance in an Asian context where social customs and traditions have traditionally worked as a support mechanism' (D'Souza 2003).

The stock of social capital created in a *guanxi* network has the character of fixed costs for its members. These fixed-cost elements, however, enable the variable costs of contacts, negotiations and implementation of transactions between club members to be reduced to a minimum (Hsing 1998: 134ff.). Since the fixed costs are higher than the variable costs, the incentive for a high intensity of interaction is an integral part of the *guanxi* system.

On the basis of this coordination mechanism, which clearly reduces the transaction costs of economic exchanges, the Chinese *guanxi* networks have advanced the development of the division of labour in the economic process (and also economic development) in Chinese society over the centuries, and they continue to exist as complementary and parallel mechanisms for ordering economic interaction.

Embedding corrupt transactions in *guanxi* networks

In a society permeated by such *guanxi* networks, an analysis of (economic) behaviour can never be absolute but must be evaluated in relation to the specific social situation. The definition of morally correct behaviour is not identical for all interacting parties but is based on the identity of the counterpart. Members of the core groups (i.e. a *guanxi* network) experience, in general, a different behaviour than non-members (Gabrenya and Hwang 1996). This is particularly important for the further analysis since the provision of certain goods or the implementation of transactions, which from the perspective of a *guanxi* relationship appear as normal and even necessary transactions within the club, from the perspective of a legal system would certainly belong to the sphere of corruption (Goudie and Stasavage 1998). Insofar as *guanxi* networks and legal systems co-exist, there is a blurring of the limits between regular economic transactions and corruption (Heberer 2001). For the individual economic actor this means that as long as no clear hierarchy exists between these two systems, and as long as *guanxi* transactions are not assigned a clearly delineated functional zone within the legal system, conflicts of interest will always arise between maintaining club discipline on the one hand and following legal statute on the other.[6] Accordingly, a not-insignificant portion of behavioural patterns that are classified as corrupt by external institutions such as the World Bank or the

OECD are important elements of the social fabric (White 1996). What is more, the network-preserving transactions – which from the viewpoint of a supra-individual, codified legal system are classified as illegal – are precisely those which establish institutions that create legal certainty in a relational, person-oriented environment. Examining the case numbers of corruption in China from this point of view, it is necessary to relativize the accusation of corruption in many areas.

It would be wrong, however, to dismiss the entire phenomenon of Chinese corruption as a problem of classification, caused by the parallel existence of two systems of order with differing functional principles and values. In Chinese society – independent of and beyond that grey zone– there is also a clear, normative differentiation of morally unimpeachable behaviour and corruption or illegal granting of advantage, etc. That is to say, corrupt behaviour aimed at achieving private advantage can very well be identified in China, and there is a considerable amount of it. A particular characteristic here is that a considerable portion of these corrupt transactions take advantage of the existence of *guanxi* networks (Lee 1991). It must be noted, however, that such transactions in interplay solely with the environment outside of the given *guanxi* networks can be classified as completely 'corrupt'. Within the network itself they serve the formation of social capital and the maintenance of relationships just as any other 'regular' transactions, and are indistinguishable from them.

It is a fundamental insight that corrupt transactions, just like all other economically based interactions, are grounded on the exchange of specific bundles of property rights and like these must deal with the cost problems of transaction initiation, of contract completion and safeguard against opportunistic behaviour of the transactions partners (Goudie and Stasavage 1998). Corrupt transactions, however, are particularly endangered by *ex post* opportunism. Since corruption payments are a form of investment, which have no value outside the transaction, the payer places himself in a potential hold-up of the receiver who can demand additional payment, or who may not – or not sufficiently – perform the agreed service, without having to fear countermeasures from the payer.

In light of the illegal character of corrupt transactions, the established, formal institutions of the national market and legal systems cannot be laid claim to (Goudie and Stasavage 1998), so that other ordering mechanisms must be utilized (Rose-Ackerman 1999; Lambsdorff 2002). The ideal solution of such a problem from the perspective of new institutional economics is the 'vertical integration' of all transaction partners under the roof of a governance structure that encompasses the entire transaction: an enterprise (Williamson 1985). This solution, however, is not suitable for corrupt transactions because of their illegal character and the fact that one party is usually part of the public administration and not internalizable.

A solution to this problem, however, seems to be available in the form of the Chinese *guanxi* networks. The suitability of *guanxi* networks for the solution of the problem of corrupt transactions is seen in the ability of this institution to transform high-risk exchanges into self-implementing contracts. At the same time, they are an approximation of an ideal solution in terms of institutional economics: with their significant investments in building the network, all participating parties document a credible commitment; they expend resources which can only lead to a pay-off if future transactions are carried out in the interests of all contracting parties. The above argumentation shows that these contractual relations are 'stable' since all participating parties must have an interest in long-term transaction relationships. Because of their high portion of such investment costs, *guanxi* networks create governance structures that enforce contract-honouring behaviour of the transaction partners, analogous to vertical integration solutions (Reja and Tavitie 2000). *Guanxi* networks thus manage to provide an infrastructure in which the transaction partners can safeguard themselves from the *ex post* opportunism of one side.

The use of *guanxi* networks for coordinating corrupt transactions not only makes sense in functional terms but is also optimal with regard to transaction-cost theory. As described above, transactions coordinated in *guanxi* networks have high fixed costs but low variable costs. For the individual this means that with a high volume of transactions the average cost of individual transactions can be lowered. There is thus an incentive to use a *guanxi* network for as many transactions as possible. The individual can use the same ordering mechanism that forms the basis for his 'regular' transactions also for transactions carried out with the clear intention of manipulating the political decision-making process for personal advantage – transactions that must accordingly be classified as 'corrupt'. In this way he cannot only save the costs of setting up a special system for coordinating corrupt transactions but can additionally also lower the average costs of *all* transactions coordinated via this *guanxi* network.

Fighting corruption in China by strengthening the formal legal system

As has been illustrated, Chinese society is permeated by *guanxi* networks. These *guanxi* networks are important for the analysis of and the fight against corruption in China in at least two perspectives. First, *guanxi* networks prevent a clear-cut demarcation of 'regular' and corrupt transactions. Transactions that are to be classified as corrupt in a non-network environment may be 'regular' in the context of network discipline. Without taking a definite stance with either of these two sets of norms and values, any analysis will be at least to some extent misleading. Second, *guanxi* networks provide a hyper-stable ordering mechanism for corrupt transactions. By embedding corrupt transactions in *guanxi* networks, the potentially prohibitively high transaction costs of 'contracting in the shadow of the law' (Lambsdorff 2003) not only can be overcome but also the average costs of all transaction conducted under the umbrella of the *guanxi* network can be reduced.

The fight against corruption in China is therefore facing a formidable challenge. How can such corrupt relationships be destabilized? One solution brought forward by Chinese politicians and academic circles is a further strengthening of the rule of law and the introduction of a formal legal system based on Western models. In the following we will therefore deal with the question as to the extent an intensified establishment of an institutionalized and codified legal system will be able to lead to a displacement of the *guanxi* networks, or whether the co-existence of two systems that offer transactional security is possible in an economy in the long run. The analysis of the complementary or substitutive position of *guanxi* networks in a legal system will therefore also deal with the question as to whether the institutional underpinnings of a large share of corrupt transactions in China will persist in the near future.

The establishment of an institutional framework that offers legal security at a supra-individual level beyond social relationships seems at first glance to offer significant advantages for economic interaction, especially with regard to transaction frequency, the free choice of transaction partners, and especially transaction costs.[7] This should lead individuals to rely on the system of *guanxi* networks no longer in order to secure their transactions since there is now no uncertainty regarding the enforcement of contractual rights. From this standpoint, *guanxi* networks should gradually lose importance and ultimately disappear once a functioning legal system gradually becomes established.

However, the superiority of a supra-individual legal system postulated here *vis-à-vis* the personalized *guanxi* networks is, at closer examination, doubtful and certainly not supportable as a categorical formulation. Supra-individual legal systems appear superior in terms of their ability to provide legal security, but this unambiguous assertion is no longer possible with respect to the transaction costs that are linked to the provision of good 'legal security'. The utility and cost-based rationale for shifting transactions once coordinated by *guanxi* networks to the ordering mechanism of a legal system appears especially doubtful, taking into account the concepts of path dependency and embeddedness.[8]

Transaction security as a public or club good

In terms of the establishment of institutional order, legal security can be regarded as a public good. In contrast, legal security provided by *guanxi* networks, as already discussed, could be labelled a club good. Seen in these terms, a couple of characteristics emerge that must be considered in the analysis. The central feature here is optimal club size. With an increasing number of club members, an effective sanctioning of infringements is no longer assured. Once the optimal size of a club has been exceeded, the costs of informing club members of individual infringements increase (Carr and Landa 1983). Sanctioning misbehaviour, which depends on the complete information of all club members regarding the trustworthiness of all others, can no longer be guaranteed under all circumstances. This could make opportunistic behaviour appear worthwhile for some individuals (Buchanan 1965: 13–14), and the function of the club as a guarantor of legal security for its members is thus challenged. With a public good, provided by a codified and institutionalized legal system, this problem does not arise (Buchanan 1965: 1–3). On the contrary, even an expansion of the number of 'consumers' of this good will not, by definition, allow any rivalry in consumption to arise. Additional users lower the per capita payments without giving rise to crowding effects (Sandler and Tschirhart 1997: 336–8). Especially in rapidly growing economies such as China, the increase in transaction partners and the advancing division of labour via specialization is a motor for this growth (North 1984: 11). With an increasing division of labour, *guanxi* networks have definite limitations because of their club character, since the optimal club size is reached much earlier than the optimal permeation of a division of labour (and accordingly the optimal number of transactions and transaction partners). In this respect the formal legal system seems to be superior to the personalistic *guanxi* networks and possesses a potential to crowd out the latter.

Fixed and variable costs of transaction assurance

As has been shown, *guanxi* networks can limit the variable costs of a transaction to a minimum. After a comparatively high initial investment in social capital for membership in the club, only marginal transaction costs (mostly limited to search costs) accrue for all further transactions. Since, however, the investments are in the form of sunk costs, these should no longer be significant in an individual's utility maximization calculations. *Guanxi* networks thus contain an inherent incentive for maximizing possible transactions, since each additional transaction has to be assessed only in terms of its variable costs. In contrast, there are opportunity costs for club membership that arise because transactions with outsiders are only possible at greatly increased costs. These costs are hence a function of the club size, and decrease as the club size increases.[9]

In an institutional legal system there are no fixed costs for the individual.[10] Legal security exists for every individual and protects every transaction. In such a system, however, there is a fundamental difference between the existence of laws, rights and claims and their enforcement.[11] The legal security granted by such a system is thus closely bound to the credibility and impartial application of sanctions (Schwartz and Tullock 1975: 75). However, if one of the supports is weakened – be it that the judiciary is not sufficiently independent or the executive is not able to enforce the imposed sanctions – the system loses its functionality in many areas.[12] It must be clearly understood that the judiciary must not only be free of preferences in a personal regard but must also give out clear signals of its credibility. A codified legal system does not establish the public good of contractual and legal security simply as a matter of course. Rather, it is the task of particularly specialized individuals to manifest this in everyday social dealings. It is not clear, however, whether precisely these specialists, who because of their institutional position have (spatially limited) monopoly power, can be exonerated of opportunistic behaviour (Brennan, Güth and Kliemt 1997: 2; Elster 1989: 100; Zou 2000).

Lastly, comparing the cost structures of *guanxi* and the legal system does not lead to a result as obvious as might be assumed. After all, it is hardly even possible to predict the possible outcome of such a calculus: the costs of establishing and maintaining a legal system are eventually financed by taxes and fees; however, it is important to note that the ordinary taxpayer is not informed what share of his taxes and fees is employed to facilitate these tasks. In addition, this intransparent cost factor any individual bears does not guarantee individual legal security, just as the existence of judges and laws does not implicate protection on a personal level. Each time an individual takes recourse to the legal system it implies bearing additional variable costs in the form of service fees for lawyers and spending time in court.

Path dependency in the use of systems of order

A reduction of the importance of *guanxi* networks for the coordination of economic transactions, and a strengthening or sole use of the legal system, is prevented to a great extent by the phenomenon of path dependency (David 1985). In the final analysis, path dependency points to competition failure in the area of institution selection owing to the lack of possibilities for setting up several parallel institutions and making a direct comparison of performance (c.f. North 1990: 92–4). Instead, decisions are made under conditions of great uncertainty for the establishment of a specific institution for which investments are made, which, in the form of sunk costs, create incentives for the retention of the institutional solution that has been chosen – even if, at a later point in time, another institution may be considered a better option (Kali 1999: 633). A change in systems of order among the competing systems is thus not made solely on the basis of weighing up the accruing costs per transaction. An economic actor with a short-tem orientation will persist in using a once-established system of order until the opportunity costs of maintaining the existing system surpass the costs of constructing a new system within the relevant calculation period.

As shown, *guanxi* networks involve a great amount of sunk costs, which account for the great inertia of this ordering mechanism. The low variable costs of using this mechanism and the high fixed costs make it extremely resistant to changing to a competing mechanism once the initial investment has been made in the social capital it is based on (Hannan and Freeman 1984: 157). This means that the performance of the Chinese legal system must be regarded as considerably superior to the *guanxi* networks for the individual economic actor to view the use of the legal system as a rational way to safeguard transactions. Alternatively, massive pressure by political decision-makers must be exerted for legal systems to displace the *guanxi* networks.[13]

Embeddedness of order mechanisms

An additional argument for the continuation of *guanxi* networks stems from their embeddedness in Chinese society as a whole (Granovetter 1985). Within the overall system, the choice and arrangement of institutions does not follow economic efficiency criteria alone but is also influenced by cultural and social factors (DiMaggio 1994: 38). As Uzzi notes:

> embeddedness is a logic of exchange that shapes motives and expectations and promotes coordinated adaptation. This logic is unique in that actors do not selfishly pursue immediate gains, but concentrate on cultivating long-term cooperative relationships.
>
> (Uzzi 1996: 693)

On the basis of their development within China over the centuries, the *guanxi* networks are strongly anchored in Chinese society and have an important function not only on the economic level but also dominate interaction on a political and social level. *Guanxi* networks themselves are an important part of the social fabric, integrally linked to other (moral and social) foundations of Chinese sociality.[14]

For Hamilton, *guanxi* networks are the primary cultural feature of China and stand, moreover, in an antagonistic relationship to the Western system based on legal rights:

> In the West, Christianity combined with preexisting institutions to produce clear jurisdictional lines of top-down personalized authority. In the economic sphere, this led to legal definitions of property and ownership. But Chinese institutions rest on relationships and not jurisdictions, on obedience to one's own roles and not on bureaucratic command structures ... [B]oth jurisdictional principles and the autonomous individual are historically absent in the Chinese worldview, and thus were not incorporated in Chinese institutions. Instead, Chinese society consists of networks of people whose actions are oriented by normative social relationships.
>
> (Hamilton 1994: 198)

In this light, it seems doubtful that a rapid replacement of *guanxi* networks – motivated by economic efficiency considerations alone – by a comprehensive legal system is likely.[15] Therefore, viewing *guanxi* and a formal legal system as opposing poles, one of which must vanish, might not be the whole story: as both exist it is fairly likely that the well established and socially well embedded one – *guanxi* – will shape the understanding of what is to be expected from a legal system (Potter 2002: 180). Thus, *guanxi* has shaped and will continue to shape what is called the legal culture of a society.[16] After all, the system of codified law already in place is an imported one due to the requirements posed by the WTO to China. As Potter points out:

> These imported forms of law may be seen to reflect changing economic and philosophical conditions of their places of origin, whereas legal conduct in China and the response of Chinese society to the imported legal regime are

dictated by local culture ... The influence of tradition on cultural response to law is a key element in the interaction of law and custom.

(Potter 2002: 181–2)

Lastly, this means that importing a legal system that is totally different from the one already working in Chinese society will pose serious problems to the enforcement of that new kind of legal system, as it is not just the state but also the legal culture that helps to enforce that legal regime.

Summarizing the above argumentation against the background of China's fight against corruption, it seems highly probable that *guanxi* networks will continue to permeate Chinese society in the near future. Therefore a main pillar for the continued widespread existence of corruption in China will remain in place.

Conclusion: the Herculean task of fighting corruption in China

Starting from the proposition that the fight against corruption should focus less on individual moral attitudes or penalties and rather try to destabilize the institutional frameworks employed to conduct corrupt transactions (Lambsdorff 2002), the conclusions to be taken from this chapter for the fight against corruption in China seem to be bleak. Due to the strong tradition of personalistic systems of order (i.e. *guanxi* networks), the classification of individual behaviour in China as 'corrupt' must, in many cases, remain relative. There is no universalistic set of norms that would condemn 'corrupt behaviour' in all circumstances. The same transaction that would be regarded as 'corrupt' from the perspective of a universalistic system of order might constitute norm-conforming behaviour when seen from the perspective of a personalistic-bound ordering system like a *guanxi* network. The fight against corruption in China would therefore have to begin with the propagation of a universal understanding of what constitutes corrupt behaviour – and in this way would have to challenge the underpinnings of one of the oldest and most widespread institutions of Chinese society.

Apart from this relative concept of corruption that derives from the parallel existence of two systems of order, another form of corruption was also identified. This is not an endogenous part of the functional mechanism of *guanxi* networks but instead takes advantage of the coordinating mechanisms of existing *guanxi* structures. In actual fact, *guanxi* networks offer a transaction cost minimizing (best practice) solution for the problem of order that corrupt transactions are confronted with. *Guanxi* networks, by binding investments in social capital, are able to transform very risky trade relationships into contracts that are self-implementing. Insofar as transaction activity within *guanxi* networks have high fixed costs and low variable costs, it is obvious that already existing *guanxi* networks transcend their normal use and are also used to coordinate illegal, corrupt transactions. In this way it is not only the average costs of all transactions carried out can be lowered; it is also possible to economize on the expenses for creating a special security mechanism for the share of corrupt transactions.

Any effort to try to fight this kind of corruption by the destabilization of the ordering mechanism (i.e. the *guanxi* networks) and the establishment of a new formal legal system can be expected to encounter considerable difficulties. The Chinese *guanxi* networks constitute hyper-stable systems of order, equipped with high institutional inertia, that make their substitution by alternative systems of order – like formal legal systems – extremely difficult.

Seen in perspective, the phenomenon of corruption in China seems to be closely linked to the institution of *guanxi* networks. As a result the fight against corruption may be regarded as a Herculean task. In order to fight corruption one of the most important institutions of Chinese society will have to be confronted and eventually subordinated to an overarching supra-personalistic system of order.

Notes

1 In the Corruption Perception Index published annually by Transparency International, the PR China was listed 66th of 133 nations, with a score of 3.4 on a scale ranging from 0.0 (highly corrupt) to 10.0 (highly clear) (Transparency International 2003).

2 Based on numerous press reports by Chinese and Hong Kong sources.

3 It has been pointed out that '[t]he simplest economic view of the state as an institution that enforces contracts and property rights and provides public goods poses a dilemma: A state with sufficient coercive power to do these things also has the power to withhold protection or confiscate private wealth' (Greif, Milgrom, Weingast 1994: 74).

4 Following this argument Xin and Pearce describe the re-emergence of *guanxi* as a transitional arrangement bridging the time gap until the formal institutional system is well established – a hypothesis the authors of this contribution do not share. Xin and Pearce (1996: 1642f) compare to this point also Guthrie (1998, 1999).

5 This is what Lee, Pae and Wong (2001: 56) call 'perceived similarity' as the founding basis of a *guanxi* relationship.

6 See also Song (1996). Moreover, in the context of the Chinese transformation process, which is only roughly controlled by the central state and otherwise based on the trial-and-error principle, the interpretation of specific behaviours as correct or incorrect is by no means always consistent. Instead, observations have shown that particular measures that were tolerated or even promoted at one point in time because they were considered useful for the economic development of a region or an industry, at a later point of time were then classified as illegal and were prosecuted. The concepts 'legal' and 'corrupt' are thus subject to a relativity that is determined by the changeable progress in the transformation process (Ding 2000).

7 As a result of his cliometric studies, North asserts: 'The move, lengthy and uneven, from unwritten traditions and customs to written laws has been unidirectional as we have moved from less to more complex societies and is clearly related to increasing specialization and division of labour associated with more complex societies' (North 1990: 46).

8 For the future viability of *guanxi* networks, see also Wang (2000).

9 See also the discussion of optimal club size, and the control costs dependent on this, in Sandler and Tschirhart (1997) and Carr and Landa (1983).

10 There are, however, overall fixed costs of a workable legal system. (Compare Schwartz and Tullock 1975: 77ff.) Although this cost must not be borne directly by the individual, they are at last covered by their taxes.

11 This is especially true in China, as Lin pointed out: 'Many tasks remain to improve the effectiveness and the efficiency of China's legal system. Topping the list is the need for a system to safeguard the fundamental principle of "independence of justice" ... Although it is written in the constitutions and other laws, it must be prevented from being eroded in practices' (J. Lin 2002: 5).

12 Despite decades of intensive efforts in establishing a codified legal system with independent courts, great uncertainty still remains in China concerning the true independent status of the court system, and thus the role of the courts as a legal arbiter (Wank 1999).

13 Such a politically induced replacement process can be associated with massive compensation payments to the 'losers' of structural change, depending on the political constellation.

14 Compare Gold, Guthrie and Wank (2002: 4), who point at such basic social models as *ganqing* (sentiment), *renqing* (human feelings), *mianzi* (face) and *bao* (reciprocity).

15 DiMaggio, however, sees a counter trend on the global level: 'If anything, relational contracting seems to be on the rise, as more firms develop "network" alternatives to conventional markets and hierarchies' (DiMaggio 1994).

16 Compare Friedman, who defined legal culture in terms of customs and opinions, and the way of thinking and doing about the law (Friedman 1975: 15). Of course this argument holds as well if the underlying legal system is based on relational networks, as in the case of *guanxi*.

References

Axelrod, R. (1983) *The Evolution of Cooperation*, New York.

Ben-Porath, Y. (1980) 'The F-Connection: Families, Friends, and Firms and the Organization of Exchange', *Population and Development Review*, vol. 6, no. 1, pp. 1–30.

Bian, Y. (1994) 'Guanxi and the Allocation of Urban Jobs in China', *The China Quarterly*, vol. 140, pp. 971–99.

Bo, Z. (2000) 'Economic Development and Corruption: Beijing beyond "Beijing"', *Journal of Contemporary China*, vol. 9, no. 25, pp. 467–87.

Bourdieu, P. (1986) 'The Forms of Capital', in J.G. Richardson (ed.) *Handbook of Theory and Research for the Sociology of Education*, New York, pp. 241–58.

Brennan, G., Güth, W. and Kliemt, H. (1997) 'Trust in the Shadow of the Courts If Judges Are No Better', *Discussion Paper, Economic Series*, no. 93, Humboldt-Universität zu Berlin.

Buchanan, J.M. (1965) 'An Economic Theory of Clubs', *Economica*, vol. 32, pp. 1–14.

Butterfield, F. (1982) *China: Alive in Bitter Sea*, New York.

Carr, J.L. and Landa, J.T. (1983) 'The Economics of Symbols, Clan Names, and Religion', *The Journal of Legal Studies*, vol. 12, no. 1, pp. 135–56.

Chan, K.-M. (1999) 'Corruption in China: A Principal–Agent Perspective', in K.-H. Wong and H.S. Chan (eds) *Handbook of Comparative Public Administration in the Asia-Pacific Basin, Public Administration and Public Policy*, vol. 73, New York, pp. 299–324.

D'Souza, C. (2003) 'An Interference of Gift-Giving Within Asian Business Culture', *Asia Pacific Journal of Marketing and Logistics*, vol. 15, pp. 27–35.

Dasgupta, P. and Serageldin, I. (1999) *Social Capital. A Multifaceted Perspective*, Washington.

David, P. (1985) 'Clio and the economics of QWERTY', *American Economic Review*, vol. 75, pp. 332–7.

Davis, H. (1995) *China Business: Context and Issues*, Hong Kong.

DiMaggio, P. (1994) 'Culture and Economy', in N. Smelser and R. Swedberg (eds) *The Handbook of Economic Sociology*, Princeton.

Elster, J. (1989) 'Social Norms and Economic Theory', *Journal of Economic Perspectives*, vol. 3, pp. 99–117.

Fan, G. and Xin, C. (1998) 'The Role of Law and Legal Institutions in Asian Economic Development: The Case of China', *Development Discussion Paper*, no. 664, Harvard Institute for International Development, Harvard University.

Fan, Y. (2002a) 'Guanxi's Consequences: Personal Gains at Social Cost', *Journal of Business Ethics*, vol. 38, pp. 371–80.

Fan, Y. (2002b) 'Questioning Guanxi: Definition, Classification, and Implication', *International Business Review*, vol. 11, issue 5, pp. 543–61.

Friedman, L.M. (1975) *The Legal System*, New York.

Gabrenya, W.K. and Hwang, K.-K. (1996) 'Chinese Social Interaction: Harmony and Hierachy on the Good Earth', in M.H. Bond (ed.) *The Handbook of Chinese Psychology*, Oxford and Hong Kong.

Gilley, B. (1998) *Tiger on the Brink: Jiang Zemin and China's New Elite*, Berkeley.

Gold, T., Guthrie, D. and Wank, D. (2002) 'An Introduction to the Study of Guanxi', in T. Gold, D. Guthrie and D. Wank (eds) *Social Connections in China. Institutions, Culture, and the Changing Nature of Guanxi*, New York, pp. 3–20.

Goudie, A.W. and Stasavage, D. (1998) 'A Framework for the Analysis of Corruption', in *Crime, Law & Social Change*, vol. 29, pp. 113–59.

Granovetter, M. (1985) 'Economic Action and Social Structure: The Problem of Embeddedness', *American Journal of Sociology*, vol. 91, no. 3, pp. 481–510.

Greif, A. (2002) 'Institutions and Impersonal Exchange: From Communal to Individual Responsibility', *Journal of Institutional and Theoretical Economics*, vol. 158, pp. 168–213.

Greif, A., Milgrom, P. and Weingast, B.R. (1994) 'Coordination, Commitment, and Enforcement: The Case of the Merchant Guild', *The Journal of Political Economy*, vol. 102, issue 4, pp. 745–76.

Guthrie, D. (1998) 'The Declining Significance of Guanxi in China's Economic Transition', *The China Quarterly*, vol. 154, pp. 254–82.

Guthrie, D. (1999) *Dragon in a Three-Piece Suit: The Emergence of Capitalism in China*, Princeton.

Hamilton, G.G. (1994) 'Civilizations and the Organization of Economics', in N. Smelser and R. Swedberg (eds) *The Handbook of Economic Sociology*, Princeton.

Hannan, M.T. and Freeman, J. (1984) 'Structural Inertia and Organizational Change', *American Sociological Review*, vol. 49, pp. 149–64.

Heberer, T. (2001) 'Korruption als globales Phänomen und seine Ausprägungen in Ostasien: Korruption und Korruptionsdiskurse', in *Project Discussion Paper of the Institute for East Asian Studies/East Asian Politics*, no. 9, Duisburg.

Heuser, R. (2003) 'Rechtskultur', in B. Staiger *et al.* (eds) *Das große China-Lexikon*, Darmstadt, pp. 606–9.

Hsing, Y.-T. (1998) *Making Capitalism in China: The Taiwan Connection*, New York and Oxford.

Hu Biliang (1998) *Fazhan lilun yu Zhongguo* [Development Theory and China], Beijing.

Hwang, K.-K. (1987) 'Face and Favour: The Chinese Power Game', *American Journal of Sociology*, vol. 92, no. 4, pp. 944–74.

Jacobs, J.B. (1979) 'A Preliminary Model of Particularistic Ties in Chinese Political Alliances: Kan-chi and Kuan-his in a Rural Taiwanese Township', *The China Quarterly*, vol. 79, pp. 286–95.

Kali, R. (1999) 'Endogenous Business Networks', *Journal of Law, Economics and Organization*, vol. 15, pp. 615–36.

Kirby, W.C. (1995) 'China Unincorporated: Company and Business Enterprise in Twentieth-century China', *The Journal of Asian Studies*, vol. 54, no. 1, pp. 43–63.

Klein, B. (1985) 'Self-Enforcing Contracts', *Zeitschrift für die gesamte Staatswissenschaft/ Journal of Institutional and Theoretical Economics*, vol. 141, pp. 594–600.

Krug, B. and Polos, L. (2000) 'Entrepreneurs, Enterprises, and Evolution: The Case of China', Paper presented at The Annual Meeting of the International Society for New Institutional Economics, Tübingen, September.

Lambsdorff, J. (2002) 'Making Corrupt Deals: Contracting in the Shadow of Law', in *Journal of Economic Behaviour and Organization*, vol. 28, pp. 221–41.

Lee, D.-J., Pae, J.H. and Wong, Y.H. (2001) 'A Model of Close Business Relationships in China (guanxi)', *European Journal of Marketing*, vol. 35, no. 1/2, pp. 51–69.

Lee, P.N.-S. (1991) *Bureaucratic Corruption During the Deng Xiaoping Era*, Hong Kong Institute of Asia-Pacific Studies, HKIAPS Reprint Series, No. 7, Hong Kong.

Liang, H. (2003) 'Die Rezeption ausländischen Zivilrechts in China', *Newsletter der Deutsch-Chinesischen Juristenvereinigung*, vol. 10, pp. 68–72.

Lin, J. (2002) 'Robe, Gavel, and Wigs too?', *China Review*, Issue 23, Autumn/Winter, pp. 4–6.

Lin, Y.-M. (2002) 'Beyond Dyadic Social Exchange: Guanxi and Third-Party Effects', in T. Gold, D. Guthrie and D. Wank (eds) *Social Connections in China. Institutions, Culture, and the Changing Nature of Guanxi*, New York, pp. 57–77.

Luo, Y. (1997) 'Guanxi and Performance of Foreign-invested Enterprises in China: An Empirical Inquiry', *Management International Review*, vol. 37, pp. 51–70.

Nee, V. (2000) 'The Role of the State in Making a Market Economy', *Journal of Institutional and Theoretical Economics* (JITE), vol. 156, no. 1, pp. 64–98.

Needham, J. (1978) *Wissenschaft und Zivilisation in China*, Frankfurt am Main.

North, D.C. (1984) 'Transaction Costs, Institutions, and Economic History', *Journal of Institutional and Theoretical Economics*, vol. 140, pp. 7–17.

North, D.C. (1990) *Institutions, Institutional Change and Economic Performance*, Cambridge.

Osland, G.E. (1990) 'Doing Business in China: A Framework for Cross-cultural Understanding', *Marketing Intelligence and Planning*, vol. 8, no. 4, pp. 4–14.

Palmer, M. (1992) 'What Makes Socialist Law Socialist? – The Chinese Case', in F.J.M. Feldbrugge (ed.) *The Emancipation of Soviet Law*, Dordrecht and Boston.

Posner, R.A. (1980) 'A Theory of Primitive Society, with Special Reference to Law', *Journal of Law and Economics*, vol. 23, issue 1, pp. 1–53.

Potter, P.B. (2002) 'Guanxi and the PR Legal System: From Contradiction to Complementarity', in T. Gold, D. Guthrie and D. Wank (eds) *Social Connections in China. Institutions, Culture, and the Changing Nature of Guanxi*, New York, pp. 179–95.

Pye, L. (1982) *Chinese Commercial Negotiating Style*, Cambridge.

Rawski, T.G. (1999) 'Reforming China's Economy: What Have We Learned?', *The China Journal*, vol. 41, pp. 139–56.

Reja, B. and Tavitie, A. (2000) 'The Industrial Organization of Corruption: What is the Difference in Corruption Between Asia and Africa?', Paper presented at The Annual

Conference 2000 of the International Society for New Institutional Economics, Tübingen, September.

Rose-Ackermann, S. (1999) *Corruption and Government: Causes, Consequences, and Reform*, Cambridge.

Sandler, T. and Tschirhart, J. (1997) 'Club Theory: Thirty Years Later', *Public Choice*, vol. 93, no. 3–4, pp. 335–55.

Schwartz, W.F. and Tullock, G. (1975) 'The Costs of a Legal System', *The Journal of Legal Studies*, vol. 4, pp. 75–82.

Senger, H. von (2003) 'Rechtspflege', in B. Staiger *et al.* (eds) (2003) *Das große China-Lexikon*, Darmstadt, pp. 609–12.

Song, X. (1996) 'Die Rationalität der Korruption in China', *Duisburger Arbeitspapiere zur Ostasienwirtschaft*, no. 28, Duisburg.

Steidlmeier, P. (1999) 'Gift Giving, Bribery and Corruption: Ethical Management of Business Relationship in China', *Journal of Business Ethics*, vol. 20, no. 2, pp. 121–32.

Tao, Z. and Zhu, T. (2001) 'An Agency Theory of Transaction without Contract Enforcement: The Case of China', *China Economic Review*, vol. 12, pp. 1–14.

Tsang, E.W. (1998) 'Can Guanxi be a Source of Sustained Competitive Advantage for Doing Business in China?', *Academy of Management Executive*, vol. 12, no. 2, pp. 64–73.

Uzzi, B. (1996) 'The Sources and Consequences of Embeddedness for the Economic Performance of Organizations: The Network Effect', *American Sociological Review*, vol. 61, pp. 674–98.

Wang, H. (2000) 'Informal Institutions and Foreign Investment in China', *The Pacific Review*, vol. 13, no. 4, pp. 525–56.

Wang, Y. (2002) *Chinese Legal Reform*, London.

Wank, D.L. (1999) 'Producing Property Rights: Strategies, Networks, and Efficiency in Urban China's Nonstate Firms', in J.C. Oi and A.G. Walder (eds) *Property Rights and Economic Reform in China*, Stanford.

White, G. (1996) 'Corruption and the Transition from Socialism in China', *Journal of Law and Society*, vol. 23, no. 1, pp. 149–69.

Williamson O.E. (1985) *The Economic Institutions of Capitalism: Firms, Markets, Relational Contracting*, London.

World Bank (1992) *China. Reform and the Role of the Plan in the 1990s*, A World Bank Country Study, Washington.

Xin, K.R. and Pearce, J.L. (1996) 'Guanxi: Connections as Substitutes for Formal Institutional Support', *Academy of Management Review*, vol. 39, pp. 1641–58.

Yan, Y. (1996) 'The Culture of Guanxi in a North China Village', *The China Journal*, vol. 35, pp. 1–25.

Yang, M.M. (1994) *Gift, Favors, Banquets: The Art of Social Relationship in China*, New York.

Zou, K. (2000) 'Judicial Reform Versus Judicial Corruption: Recent Developments in China', in *Criminal Law Forum*, vol. 11, pp. 323–51.

11 Inefficient property rights and corruption

The case of accounting fraud in China

Sonja Opper

Introduction

Within the economic literature on corruption, the idea that 'different political systems foster different levels of corruption' (Ali and Isse 2003) has been receiving increasing attention. Causal explanations on the emergence and pertinence of corrupt transactions no longer focus on the specification of contracts, but have shifted their attention to the role of the institutional environment as an important explanatory factor of corruption. In other words, the new research has shown a tendency to consider the idea that the outcome of transactions is not solely determined by the structure and quality of institutional arrangements at the micro-level, but also by the entrenched institutional environment. The preliminary account suggests that environments characterized by institutional deficiencies seemingly offer fertile grounds for corruption (World Bank 2002). This account is supported by the fact that high national corruption levels heavily burden almost all transition economies, typically characterized by a hybrid and weak institutional environment.

The assumed connection between a country's institutional quality and the resulting incentives for corruption suggests that thorough analysis of the institutional environment may offer further insights into the underlying causal mechanisms for and appropriate remedies against widespread corruption. This chapter will follow preliminary evidence (Broadman and Recanatini 2002; Kaufmann 2001; Hellman *et al.* 2000) suggesting that the quality of national property rights arrangements may be regarded as an important institutional determinant of national corruption levels.[1] Based on the theoretical framework provided by property rights theory, possible links between inefficient property rights and incentives of corruption will be explored. In order to exemplify the diverse links between property rights arrangements and corruption this chapter will draw on corruption in China's accounting business as a most informative but also globally important case study.

This specific case was chosen for two main reasons. First, China's economic system as we know it today is representative of transition regimes, characterized by deficient institutions. China's government has taken a unique reform path, embedding market-oriented reforms in a stable socialist political environment still characterized by socialist attributes, such as the persistence of collective ownership in central parts of the economy. A hybrid ownership system has emerged with property rights that can by no means be considered efficient. China's national property arrangements thus provide an excellent opportunity to study the relationship between inefficient property rights and corruption. Second, corruption in the accounting sector is particularly fitting for an examination of the diverse effects of inefficient property rights, as interests of shareholders, managers, employees and regulators are closely intertwined.

The analysis of corruption in China's accounting business is not a mere academic exercise. Due to China's high level of integration in the world economy, the findings are of global relevance. Corruption in the accounting business not only affects national growth perspectives but global financial health as well.[2] China is among the top ten export nations in the world, and foreign capital inflow during the period from 1999–2000 reached US$290 billion, with a lion's share of more than 70 per cent accruing from foreign direct investment. There are already more than fifty Chinese companies listed at the Hong Kong Stock Exchange and more than twenty companies listed at NYSE and NASDAQ. Future capital demand for enterprise and banking reforms, as well as for financing the social security system, will accelerate the demand for international borrowing. In spite of the Asian crisis and the more recent collapse of financial information credibility, little attention has been paid to this specific field of corruption in China. A major reason for the lack of international interest is certainly China's painless survival of the Asian crisis. China's soft landing was not attributable to a superior economic policy and a mature institutional environment compared to neighbouring countries, however. China was simply less exposed to the crisis due to highly regulated national financial markets and comparatively tight capital controls. With increasing global integration following China's WTO entry, the soundness of financial information will gradually develop into a decisive determinant of China's performance and prosperity in the world economy.

In line with the widespread definition of corruption, manifestation in accounting is considered to be the abuse of office (provision of illegal services) for private gains (Bardhan 1997: 1321). Corruption within accounting and auditing procedures refers to two different phenomena:

1   The management may bribe providers of accounting and auditing services to falsely report business information, which creates a disadvantage for all company shareholders.
2   The management and large shareholders may collaborate and misreport information in an attempt to exploit only a part of the shareholders and other stakeholders. One example would be false information in the context of new share issuance.

The economic costs of corruption in accounting service provision accrue on two levels. First, the payment of bribes increases transaction costs; second, false reports cause follow-up costs in the form of inefficient capital allocation by shareholders and creditors. Typically, follow-up costs exceed the total of bribes considerably. Rose-Ackerman (1999: 49) pointed out that the individual size of a bribe might decrease in the course of increasing competition, as the briber may turn to another bribee to achieve illegal services. If charges for the service itself are high, and competition is fierce, the bribe price may actually fall close to zero and the whole business offers fraudulent services almost for free or at comparatively low additional bribe prices. Such a situation seems to prevail in China's accounting and auditing business, with auditing contracts worth between RMB 200,000–500,000. Accountancy and auditing firms thus find themselves under heavy pressure to defer to the wishes of their client firms.[3]

The next section provides theoretical and empirical underpinnings to analyse the impact of property rights arrangements on the level of corruption (pp. 200–4). Then, China's accounting reforms and current corruption levels from a property-rights perspective are evaluated (pp. 204–11). Based on a brief summary of the current accounting system, inefficient property rights systems and weak civil rights will be interpreted as major factors determining the persistence of commercial corruption in financial accounting and auditing. The analysis will place a special focus on accounting and auditing fraud in China's listed companies, as these companies currently set the formal standard of corporate governance and capitalist firms in China. Based on this groundwork, the next section (p. 211) evaluates the viability of ongoing attempts to reduce corruption and financial fraud. A section on perspectives concludes the chapter (pp. 213–140).

Explaining corruption: a property rights perspective

While most institutional studies on corruption concentrate primarily on the principle–agent aspect of corruption and investigate potential incentives to align the agent's interests with those of the principal (Rose-Ackerman 1978; Klitgaard 1988), it is important that the neglected property rights aspect of corruption be brought to attention. 'Property rights define the accepted array of resource uses, determine who has decision-making authority, and describe who will receive the associated rewards and costs of those decisions' (Libecap 2001). The clarity, structure and protection of property rights are central determinants for efficiency in all types of interpersonal transactions, whereas incomplete or ill-defined property rights give rise to diverse forms of illicit economic behaviour such as looting, rent-seeking activities and corruption. It is assumed here that an efficient system of property rights includes universality (all resources are privately owned), exclusivity (all benefits and costs accrue to the owner), transferability (all property rights are transferable in a voluntary exchange) and enforceability of property rights (security from involuntary seizure or encroachment).

Among others, Kaufmann (2001) has stressed the causal link between property rights and corruption. He has shown that high-capture economies have a significantly lower level of firms with secure property rights than low-capture economies. Hellman *et al.* (2000) also found that insecure property rights and contract rights are connected with higher levels of administrative corruption. Generally speaking, efficient property rights arrangements ensure that any stakeholder negatively affected by corrupt activities, has both incentives and devices to fight corruption independent of state-led anti-corruption activities. The constraining effect of an efficient property rights system on corruption levels rests on three major, mutually reinforcing causal mechanisms.

1 Efficient property rights arrangements constrain the scope of corruption

Diluted property rights indicate an unclear separation of rights and powers between the state, its regulatory organs and economic actors. In this way, corruption levels may be affected by two distinct mechanisms. First, blurred distinctions of authority between the state and private actors will *ceteris paribus* multiply the transactions influenced by state representatives and bureaucrats and thereby broaden the potential scope of corruption. Assuming a given ratio of potential bribers and bribees (constant probability of being corrupt), a higher proportion of transactions involving actors with blurred authorities will *ceteris paribus* increase the total level of corruption. On the flip side, a high proportion of transactions involving actors with secure property rights and clear authorities will reduce the chances for illicit and corrupt behaviour and may thereby constrain national corruption levels. Second, close connections between economic actors and regulatory institutions may reduce the regulators' incentives to detect corruption. The resulting lower detection rate will in turn reduce the expected costs of corruption and individual incentives for corruption will increase.

2 Efficient property rights arrangements strengthen incentives for private monitoring

The efficiency of transactions is usually higher in a zero-corruption world. From this perspective, negatively affected stakeholders should have incentives to mitigate and counteract corrupt activities. This implies that negatively affected stakeholders act under hard budget constraints and personally benefit from reduced transaction costs in a zero-corruption paradigm. Only residual claimants have material incentives to monitor their agents and to reduce corruption. In addition, the quality of stakeholder monitoring is largely determined by corporate governance structures. That individual incentives of property owners and their capacity to monitor their agents effectively increase with the size of ownership shares can be derived from the corporate governance literature (Shleifer and Vishny 1986). Based on this observation, we can conclude that the effectiveness of anti-corruption activities (as part of stakeholder monitoring) will increase with ownership concentration. On the other hand, representatives of collectively owned firms, typically characterized by soft budget constraints (Kornai 1992), have little or no individual incentives to fight corruption. The costs of corruption are socialized, while any personal efforts on the part of management and employees to mitigate corruption will not be rewarded. The general public as the true owners of the firm have no incentives to engage in monitoring, as it is not clear who would gain from reducing corruption. Briefly, the arrangement of collective ownership offers briber and bribee a convenient environment for collusion and theft at public expense. Exclusive and secure property rights are therefore likely to be connected with intensified monitoring activities. Given a constant probability of successful detection of corrupt activities, the resulting level of national corruption should fall.

3   *Efficient property rights arrangements provide instruments of self-regulation*

Efficient property rights are enforceable rights. That is to say, property rights include the existence of legal devices and independent, effective courts. These safeguard mechanisms provide affected stakeholders with important tools to seek litigation, whenever individual property rights are violated. Expected costs of illicit and corrupt behaviour will thereby increase, and the optimal level of corruption should fall, within a given probability of detection. As these individual anti-corruption measures are independent of state-led anti-corruption campaigns or monitoring activities, their result is not affected by corruption within the state bureaucracy. The major problem of 'corruption in monitoring' (who monitors the corruption agency?) is not a concern, since sanctioning of corruption (i.e. the initiation of a court-procedure) is the sole responsibility of individual affected stakeholders and not the state.

The following simple econometric exercise supports the close connection between the quality of property rights arrangements and corruption. A linear regression model (OLS) is employed to estimate the effect of property rights protection on national corruption levels for a cross-sectional sample covering 88 countries in the year 2000. The corruption perceptions index (CPI-index) calculated by Transparency International is applied to proxy national corruption levels. The original index values range between 1 and 10, whereas a value of 10 signals the lowest level of perceived corruption. The property rights index is taken from the Index of Economic Freedom, which is calculated by the Heritage Foundation. Index-values range from 1–7, within 1 indicating the highest degree of property rights protection. The empirical literature suggests that the constraining effect of property rights depends on the free and unbiased flow of related information. To proxy the quality of the market for information, and also the quality of democratic processes, the freedom of press-index provided by Freedom House is employed. Freedom House provides an index ranging from 1–100, with low values signalling a high degree of press freedom. For conformity, all indexes were converted into a scale of 1–7. Available empirical evidence on determinants of corruption suggests that incentives for corruption are lower in economically more developed countries (Broadman and Recanatini 2002). In order to control for this developmental effect, the per capita gross national income (World Bank 2002) is included as a control variable.

Table 11.1 presents estimation results. OLS-estimates confirm that the perceived level of national corruption is significantly (1 per cent level) constrained by efficient property rights. Furthermore, estimates suggest that the quality of information supply does not have an independent constraining effect on national corruption levels. To check the robustness of results the model was re-estimated under the inclusion of several additional institutional variables covering major institutional determinants (freedom of trade, government intervention, democracy) discussed in the literature. The extended model, however, does not yield qualitatively different results for property rights. Property rights still significantly constrain corruption, though the estimated slope coefficient is slightly smaller. Still, caution should be exercised when interpreting these results, as small sample size and simple model specification do not suffice for general conclusions. Simultaneity is likely to be a problem as well. If a deficient institutional environment causes high levels of corruption, it is not less likely that corruption will impede the development of the institutional environment. The standard prescription to deal with this 'simultaneity' problem is the use of instrumental variables. It was not possible, however, to find appropriate instruments for the given explanatory variables.[4] It must therefore be assumed that the results are tainted by reverse causality and cannot provide conclusive evidence on the relationship between corruption and the quality of property

Table 11.1 Property rights protection and corruption levels, 2000

Independent variables	CPI	CPI
Log (pc GNI)	0.3525***	0.3510***
	(0.0705)	(0.0673)
Log (property rights)	−1.0851***	−0.9583***
	(0.2298)	(0.2410)
Log (press freedom)	−0.0358	−0.0279
	(0.1489)	(0.1353)
Log (regulation)		−0.3465
		(0.3024)
Log (freedom of trade)		−0.3934***
		(0.1323)
Log (government interventions)		0.2442*
		(0.1293)
C	0.4100	0.9063
	(0.7218)	(0.7789)
N	88	88
R²	0.8537	0.8764
Adj. R²	0.8485	0.8673
F-statistic	163.4223***	95.7442***

Notes
White Heteroskedasticity-consistent standard errors are reported in parentheses.
*** significant at 1 per cent level.
* significant at 10 per cent level.

rights. The estimates should therefore only be treated as indicative results, supporting the existence of a close link between property rights and national corruption levels.

Financial accounting in China

Based on theoretical and empirical evidence, the previous section corroborated the assumption that there is a causal link between the quality of property rights and corruption levels, leading to severe doubts about the ability of a socialist-shaped portfolio of governance mechanisms to limit and mitigate corruption effectively. Referring to the specific example of corruption in the accounting and auditing business, the following section highlights the respective causal mechanisms between inefficient property rights and accounting fraud.

This section starts with a brief overview of China's formal accounting framework, and then applies a property rights perspective to exemplify the above-characterized causal links between inefficient property rights and high corruption levels in the accounting business.

China's formal accounting framework

The implementation of an internationally comparable accounting system was accomplished with 'The Accounting Standards for Business Enterprises' (ASBE), which came into effect on 1 July 1993. The ASBE are supplemented by a series of specific rules, which are broadly in line with the spirit and intention of the International Accounting Standards (IAS).

In spite of these considerable efforts at harmonization, however, the Chinese system has retained some national characteristics that are noteworthy in their potential to facilitate accounting fraud. While revenues should be measured at the fair value of the consideration receivable according to IAS 18.9, revenues are valuated according to the amount stipulated in the contract (see ASBE: Revenue, sentence 6). This rule clearly provides certain leeway for manipulation, which is particularly easy to exploit in the case of transactions between related parties such as companies that are part of the same business group. Although an official explanation of the soundness of the contract price is requested, in case of significant deviation from the fair value, abuse of this rule is widespread (Tenev and Zhang 2002: 123).

Second, the Chinese definition of assets is not consistent with the regulations specified by IAS and US-GAAP. In contrast to IAS and US-GAAP, which both specify assets as resources promising future economic benefits, China's regulations simply define assets as 'economic resources, which are measurable by money value' (see ASBE, Art. 22). The existence or expectation of future economic benefits is not a material factor. Third, the strict adherence to the principle of 'historical costs' in the case of asset evaluations is striking (ASBE, Art. 19). Even securities and inventories are valued according to 'historical costs' (Arts. 26, 28) and re-evaluations of assets are only possible in exceptional cases (ASBE, Art. 19).[5] Overall, the principle of historical cost accounting may easily lead to a significant over-valuation of assets. Finally, the depreciation of doubtful claims depends on official approval by relevant local authorities and bureaucrats, whose political and individual objectives may easily conflict with a sound evaluation of the creditworthiness of firms under their administrative responsibility.[6]

On the whole, China's accounting system in its current structure still has significant national characteristics, which all contribute to the overvaluation of the financial situation of business enterprises and facilitate accounting fraud in China. Chen *et al.* (1999) estimate that even legally calculated reported earnings of China's listed companies are overvalued by 20–30 per cent compared to accounting under IAS. The system's inherent tendency to overvalue enterprise performance is reinforced by China's Company Law and Securities Law which both provide additional incentives 'to create' profitable company accounts, as diverse company rights are delineated from the fact that a company has been profitable over a certain period of time. Only profitable firms are considered for an IPO (Company Law, Art. 152) and may remain listed at China's Stock Exchanges, and only profitable firms are eligible for further rights issues (Company Law, Art. 137.2) and the issuance of company bonds (Art. 161.3). Though these specifications were certainly motivated by the government's intent to protect investors from unprofitable investments, the de facto effect is just the opposite (Neoh 2000). Incentives to suppress negative news and to fabricate positive accounts increase.

Determinants of financial corruption: a property rights perspective

As with all illegal activities, reliable data on de facto corruption levels are not directly available, since most of the cases of financial fraud and corruption remain undetected. Sample surveys give only a rough idea of the potential amount of malfeasance in financial accounting and auditing. An investigation of 1,290 state-owned enterprises (SOEs) conducted by the State Auditing Bureau in 2000 revealed that about 68 per cent of companies' accounts contained serious falsifications.[7] Due to more advanced corporate governance mechanisms, irregularities in listed companies are estimated to be less, though they are still severe. According to a small panel-survey of 32 financial reports of listed companies conducted by the State Auditing Bureau, 14 accountancy firms had allowed major inaccuracies in listed companies' accounts to pass unchecked during the audits.[8] Based on these findings the State Auditing Bureau states that the disguise of false information in financial statements is one of the central deficiencies of today's auditing business in China.[9]

It is obvious that the dearth of company-level data does not allow for econometric tests supplying direct empirical evidence on the interconnection between property rights and accounting fraud. My arguments will therefore be necessarily constrained to an analytical and speculative approach, which builds on an institutional analysis of China's accounting sector. However, it is to be assumed that the incentive-based evaluations derived within the analytical framework of the property rights approach have a solid prognostic capacity. In light of the three major links between the quality and structure of property rights arrangements and the emergence of corruption (see Chapter 2, this volume) that have been illustrated here, a three-step analysis of China's accounting business and its relevant institutional environment is applied to exemplify the impact of inefficient property rights on corruption.

Blurred rights between state agencies and the economic sector

We have operated under the assumption that the scope of corruption is constrained by a clear separation of rights and powers between the state, its regulatory organs and economic actors. Against this background, the detection of corruption in China's financial accounting and auditing business is certainly hampered within the typically close business networks between enterprises, managers, Certified Public Accountants (CPAs) and responsible government and supervisory departments. Collusion between enterprises and auditing firms was facilitated and discovery of financial fraud less likely, as auditing firms did not become independent from the Ministry of Finance and the government before 1998. It is reported that government departments even use their power to interfere in the work of professional service companies. Other departments set up their own companies to use their administrative power in the pursuit of economic benefits. Though these links between companies and government departments have been formally severed during the last years, it is doubtful whether established personal networks are affected by mere formal changes. Both local governments and local party committees continue to influence the management's choice of accounting and auditing firms (Opper et al. 2002). It may be suspected that the underlying intent is to keep service provision and related rent-seeking opportunities within established personal networks.

A temporary attempt to import reputation by competition with international accounting firms was quickly blocked by national interest groups. Shortly after the promulgation of rules (December 2001) requesting companies to undergo supplementary audits by foreign auditing firms in the case of an IPO or additional share offerings, the implementation was suspended due to severe national resistance by the domestic auditing industry. The official explanation of the drawback was that the Enron case had proven that foreign accountancy and auditing ethics were in fact not superior to China's business ethics.[10] Empirical studies, however, give evidence quite to the contrary. According to Chen et al. (2001), Big5[11] auditors actually serve as an effective means of reducing the earnings gap between accounting based on China's standards and those specified by IAS.

Weak incentives for private monitoring

The second causal mechanism builds on the theoretically and empirically well-founded fact that property rights arrangements determine the individual motives and incentives of economic actors and thus have a significant impact on economic performance. Control of and measures against corruption as an important source of efficiency losses are usually part of any efficiency oriented and profit-maximizing corporate governance regime. The effectiveness of such measures will largely depend on the prevailing ownership structure. In order to clarify shareholders' incentives to detect and mitigate corrupt behaviour in China's accounting and auditing business it is therefore worthwhile to shed some light on the property rights structure of China's stock-listed companies.

From corporate governance literature it is well-known that two major factors affect shareholders' incentives to monitor and supervise management activities. The first is the profit-maximizing motive. The more profit-oriented a shareholder is, the stronger his/her incentive to control management malfeasance. In addition, shareholder activity depends crucially on the expected benefits and costs calculus. A profit-motivated shareholder will not undertake any control activities if the expected benefits do not cover the costs involved. Since monitoring benefits are to be shared with all shareholders, whereas monitoring costs accrue to the individual shareholders who take actions, rational stockowners holding only small residual claims are likely to be free-riders, leaving the task of management control and supervision to larger shareholders (Shleifer and Vishny 1986).

China's stock market is highly segmented, with four different types of shares: state shares, legal person shares, A-shares and B-shares, with the first three types each making up on average of about 30 per cent of total company shares.[12] The majority of large shareholders, however, is to be found among the groups of holders of state-shares, legal person-shares and B-shares, while individual holders of A-shares are imposed with a legal limit of 0.5 per cent of total shares.[13] Recently, institutional investors are also holding A-shares, but their holdings are still quite limited. We may therefore assume that holders of A-shares are likely to take a free-rider position and leave active control activities to holders of larger shares.

Incentives to perform an efficiency oriented active monitoring are obviously weak for holders of state shares. State shares are obtained by an institution acting as a representative of the central government, and bought on behalf of the state in exchange for its capital contribution. The institutions holding state shares are mainly state asset management agencies charged with the responsibility of preserving and increasing the value of state property. In light of the findings of property-rights theory, it is evident that the monitoring incentives of these institutions are usually weak. First, officials of state asset management agencies are unlikely to receive personal benefits from effective monitoring. Second, state shareholders do not operate under hard budget constraints and will be bailed out by the state treasury if companies suffer financial distress as a result of malfeasance in financial accounting and auditing. Accounting fraud is even supported, or at least tolerated, by the responsible holders of state shares (like local governments and asset management bureaux). Since managers of state assets have the duty to protect and increase state property, creative book-keeping with the purpose of overvaluation of assets and earnings may well be in the interest of asset managers.

Unlike state shareholders, holders of legal person-shares operating under independent accounting systems are formally responsible for their profits and losses, which means that they are therefore likely to have stronger profit motives and monitoring incentives.[14] Furthermore, since legal persons usually hold large portions of shares they are unlikely to free-ride and will perform monitoring activities (Xu and Wang 1999; Qi *et al.* 2000). According to a recent survey conducted by the Shanghai Stock Exchange, the average shareholding of the top ten shareholders holding legal person-shares is about 20 per cent. Legal persons holding large portions of shares often hold seats on the BoD, which allows them to monitor the accuracy of financial accounting directly (Xu and Wang 1999).

Finally, the B-share market is open to trading for foreign individuals, institutional investors and Chinese nationals capable of trading in foreign currency. Foreign investors are predominantly non-state investors operating under hard budget constraints and who have strong incentives to maximize the return on their investment. Stock market statistics indicate, however, that at the end of 1999 the majority of foreign investors were individuals, while only about 5 per cent of B-share holders were institutional investors (China Securities Regulatory Commission 2000). Second, effective monitoring by foreign investors may be impeded by information costs, owing to their unfamiliarity with China's dynamic development and rapidly changing regulatory framework. Overall, the capacity of foreign investors to serve as a strong force of monitoring and supervision of financial soundness is limited.

In sum, only national institutional investors might have both the capacity and the incentive to serve as effective monitors. However, it is also the powerful institutional investor which may feel tempted to collaborate with management and mask true firm performance in order to expropriate small shareholders. If this specific type of corruption occurs, the group of potential monitors further shrinks to the group of 'honest' investors among the institutional shareholders.

Another major group of stakeholders with a natural interest in monitoring the credibility of financial information are creditors, such as commercial banks and other lending institutions. Banks can serve as an important external force to discipline corporate performance. In China's socialist market economy, however, the banking sector is also plagued by incentive problems resulting from non-exclusive property rights. In spite of increasing competition in the banking sector, state banks still dominate with an overall share of state-bank credits reaching about 80 per cent, and state involvement in the banks' credit policy is still widespread (Zhu 1999; Leung and Mok 2000). Park and Sehrt (2001) provided empirical evidence that the ratio of political loans did not decrease during economic reforms and that lending decisions are not based on fundamental company data. Since the state banking system is for all intents and purposes under the protection of the Ministry of Finance (Steinfeld 1999: 61; Wilhelm and Saywell 1999), banks do not have the material incentives to oppose political involvement or to optimize their lending decisions. It is evident that the specific incentive situation delineated from the property rights structure of China's banking systems does not give sufficient incentives to monitor and control the reliability of financial data provided by debtors. Malfeasance is likely to pass unchecked and insider control can lead to serious economic distortions.

The quality of legal devices

The degree of individual discretion in decision-making processes, and the resulting leeway to use an official office for private gains, depends significantly on the opaqueness of transactions. Transparency, however, depends on system-inherent formal and informal incentives to perform monitoring activities, as well as on the availability of appropriate monitoring devices capable of protecting individual property rights. The third causal link between the quality and structure of property rights arrangements and national corruption levels therefore rests on the provision of legal instruments for self-regulation, providing individual economic actors with effective devices to protect their ownership rights. As long as legal devices for third-party monitoring are not sufficient, it is almost certain that asymmetric information will be exploited by opportunistic actors.

The original version of the Accounting Law (1985) did not stipulate any personal responsibility of the enterprise management for the soundness of financial accounting. It was not until 1999 that the new amendments to the Accounting Law (Art. 4) introduced a personal responsibility for the management and persons involved in the accounting process (Arts. 42 and 43). The responsibility for the enforcement of the Accounting Law is assigned to the financial department of the relevant local government (Art. 7). However, with regard to the specific shareholder structure, it should be evident that local governments do not necessarily have a strong interest in sound financial accounting and reporting of local enterprises. In addition, the shared responsibility of different persons involved in enterprise accounting had contra-productive effects. It was almost impossible to identify a single responsible person in case of financial fraud.[15] This drawback was finally abolished in the new Accounting Law which came into effect on 1 July 2000. Since then, the leader of a company is responsible for the accounting behaviour of its unit.

In the case of financial irregularities, auditing firms may be punished with disciplinary fines according to Art. 39, Law of the Certified Public Accountants of the PRC (13 October 1993). Income derived from illegal activities, which have been committed intentionally, may be confiscated and additional fines may range from two to five times the amount of illegal income. However, with regard to the low probability of detection, fines will hardly suffice to deter illegal activities (Rose-Ackerman 1999). Additionally, depending on the severity of the delict, the Criminal Law may also be applied. According to Art. 229, accountants and auditors who intentionally provide false certificates may be sentenced to up to five years of fixed-term imprisonment or criminal detention and a fine.[16] Confiscation of illegal incomes is also regulated in the Company Law (Art. 219(1)).

Independent from the Criminal Law, Article 108 of China's Civil Law provides shareholders with a legal foundation for grievances.[17] The right to file a lawsuit against a listed company, however, is only granted if companies have lied in their information disclosure and if the China Securities Regulatory Commission (CSRC) has already decided that financial fraud has been committed and punishment has been passed down.[18] Thus lawsuits do not actually serve as an independent means of controlling and sanctioning financial malfeasance; rather, they depend on previous activities by the CSRC, which can thereby influence the total amount of pending lawsuits and the resulting investment climate at the stock exchanges (Opper 2003). The power of market supervision is de facto concentrated in the hands of the governments and its regulatory body, while the legal devices of individual shareholders to monitor financial soundness and accuracy are constrained.

Legal shareholder protection is further weakened by the fact that the burden of proof is placed on the shareholder. That is, shareholders have to prove that a fall in stock prices is without doubt caused by financial fraud and the infringement of accounting and disclosure rules. Due to the highly asymmetric information between shareholders and firms, shareholders usually have poor chances of protecting their interests. High costs of civil lawsuits and the exclusion of class action are additional factors contributing to the overall weak position of minority shareholders.[19]

Finally, it must be emphasized that the paltry level of stakeholder protection is reinforced by the low degree of legal independence, which inevitably leads to weak and arbitrary law enforcement. There have been far-reaching legal reforms and new definitions of the party/legal relations since 1982, which explicitly forbid local party committees to replace the formal law with directives of local party secretaries. Despite these important gains, however, the legal system is anything but independent from the Party. Local courts are still restricted to a subordinate position in relation to the local party committees (Zheng 1997; Findlay 1999). Such subordination allows local party committees to provide political guidance that the local courts would hardly dare oppose. The Party's Political and Legal Affairs Committee represents a major organizational device utilized by the party committees, and it exercises control over the legal system by reviewing local legal matters (Jayasuriya 1999). It has in fact been observed that judges report directly to district party committees and discuss major cases before they come to court (Liou 1998). In general, political interests prevail over legal justice if they reach disparate conclusions.

Overall deterrence of criminal behaviour is a function of the probability of detection and the following enforcement of available legal provisions leading to de facto punishment (Becker 1968). In this light, the current deterrence effect is at best weak if not non-existent. Detection of accounting fraud still has the status of precedents, basically instrumentalized to deter malfeasance and corruption. Though incidents of false disclosure are frequently reported, creating the idea of active supervision and monitoring activities, publicity of detected cases is far higher than the de facto probability of discovery.[20] In 2001 the CSRC only handled 33 cases concerning fabrication of financial statements. Not more than eight listed companies (less than 1 per cent of all listed companies) and 21 CPAs involved in these cases got punished.[21] Thus, in sharp contrast to the current hoopla in the financial press and the frequent reassurance of all regulatory and supervisory bodies involved in the financial service industry, law enforcement and de facto probability of discovery and punishment in the case of malfeasance remain exceptionally low.

Remedies and their viability

Building on the arguments derived from property rights theory, the previous section has exemplified three major causal mechanisms, which facilitate corruption in the accounting and auditing business. Based on this groundwork, this section deals with the resulting question as to whether the foreseeable future promises a respective change in government politics and a strengthening of property rights. Will property rights be redistributed in favour of individual stakeholders in order to strengthen independent activities, or will China proceed on its socialist-style development path, leaving responsibility for the corruption problem basically to the state-led anti-corruption campaigns?

The following catalogue of recent anti-corruption measures clearly indicates that the Chinese leadership basically sticks to its socialist tradition of state-led anti-corruption campaigns instead of strengthening individual property rights.

Strengthening bureaucratic supervision

The Chinese Institute of Certified Public Accountants (CICPA), the national organization of certified public accountants, envisions the intensification of audit reviews of listed companies to combat fraudulent accounting and auditing practices. The major focus of these campaigns is to investigate whether CPA firms and their CPAs have abided by relevant rules in conducting audits, whether they have gone through the necessary auditing process and whether their auditing opinions are appropriate. Special attention shall be paid to listed companies which have recently changed their CPA firm. The recent international history of periodic anti-corruption campaigns has produced dismal results. In order to be effective campaigns to end corruption must convince a critical number of bribers and bribees that corruption is not cost effective (Bardhan 1997: 1337). One cannot hope to convince anyone with the ongoing campaigns in their present form, however. Due to scarce personnel and financial resources, the local CPA associations are only asked to pick one or two of the local CPA firms for closer examination. Thus, a wide coverage of the measure, with a significant increase of detection of fraudulent accounting, is not to be expected.[22]

In addition to these official campaigns, Shanghai, China's Commercial Centre, has started a local initiative and set up special files to track the credit standing of the city's 84 accounting firms with approximately 2,500 accountants. The project was initiated by the city's CPA Association and the Shanghai

Credit Information Service. Records of fraudulent practices and penalties will be publicized in local newspapers and websites to increase transparency over business ethics in the accounting business.[23] However, the effectiveness of the measure depends on the success rate of the above-mentioned anti-corruption campaigns and does not act as an independent force to fight corruption.

Moral persuasion and educational campaigns

Also in line with China's historical path of anti-corruption campaigns is the implementation of 'educational measures' aimed at increasing moral and ideological standards. In this sense, the government seems to have an inherent tendency to favour the 'moralist position' in corruption policy, which emphasizes that effective corruption control will not be achieved unless fundamental changes of values and norms are effected by active moral reform campaigns (Bardhan 1997). Current educational measures are applied with the intent to increase business morals and ethics. Frequent requests of the CICPA also work to remind CPA firms to be honest in auditing accounting statements.[24] It is needless to stress that moral persuasion is a weak instrument when it comes to the mitigation of criminal activities of opportunistic individuals. Also, those requests are simple reminders of what has been national law since 1993 (The Law of the Certified Public Accountants of the PRC, Art. 21). Activities of the CICPA, which recently formed an expert technical aid team to provide CPAs with accounting and auditing assistance, get even less to the root of corruption in accounting and auditing services. The central task of the expert group is to solicit opinions on major key issues in accounting practice.[25] This expert group can only tackle problems arising from unintentional malfeasance, but is by no means equipped to tackle the widespread intentional accounting fraud.

Redefinition of business relations

A significantly weaker tier of current anti-corruption activities targeting financial fraud concentrates on the redefinition of business relations between client and accounting and auditing firms. It was recently promulgated that CPAs conducting auditing for listed companies should not act concurrently as the financial adviser to the companies or take posts in the companies that may lead to conflicts of interest.[26] This rule basically states the obvious and is hardly more than a repetition of regulations which are already covered by the 'Law of CPAs' (Art. 18). In a related measure the CSRC attempts to increase transparency of payments to accountancy firms. According to most recent regulations, listed companies' payments to accountancies should be highly transparent and structured in a way that does not 'damage moral standards or quality control'. Accounting firms are asked not to collect any payments other than the service charges, and should not accept non-cash payments, such as shares in their clients' companies.[27] Again, the rules basically state the obvious and do not seem to provide an effective measure against corrupt transactions within established business networks involving clients and accounting firms. The call for financial transparency is already covered by the 'Law of CPAs' (Art. 22).

In summary, in all recent attempts to mitigate corruption in financial accounting and auditing it is quite obvious that the leadership sticks to its strong tradition of relying on state controls and supervision, instead of supporting the generation of independent controls by market forces and non-state actors, which would clearly reduce incentives to pay and receive bribes. Particularly, shareholder rights remain weak since shareholders do not have the necessary devices to control and sanction financial fraud independent of activities on the part of the responsible regulatory bodies. The success of the bureaucracy-based approach implicitly relies on the assumption that bureaucrats authorized to check on the illegal behaviour of economic actors are less vulnerable to the abuse of their office for private gains. But regulatory bodies are themselves highly susceptible to bureaucratic corruption, as frequent anti-corruption campaigns within government departments and administrative offices prove.

Perspectives

The key objective of this chapter has been to investigate the interconnectedness of property rights and corruption. It has been shown that inefficient property rights are likely to broaden the potential for corruption, reduce incentives to mitigate corruption, and are also connected with restricted legal devices for individual corruption control. Based on the case of corruption in China's accounting and auditing business, it has been illustrated how each of the detected causal mechanisms may facilitate corruption.

Chances for a clear-cut change towards efficient property rights arrangements as a basis for increasing individual oversight on corrupt activities are certainly minimal. Since the Chinese government clearly sticks to the socialist character of a market economy, with collective ownership as an important part of the national economy, a continuation of the current trajectory is likely. Political and economic constraints delineated from the government's adherence to the idea of socialist ownership indicate that state-led anti-corruption campaigns in the accounting and auditing business will be a short-term priority of a rational government.

First of all, the state as shareholder has a strong interest to avoid losing investors' trust, since a sudden, uncontrolled revelation of accounting and auditing fraud could easily result in a severe stock market crash destroying huge amounts of state assets. In addition to the state's direct shareholder interests as a stock owner, the government's concern includes China's overall economic stability. Even the currently tightly controlled level of state-led financial fraud detection already contributes to an increasing uncertainty among investors.[28] In view of China's needed GDP growth of about a minimum of 8 per cent per annum, severely burdened social security systems and increasing urban unemployment, the government will hardly be tempted to let corruption control in the financial sector slip out of its hands. A shock-therapy-like sudden clean-up in the accounting and auditing business and the concomitant loss of investors' trust could provoke a severe downsizing of China's short- and mid-term growth perspectives, which are regarded as the central economic precondition of social and political stability. Last but not the least, ongoing reforms of SOEs and their restructuring, auctioning and stock listings critically depend on the unbroken trust of investors in available financial information. If investors' trust is undermined and the supply of private capital decreases, it could bring China's reform efforts to a sudden halt and lead to a further postponement of urgently needed reforms in the state-owned production sector.

Briefly, current constraints effectuate a continuation of the gradualist, state-led and controlled approach of a financial sector clean-up. However, this approach does not come without costs and bears severe risks. First of all, the gradual, state-led clean-up is connected with high economic costs, since inefficient capital allocation persists due to false financial information. As to the risks of the chosen approach, it is doubtful that state-led anti-corruption measures offer an effective portfolio to mitigate commercial corruption in a network-based society with a high degree of collusion and corruption among politicians, bureaucrats and economic actors. In addition, private shareholders in China's increasingly liberalized market economy will gradually demand higher protection of shareholder rights and will be less willing to leave major monitoring rights solely to the state. That is, the short-term political intent to keep corruption control under the government's responsibility does not rule out that the market might nonetheless experience a sudden loss of investors' trust. Hence, it is not unthinkable that China's ideal of a costless clean-up in the accounting and auditing business is deemed to fail.

Notes

1 This specific focus should not imply that other institutional determinants are not very important as well.
2 As Bottelier (1998) has stressed: 'Financial fraud is a particularly pernicious kind of corruption. It can undermine the soundness of financial institutions and contribute to systemic crisis. It is often associated with poor accounting standards, weak supervision of financial institutions, cronyism and nepotism. The Asian financial crisis has underlined that successful participation in global capital markets requires the enforcement of rigorous regulatory standards with zero tolerance for corruption.'
3 See 'China Audit Bureau – Accountancies Allowing Listed Firms to Doctor Results', <www.p5w.net>, 29 November 2001.
4 The common use of lagged explanatory variables seems to promise no significant amelioration of the simultaneity problem, as the institutional environment rarely shows significant short-term changes.
5 ASBE, Art. 19 postulates: 'The values of all assets are to be recorded at historical costs at the time of acquisition. The amount recorded in books of account shall not be adjusted even though fluctuation in their value may occur, except when State laws or regulations require specific treatment or adjustments.'
6 According to IAS the valuation rate of doubtful claims is calculated as the likely value of the claim (= nominal value*probability of realization).
7 See 'China 68 per cent of State Firms Falsify Accounts – Audit Bureau Survey', <www.p5w.net>, 26 January 2001.

8 See 'China Auditing Bureau Finds Major Falsifications in Listed Firms' Reports', <www.p5w.net>, 27 December 2001.

9 See 'National Audit Office's Random Inspection on CPAs Gets Worrisome Results', <www.p5w.net>, 26 December 2001.

10 See 'CSRC Issues Rules Requiring Domestic/Overseas Audits Before IPOs/Share Offers', <www.p5w.net>, 31 December 2002, and 'CSRC Suspends Implementation of Foreign Audit Requirement for A-share Firms', <www.p5w.net>, 4 March 2002.

11 The 'Big5' include Arthur Andersen, Deloitte Touche Tohmatsu, Ernst & Young, KPMG and PricewaterhouseCoopers.

12 Employee shares, H-shares, N-shares and L-shares are left out due to their minor quantitative importance.

13 See 'Gupiao faxing yu jiaoyi guanli zanxing tiaolie' (22 April 1993), Art. 46.

14 It should be noted, however, that legal person-shares are not exclusively held by private enterprises but also by SOEs. Unlike conventional SOEs administered under a centralized budget, these SOEs are commercial entities operating with independent accounting. It may therefore be assumed that these firms have stronger profit motives and face harder budget constraints than traditional SOEs (Xu and Wang 1999; Qi *et al.* 2000).

15 See 'Accounting Cheats to be Brought to Book', *Asia Times*, 2 April 1999, <http://www.atimes.com/china/AL02Ad01.html>.

16 <www.qis.net/chinalaw/prclaw60.htm>.

17 The Company Law does not provide shareholders with a comparable device. Though shareholders are entitled to file a lawsuit against management and board of directors in case of violation of laws and regulations, the Law does not imply compensation of financial losses suffered from these infringements. According to Art. 111, shareholders can only file a lawsuit asking to stop any illegal acts.

18 See 'New Rules Backs Small Investors', *China Daily* (Internet Edition), 16 January 2002.

19 Ibid.

20 See for instance, 'CSRC Penalizes 4 Listed Firms for False Disclosure', <www.p5w.net>, 20 May 2002.

21 'CSRC to Continue Fight Against False Disclosure', <www.p5w.net>, 28 March 2002.

22 'CPA Association to Check on 2001 Results Audits', <www.p5w.net>, 5 July 2002.

23 'Shanghai Sets up Credit System for CPAs', <www.p5w.net>, 9 September 2002.

24 See 'CICPA Urges Honesty among CPAs Ahead of Auditing of Annual Reports', <www.p5w.net>, 13 November 2001.

25 'CPA Association to Combat Accounting Frauds', <www.p5w.net>, 1 August 2002.

26 'CICPA Urges Honesty Among CPAs Ahead of Auditing of Annual Reports', <www.p5w.net>, 13 November 2002.

27 'CSRC Issues Rules on Listed Companies' Payments to Accountancy Firms', <www.p5w.net>, 1 August 2002.

28 See <www.p5w.net>: 'Falsified Figures "Cancer" in State Firms', 26 November 2001.

References

Ali, A.M. and Isse, H.S. (2003) 'Determinants of Economic Corruption: A Cross-Country Comparison', *Cato Journal*, vol. 22, no. 3, pp. 449–66.

Asia Times, <http://www.time.com/time/asia>.

Bardhan, P. (1997) 'Corruption and Development: A Review of Issues', *Journal of Economic Literature*, vol. 35, no. 3, pp. 1320–46.

Becker, G. (1968) 'Crime and Punishment: An Economic Approach', *Journal of Political Economy*, vol. 76, pp. 169–217.

Bottelier, P. (1998) 'Corruption and Development. Remarks for the International Symposium on the Prevention and Control of Financial Fraud', Beijing, <http://www.worldbank.org/html/extdr/offrep/eap/pbsp101998.htm>.

Broadman, H.G. and Recanatini, F. (2002) 'Corruption and Policy: Back to the Roots', *Policy Reform*, vol. 5, no. 1, pp. 37–49.

Chen, C.J.P., Gul, F.A. and Su, X. (1999) 'A Comparison of Reported Earnings Under Chinese GAAP vs. IAS: Evidence from the Shanghai Stock Exchange', *Accounting Horizons*, vol. 13, no. 2, pp. 91–111.

Chen C.J.P., Chen, S. and Su, X. (2001) 'Is Accounting Information Value-Relevant in the Emerging Chinese Stock Market?', *Journal of International Accounting, Auditing & Taxation*, vol. 10, no. 1, pp. 1–22.

China Daily, <http://www.chinadaily.net>.

China Securities Regulatory Commission (2000) *China Securities and Futures Statistical Yearbook*, Beijing.

Findlay, M. (1999) 'Independence and the Judiciary in the PRC: Expectations for Constitutional Legality in China', in K. Jayasuriya (ed.) *Law, Capitalism and Power in Asia*, London, pp. 281–99.

Freedom House: Freedom in the World Country Ratings 1972–73 to 2000–01, <http://www.freedomhouse.org>.

Hellman, J., Jones, G. and Kaufmann, D. (2000) 'Seize the State, Seize the Day. State Capture, Corruption, and Influence in Transition', *The World Bank, Policy Research Working Paper*, no. 2444.

Heritage Foundation, <http://www.heritage.org>.

Jayasuriya, K. (1999) 'Corporatism and Judicial Independence Within Statist Legal Institutions in Asia', in K. Jayasuriya (ed.) *Law, Capitalism and Power in Asia*, London, pp. 173–204.

Kaufmann, D. (2001) 'Privatization, Corruption's Curse or Cure? Revisiting Some Notions and Evidence', Workshop Session, 10 October, Tenth IACC, Prague, Czech Republic.

Klitgaard, R. (1988) *Controlling Corruption*, Berkeley.

Kornai, J. (1992) *Socialist Systems*, New York.

Leung, M.-K. and Mok, V.W.-K. (2000) 'Commercialization of Banks in China: Institutional Changes and Effects on Listed Enterprises', *Journal of Contemporary China*, vol. 9, no. 23, pp. 41–52.

Libecap, G.D. (2001) 'A Transactions Costs Approach to the Analysis of Property Rights', Working Paper, 12 April, 2001, <http://www.bpa.arizona.edu/~libecap/workingpapers.html>.

Liou, K.T. (1998) *Managing Economic Reforms in Post-Mao China*, London.

Neoh, A. (2000) 'China's Domestic Capital Markets in the New Millennium, Part II', *China Online*, 23 August.

Opper, S. (2003) 'Enforcement of China's Accounting Standards: Reflections on Systemic Problems', *Business and Politics*, vol. 5, no. 2, pp. 153–75.

Opper, S., Wong, S.M.L. and Hu, R. (2002) 'Party Power, Market and Private Power: CCP Persistence in China's Listed Companies', in K. Leicht (ed.) 'The Future of Market Transition', *Research in Social Stratification and Mobility*, vol. 19, pp. 103–36.

Panorama Network, <http://www.p5w.net>.

Park, A. and Sehrt, K. (2001) 'Tests of Financial Intermediation and Banking Reform in China', *Journal of Comparative Economics*, vol. 29, pp. 608–44.

Qi, D., Wu Woody, and Zhang Hua (2000) 'Shareholding Structure and Corporate Performance of Partially Privatized Firms: Evidence from Listed Chinese Companies', *Pacific-Basin Finance Journal*, vol. 8, pp. 587–610.

Rose-Ackerman, S. (1978) *Corruption: A Study in Political Economy*, New York.

Rose-Ackerman, S. (1999) *Corruption and Government. Causes, Consequences, and Reform*, Cambridge.

Shleifer, A. and Vishny, R.W. (1986) 'Large Shareholders and Corporate Control', *Journal of Political Economy*, vol. 94, no. 3, pp. 461–88.

Steinfeld, E.S. (1999) *Forging Reform in China: The Fate of State-Owned Industry* (2nd edn), Cambridge.

Sussman, L.R. and Karlekar, K.D. (2002) 'The Annual Survey of Press Freedom 2002', Freedom House, New York, <http://www.freedomhouse.org/research/pressurvey.htm>.

Tenev, S. and Zhang, C. (2002) *Corporate Governance and Enterprise Reform in China. Building the Institutions of Modern Markets*, World Bank and the International Finance Corporation, Washington, DC.

Transparency International, <http://www.transparency.org>.

Wilhelm, K. and Saywell, T. (1999) 'Mission Critical', *Far Eastern Economic Review* (Internet Edition), 9 September.

World Bank (2002) 'Building Institutions for Markets', *World Development Report 2002*, Washington, D.C.

Xu, X. and Wang, Y. (1999) 'Ownership Structure and Corporate Governance in Chinese Stock Companies', *China Economic Review*, vol. 10, no. 1, pp. 75–98.

Zheng, S. (1997) *Party vs. State in Post-1949 China*, Cambridge.

Zhu, T. (1999) 'China's Corporatization Drive: An Evaluation and Policy Implications', *Contemporary Economic Policy*, vol. 17, no. 4.

12 Corruption in international trade – pleading for a responsible WTO

Peter Eigen[1]

Introduction

The mission of the World Trade Organization (WTO) rests on the credo that barriers to trade are barriers to development. I share this belief. And yet, like other civil society organizations worldwide, Transparency International (TI) is concerned about the WTO's single-minded concentration on the removal of trade barriers and its low attention to the development-obstructing phenomena that can accompany trade liberalization.

Unchecked global market forces can lead to exploitation, deepen poverty and fuel conflict. Strong, responsive governments, able to play an effective role in preventing or at least correcting such undesired globalization outcomes, are essential if trade liberalization is to foster sustainable development. For this reason, TI is particularly concerned about the unrestrained spread of cross-border trade corruption. Its corrosive effects on the integrity of governments vastly weaken the correlation between global trade expansion and societal well-being. TI therefore strongly urges the WTO to recognize the fight against cross-border corruption as one of its major and immediate responsibilities.

The explicit purpose for which the WTO was founded was to liberalize trade worldwide; but the maximizing of global trade is not an end in itself. Even the staunchest proponent of neo-liberal economics would not quarrel with the claim that the goal of trade liberalization is to contribute towards economic and concomitant human development. Yet while the WTO has certainly succeeded in stimulating the volume of international trade, the promise of increased, equitably distributed welfare gains for all remains unfulfilled. Instead, the rapid expansion of transnational trade has extended the opportunities for, and the negative effects of, unfettered competitive practices while substantially increasing the damages by trade-related corruption. If the WTO is to help ensure that global trade fosters development, or at the very least that grand corruption does not seriously impede it, then it must part with the widespread assumption that trade liberalization automatically bolsters development.

This chapter attempts to show how global corruption counteracts the WTO's efforts to expand world trade and enhance worldwide development. It argues that the WTO would not be alone in the attempt to contain corruption in international trade. To the contrary, the WTO would find many allies among governments, business and civil society that support a more proactive stance against corruption. It presents anti-corruption tools developed by coalitions of government, business and civil society, and their relevance and usefulness to the WTO system.

Corruption distorts competition, impedes trade, undermines development

Behind WTO's worldwide drive for the removal of trade barriers lies the basic assumption that free trade fosters competition, and through it a more efficient production and distribution of goods and services for the benefit of *all*. It is well beyond the scope of this chapter to discuss the potentials and limitations of competition policies to achieve the purported effects. Suffice it to say that a well-designed competition policy and corresponding institutions are essential for competition to function in the described mode. Where the political will and the appropriate institutions for promoting competition are weak, corruption can flourish (Transparency International 2000: 259–68).

Corruption, however, encourages competition in bribery rather than competition in quality and in the price of goods and services. By inhibiting the development of a healthy marketplace and the optimal allocation of scarce resources, and by instigating mismanagement in public institutions, corruption distorts and endangers both economic and social life and undermines development. Ultimately, it denies an increased quality of life to the most vulnerable members of society.[2]

Competition in a corrupt environment destroys the premise that the best offer in terms of price and quality will win the day. Where bribe offering and bribe taking determine choices, the products selected are not those that best serve the individual buyer or the public at large, but those that maximize bribe revenues. In the vicious circle of competition in bribes, the only winners, if any, are the corrupt. As the likelihood of increasing one's market share by offering bribes is highest in the public sector, the global costs of corruption-induced trade distortions can hardly be overestimated.

Empirical evidence

Like most fast-profit-seeking activities, corruption is not without its risks. The risk of being caught and punished increases with the number of transactions, the number of people involved, the duration of the transaction and the simplicity and standardization of the procedure. Because the risk does not clearly increase with the value of a transaction, large one-off purchases create a more efficient base for a kickback. This biases the decisions made by corrupt politicians and bureaucrats in favour of capital-intensive, technologically sophisticated and custom-built products and technologies.[3] This is particularly true for arms purchases.

The resultant distortions in public expenditures and investment – away from education, primary health and other human development fostering activities towards oversized public works and arms deals – should be seen as one of the most pernicious crimes against humanity in our times. Such heinous crimes of corruption cannot be contained, much less eliminated, by merely exposing individual perpetrators, shaming greed-guided transnational businessmen, or blaming developing-country elites. Only a concerted, worldwide coalition of 'public-good-minded' institutions and people can hope to organize the systemic approaches measuring up to the challenge of combating transnational corruption.

As reports of grand corruption associated with oversized public works and deadly arms deals unfold in the news media and fuel the arguments of anti-globalization protesters, myriad occurrences of petty corruption exasperate businessmen and investors going about their daily transactions. If an import licence can be obtained only by bribing public officials and a phalanx of corrupt inspectors, and if foreign investors are compelled to spend inordinate amounts of time and money to 'negotiate' entry regulations, the prospect for trade-fostered development will be undermined. Numerous studies have shown that corruption, no less than other non-tariff barriers, constitutes a serious deterrent to trade. Kaufmann and Wei (1999) showed that petty corruption, instead of speeding up administrative processes, increases the time managers have to waste negotiating with bureaucrats. The adverse incentives created in a corrupt environment breed further obstacles: designing artificial bottlenecks emerges as a method for exacting a corrupt payoff; service delivery is slowed down deliberately, forcing the payment of speed money.

Djankov *et al.* (2000) present a fascinating study of the nature of entry regulation. They determine the number of procedures required to start a new business for a cross-section of 71 countries, along with the necessary time and official costs. The authors find a strong correlation of these variables with a country's level of corruption. A similar conclusion is drawn by Gatti (1999), who argues that a highly diversified trade tariff menu fuels bribe-taking behaviour, whereas uniform trade tariff rates limit public officials' ability to extract bribes from importers. She reports a positive association between the standard deviation of trade tariffs and the level of corruption for a small sample of 34 countries. Broadman and Recanatini (1999) show for a sample of transition economies in Europe and Central Asia that higher barriers to market entry are associated with higher corruption.

Overall, high levels of corruption are a major deterrent to international flows of trade and investment. Wei (2000) investigated bilateral FDI flows between 14 source and 45 host countries in 1990 and 1991 and ascertained that corruption had a significant negative impact on FDI. According to his findings, an increase in the corruption level from that of Singapore to that of Mexico is equivalent to raising the tax rate in the host country by over twenty percentage points. Most recently, Lambsdorff (2003a) proves an adverse impact of corruption on total capital inflows, arguing that corruption adversely affects a country's tradition of law and order, rendering property rights insecure and alienating investors. An increase in corruption by one point on a scale from 10 (highly clean) to 0 (highly corrupt) decreases net annual capital inflows by 0.5 per cent of GDP. An improvement with regard to corruption by 6 points of the Transparency International Corruption Perceptions Index – for example, Tanzania improving to the level of the United Kingdom – would increase net annual capital inflows by 3 per cent of GDP. The implications are clear: investors tend to stay away from countries with high corruption levels. It is equally apparent that countries most in need of foreign investment tend to be those that suffer most from widespread corruption.

A race to the bottom?

Although corruption is as old as it is widespread, it is neither a natural phenomenon nor may it be considered an unavoidable evil. While hard evidence on the incidence and magnitude of corruption is difficult to find, reliable surveys do indicate that the problem varies widely across countries and business sectors, and that even within countries some public agencies (e.g. customs and tax collection) are more prone to corruption than others. All this suggests that remedies are possible.

Until a few years ago economists generally agreed that the propensity for international bribery by the private sector could not be meaningfully measured. Striving for maximum profit would induce all competitors to behave equally (e.g. to pay bribes in a bribe-demanding environment). Thus the playing field could be seen to be relatively even, even if it meant competing in an environment where corruption was rife. No competitor would abstain from paying bribes in what might emerge as 'a moral race to the bottom'. If corruption increased individual profits, moral arguments against corruption would become troublesome to implement because firms adhering to such claims lose market shares. It would be the moral claims that distort what was formerly a level playing field.

From such a viewpoint, only concerted efforts could help overcome the resulting 'prisoners' dilemma'. Leading this concerted effort is a laborious task because individual players would tend to only pay lip-service to the fight against corruption, while individual incentives would induce them to continue with the payment of bribes, this being their dominant strategy. Effective sanctions would have to be devised in order to keep all competitors and stakeholders in line. Many multinational institutions were sceptical at the beginning of Transparency International's work a decade ago as to whether leading such an international initiative would be worth the effort. I will report about this process on pp. 224–6. Those who believed that the fight against corruption resembles a prisoner's dilemma must acknowledge now that concerted efforts were successfully organized in the past. But there is even more promising evidence, showing that paying bribes is for many firms no longer the dominant strategy.

The viewpoint that all competitors behave equally does not withstand empirical investigation. TI's Bribe Payers Index, first published in 1999, and updated in May 2002, contradicts this notion (Transparency International 2002). The

2002 survey was conducted among 835 business leaders, executives at chartered accountancies, bi-national chambers of commerce, national and foreign commercial banks and commercial law firms, in 15 emerging markets around the world. The results showed that companies from some countries are seen to be significantly more prone to bribe to gain business abroad than companies from other countries. Table 12.1 shows the world's top exporting countries ranked by their perceived willingness to offer bribes in the surveyed emerging market economies. A score of 10 would mean entirely corruption-free; a score of 0 would mean relying almost entirely on corruption to enter or retain market shares when doing business abroad.

Further research based on bilateral trade data bears out the hypothesis that those exporting countries that are prone to offering bribes can obtain a competitive advantage in corrupt import markets, resulting in higher market shares there. By contrast, in clean import markets such a competitive advantage cannot be achieved by paying bribes (Lambsdorff 2001).

One of the reasons for these differences between exporting countries can be the difficulties in arranging corrupt deals. Corruption goes along with large transaction costs, particularly because one cannot seek corrupt partners by open advertising. Instead, the secrecy necessary to carry out corrupt transactions increases the costs for contracting and negotiating. In addition, because corrup-

Table 12.1 TI bribe payers index, 2002

Rank		Score
1	Australia	8.5
2	Sweden	8.4
	Switzerland	8.4
4	Austria	8.2
5	Canada	8.1
6	Netherlands	7.8
	Belgium	7.8
8	United Kingdom	6.9
9	Singapore	6.3
	Germany	6.3
11	Spain	5.8
12	France	5.5
13	United States	5.3
	Japan	5.3
15	Malaysia	4.3
	Hong Kong	4.3
17	Italy	4.1
18	South Korea	3.9
19	Taiwan	3.8
20	People's Republic of China	3.5
21	Russia	3.2
	Domestic companies	1.9

Source: *Transparency International* (2002).

tion does not allow for legal recourse, in exchange for a bribe firms only obtain the vague promise that a corrupt service will be delivered in the future. The standard strategies for coping with these risks, such as carrying out corrupt deals only in trenches, or with established business partners or employing middlemen, are not without costs and usually add to the large transaction costs of corrupt agreements. Even when employing these mechanisms, firms can never be safe after paying a bribe. In many cases, corrupt services are not delivered and those paying bribes are blackmailed instead afterwards.

Whether it actually pays to engage in corrupt transactions thus becomes a more difficult question. If firms lack the necessary know-how and know-who, they prefer to compete with legal means. Other firms may fear for their international reputation, in particular with their customers. If known to resist demands for bribes, they may also be safe from blackmail. Those pressurizing firms in their zeal for illegitimate income may spare those firms who are known to reject such a request under all circumstances. Finally, a firm's employees often misuse the secrecy surrounding corrupt agreements to pocket parts of the bribes for themselves. Allowing one's employees to engage in corrupt transactions often acted like an invitation to defrauding the firm itself. New sanctions, such as black listing by the World Bank or other important financiers and customers, add to the risk of bribing.

As a result, paying bribes is not necessarily the dominant business strategy. Leading a concerted effort to containing corruption is not the arduous task one would expect from a prisoner's dilemma. Instead, many individual players from government, business and civil society are strongly supportive in the fight against corruption. They do not merely pay lip service to integrity but are willing to take leadership roles in the fight against corruption.

Perhaps less surprising than the differences among exporters from different countries, and their propensity to bribe, are the differences between the main sectors of international trade and investment. Certain sectors, such as public works/construction, and the arms and defence industry, are particularly prone to bribery, whereas others, such as agriculture, are less so (Table 12.2). These

Table 12.2 Bribery by business sector

Business sector	Score	Business sector	Score
Public works/construction	1.3	Heavy manufacturing	4.5
Arms and defence	1.9	Banking and finance	4.7
Oil and gas	2.7	Civilian aerospace	4.9
Real estate/property	3.5	Forestry	5.1
Telecoms	3.7	IT	5.1
Power generation/transmission	3.7	Fishery	5.9
Mining	4.0	Light manufacturing	5.9
Transportation/storage	4.3	Agriculture	5.9
Pharmaceuticals/medical care	4.3		

Source: *Transparency International* (2002).

differences may relate to the proceeds that can be attained with the help of corruption, on the one hand, and the institutional difficulties in arranging corrupt deals on the other. Public construction and arms deals promise large side payments and make these sectors highly lucrative for those seeking extra income.

While globally the WTO has succeeded in stimulating the volume of world trade, corruption has been shown to undermine the presupposed positive effects of trade on sustainable development. These findings do not negate the proposition that free trade *can* induce economic growth and development. What they demonstrate is that trade liberalization does not automatically ensure development. Corruption has been shown to be a major obstacle, at best 'merely' obstructing, at worst totally destroying, development opportunities. In any event, it debilitates government as a regulator and protector of the common interest – as the key actor in maintaining the social market economy. New corrective policies, including corruption-control measures, urgently need to be designed and implemented to strengthen the WTO's effectiveness for trade-fostered development.

Corruption control as a trade commitment

International efforts to contain corruption

Corruption has emerged as a central topic on the international agenda. The UN Conference on Financing for Development, held in Monterrey in March 2002, was no exception. A succession of heads of state, finance and development ministers, not to mention the leadership of the World Bank and IMF, stressed the importance of controlling corruption. Differences regarding the relative contribution of trade and aid abounded, but not with respect to corruption. Here the judgement was universal: wherever corruption reigned, development aspirations would remain a hopeless dream. Indeed, if the prevalent notion of political correctness had not disallowed overt reliance on 'conditionality', the control of corruption as a *sine qua non* for increasing development aid and private investment would most certainly have figured even more prominently in the 'Monterrey Consensus'.

The broad anti-corruption consensus manifest at Monterrey hardly comes as a surprise. Awareness and solid documentation on the worldwide pervasiveness of corruption and its dramatically detrimental effects on developing economies and societies had been growing steadily since the mid-1990s. To date, most international organizations and agencies have at least declared their intent to join the fight against corruption.

In a remarkable reversal from its hands-off-stance concerning corruption, the World Bank declared war on corruption in 1996. Arguing for the first time that corruption is above all an economic issue and therefore its legitimate concern, the Bank has since engaged in a comprehensive fight against corruption, both internally and in the countries it works with. The IMF as well, although opting for a less proactive approach, has taken up the fight against corruption as a central component of its lending policy.

As business has become increasingly global and the systematic and large-scale bribery by exporting companies has become obvious, it has proved to be more and more unrealistic to regard corruption as the preserve of developing countries to be addressed only by them. The 1997 OECD Convention on Combating Bribery of Foreign Public Officials in International Business Transactions was a landmark in addressing the 'supply' side of international bribery. This Convention came into force in 1999 and has since been ratified by 34 states (29 of the 30 OECD member countries[4] plus Argentina, Brazil, Bulgaria, Chile and Slovenia). The Convention requires all parties to criminalize the bribery of foreign public officials, and to provide mutual legal assistance to facilitate inquiries into suspected violations. Furthermore, it foresees intrusive 'country inspections' at regular intervals to help ensure that each country is playing a full role in respecting the objectives of the convention.[5]

Several regional agreements, similar in content and aim to the OECD Convention, were initiated around the same time, or followed suit. In 1996, for instance, the Organization of American States (OAS) agreed on an 'Inter-American Convention Against Corruption'. Around one year later, the European Union tackled the issue, enacting the convention on the 'Fight Against Corruption Involving Officials of the European Communities or Officials of Member States of the European Union', which purports to penalize both active and passive corruption. Although rather modest, this convention has yet to be ratified by the majority of its 15 signatories.

The Council of Europe, now an important trendsetter in international law, went much further by concluding both the 1999 Criminal Law Convention on Corruption and the 1999 Civil Law Convention on Corruption. Under the Criminal Law Convention, which entered into force in July 2002, each party commits to enacting a range of measures at the national level to counter corruption in public life, in public administration and in the private sector. Furthermore, corporations are to be rendered subject to criminal law and measures introduced to facilitate the gathering of evidence and the confiscation of proceeds. Similarly to the OECD Convention, the implementation of the Criminal Law Convention is to be monitored. For this purpose, the 'Group of States against Corruption' (GRECO) was established. Its members will monitor not only this Convention but also other measures developed by the Council of Europe as part of its action plan against corruption.

These conventions constitute the most important formalized agreements of international cooperation for fighting corruption. Other international mechanisms to counter global corruption include measures taken to check money laundering, the activities of Interpol, and a multiplicity of mutual assistance agreements entered into between states.[6] In 2003, the noose is about to be tightened further around international corruption. In recognition of the fact that global institutions must play their full role in containing the global menace of corruption, a UN Convention against Corruption has now been drafted and is scheduled to be signed in December 2003 in Mexico.

Efforts to combat and control corruption must continue and become more effective. The WTO could play an important part in underpinning and assisting these efforts around the world.

What will be the role of the WTO?

Notwithstanding the commendable efforts of governments and international organizations to criminalize and thus to contain corruption, the rapid expansion of transnational trade continues to expand the opportunities for cross-border grand corruption vastly. And as is well known, where institutions are weak corruption can flourish. And where the risk of being caught is small and the gain disproportionately large, corruption does flourish. This is certainly the case in the global trade arena. As the empirical evidence presented has shown, cross-border trade corruption continues to be pervasive, and the need for trade-focused corruption *prevention* policies and mechanisms remains undiminished.

What is to be the role of the WTO in combating corruption in the global trade arena? If trade is essential for development, can the WTO remain inactive while corruption-fraught trade threatens to exacerbate poverty and underdevelopment? Do the WTO statutes allow a more proactive role in combating corruption? Does the professed or implied mission demand it? How can the WTO build upon the experience of existing international anti-corruption mechanisms to expedite the development and implementation of its own, long overdue corruption-control system?

What role can the WTO play in fighting corruption? The control of corruption in international trade has been an essential mandate of the GATT since 1947. In TI's view, ensuring that trade liberalization comes to mean corruption-free trade is intrinsic to WTO's mandate. By virtue of its declared purpose and actual agenda, the WTO is well positioned to serve as both architect and universal guardian of global free trade. As such, not only is it ideally placed, but is also obliged to assume leadership in eliminating those obstructions to the free flow of trade that distort competition and with it an equitable distribution of the benefits of global trade. Cross-border corruption unquestionably constitutes an obstruction to free trade; it vastly diminishes the very benefits for which trade liberalization is purportedly pursued. Article X includes language designed to promote greater transparency of laws, regulations, judicial decisions and administrative rulings related to trade; unfortunately it has not been widely used. The 1994 Uruguay Round Agreement did not explicitly address corruption. In recent years, WTO members began discussing the potential anti-corruption effects of the existing trade rules. According to a WTO working paper, 'Article X's paramount objective is the attainment of transparency.' If the development goals of the Doha Ministerial Declaration are to be met, then the WTO must move promptly to improve them and make them more effective.

And yet, to this day, the WTO remains the only major organ of economic governance without an identifiable corruption-control policy.

If the promises of trade-fostered development, untiringly espoused by the WTO since its foundation, and most recently emphasized as the Doha Development Agenda, are to stand any chance of serving as anything more than further fodder for 'Globalphobia', then intelligent policies and pragmatic measures for controlling trade-related corruption must start to feature prominently in the WTO work programme. Since Seattle, scepticism, fear and outright opposition have unremittingly accompanied WTO's efforts to further expand international trade. The fear of many civil society activists – that international trade is the captive of powerful multinational corporations in an unholy alliance with corrupt government leaders – can only be addressed by designing and articulating a high-profile anti-corruption strategy driven by the WTO. It seems quite safe to predict that the manifest resistance to further trade liberalization, particularly persistent among many developing countries, as well as among southern and northern NGOs, will not be overcome unless the link between trade and sustainable development is not only verbally espoused but also strategically supported.

Hence, one important element of such strategic support for trade-fostered development could be the design of effective WTO policies and commensurate measures to combat and thereby to significantly reduce the incidence and impact of trade-related corruption. The WTO should not hesitate any longer to commit itself to a full-fledged policy and programme of corruption control in global trade transactions.

Taking into account the scope of existing international and national efforts to contain corruption, and with due concern for the requirements of the majority of the WTO's membership, a focus on prevention, insofar as this is possible, rather than on criminalization, suggests itself. Particularly for poor countries, the prevention approach is crucial. Although misuse of resources needs to be avoided everywhere, in poor countries overpriced and misallocated investments of fungible resources in one area all too frequently mean starving another area. In practice, as documented, corruption invariably promotes inflated infrastructure investments while basic needs such as primary education and health care – where the pickings for the corrupt are on a much reduced scale – tend to fall by the wayside. Morally, economically and politically the long-term costs of postponed or forgone human development opportunities are staggering. Preventing irreparable social and economic damage should be a prime objective of the WTO's anti-corruption policy.

In terms of practicality and cost, the prevention approach seems preferable, as its implementation can be relatively inexpensive. Transparency, public awareness and a system of people-centred, voluntary and thus well-accepted rules can help stop corruption in its tracks. Prosecution and punishment are, by comparison, costly and complex, requiring a professional judicial and policing apparatus. Of course, punitive action cannot be dispensed with altogether; but the better the prevention the less formalized costly enforcement will be necessary.

Furthermore, an enforcement system raises controversial questions. What is to be the role of the WTO in an enforcement system? Is it to be 'a global corruption policeman'? Or would a cooperative framework to counter abusive and corrupt practices adversely affecting international markets be more suitable for an intergovernmental organization? Clearly such and many other key questions will need to be thoroughly considered when designing an anti-corruption system specifically suited to the special strengths and weaknesses of the WTO. Preliminary analysis of a variety of international anti-corruption efforts, however, does suggest that a system designed to prevent corruption from occurring in the first place, rather than one relying on penalties after the event, will, without doubt, be superior not only for poor countries but for the WTO membership as a whole.

A further important lesson to be drawn from international anti-corruption efforts is, that the most recent and promising ones are the offspring of what until recently have been deemed strange bedfellows: the private sector and civil society organizations; governments and civil society organizations; and an occasional *ménage à trois* of the aforementioned. Indeed, coalitions of stakeholders have been at the forefront of the anti-corruption, good governance and accountability movement. Anti-corruption strategies could be conceptualized, specific corruption control tools developed and international agreements forged more or less by virtue of the fact that a broad-based coalition of business, government and civil society organizations reached agreement on what needed to be done and how. Thus, for example, the International Chamber of Commerce combined with Transparency International (TI) in their successful campaign for the now highly regarded OECD Anti-Bribery Convention. Ever since, TI has participated in the OECD 'country inspections' monitoring – together with government and private sector representatives – compliance with the convention. The creativeness and results-orientation of these new coalitions is also evident in such joint products as corporate anti-bribery principles, the banking sector's initiative to curtail money laundering, known under the name of the 'Wolfsberg Principles',[7] and the rapid spread of corporate social reporting.

The moral of these developments is twofold. First, there is neither need nor justification for the WTO to go it alone in designing its anti-corruption policy and implementation mechanisms. A variety of multi-stakeholder coalitions have demonstrated that they can produce solid substantive results and, most importantly, can be relied upon to ensure a comparatively wider acceptance than unilaterally produced solutions. Second, the existing anti-corruption principles, conventions and agreements constitute an impressive body of efforts attempting to deal with some of the negative fallout of globalization. However, their practical impact on cross-border trade corruption thus far has been limited and will most certainly not be up to the challenges posed by further trade liberalization and concomitant opportunities for abusive practices. And even though – with some conspicuous recent exceptions – private sector anti-corruption and accountability standards are on the increase, their cumulative effect cannot be expected to be more far-reaching than anti-corruption conventions and agreements.

If globalization is not to destroy itself, it must be better managed for the benefit of all. Patchwork approaches to global problems may be considered a highly useful field for experimentation, but corruption in international trade and its manifold aberrations demand a holistic approach, one that combines global reach and trade system acumen with social and political sensitivity. Such a solution cannot be achieved without WTO leadership, resources and the conviction that system reform must not be postponed any longer. The opportunity for active engagement is most propitious: governments are keen to introduce new anti-corruption rules applying to cross-border trade, and the assistance of the WTO should be most welcome to them.

Transparency in government procurement and services

The WTO, in contrast to its global sister organizations the UNDP, World Bank and the IMF, has not so far identified corruption as one of its concerns, much less as one of its core responsibilities. Nonetheless, some initiatives and new agreements presently under preparation could become highly useful tools for reducing corrupt practices. One potential agreement, Transparency in Government Procurement, merits special attention in TI's view. On the one hand, it is a prime example of the WTO's high potential for reducing opportunities for corrupt practices in a key area of world trade. On the other hand, it mirrors the institutional bind in which the WTO is caught, a bind that restricts the WTO's capacity for dealing with the global issues entailed in its mandate.

There is probably no more straightforward way of reducing corruption in the multilateral trade system than tackling government procurement. Annual budgets for government purchases worldwide have been estimated by the OECD to run up to about US$5 trillion. A large share of these expenditures goes on essential public services, such as utilities and transport, education and health. And yet these economically and socially important investments, involving as they do major shares of countries' budgets, are often spent in shockingly wasteful ways (OECD 2002).

Reviewing global experience, experts have found that far too many government investments and purchases are uneconomical, either not needed at all, oversized, ineffective or too costly to operate. Too often, the true cost of an investment or purchase is not made public at the outset for fear of not obtaining the necessary administrative or parliamentary approvals if the full cost were known. Actual costs emerge only slowly during the implementation process, usually when it is too late to reverse an original decision because too much of the investment has already been implemented. The reasons for such misallocation of resources can include outright incompetence. But more often than not, unethical officials, frequently in collusion with unethical consultants, suppliers and contractors, have influenced and manipulated faulty project choices and investment decisions. There is widespread evidence that full transparency of the government decision-making processes – from the point of conceptualization of an investment or purchase until the completion of implementation coupled with appropriate monitoring throughout – will bring economic, design or operational faults to light and mobilize public opinion against such wastage of resources.

Practical experience also demonstrates quite convincingly that in public procurement the use of competitive bidding under transparent conditions reduces the risk of manipulation and corruption. As a rule, competitive transparent procurement practices result in lower prices for the goods or services acquired, since the prices are determined by competition on the basis of quality and price rather than by bribery and corruption. Such open procedures are well worth the effort. Experts estimate that where corruption is systemic, it can add 20–30 per cent to the costs, and on top of that results in inferior-quality purchases.[8] It can even result in wholly wasted investments. In exceptional cases, the costs, or conversely the savings, can be much higher. Thus for example, in this year's celebrated Karachi Water and Sewerage Board (KW&SB) investment project, the mutual no-bribes 'TI-Integrity Pact', agreed by TI-Pakistan, the KW&SB and consultant bidders, resulted in a winning consulting bid 75 per cent lower than the reserved funds allocated based on experience in World Bank financed projects.[9]

Providing for more transparency in procurement is as much in the interest of the seller as of the buyer. Many companies offering goods or services have discovered that operating in a non-transparent market, where corruption thrives, is significantly more expensive (costly bribes), inherently unreliable (the influence and the advantage purchased by bribes cannot be enforced by legal action, and with democratization the longevity of any particular regime can no longer be assumed) and increasingly risky (in terms of likely criminal prosecution, financial, personal and reputational disadvantages). They are also finding that corruption scandals can serve to tarnish the brand-names they have spent fortunes to promote. More and more companies thus welcome a market without bribery. In several business sectors with global activities, the major actors have recognized the advantage of a corruption-free competition and are in the process of negotiating 'common competition standards', which would of course be much more likely to be effective if those companies competed in a fully transparent procurement environment.

But the international procurement environment is a far cry from full transparency. Although many countries have good procurement rules in the books, they are routinely circumvented and thus largely useless. Escape clauses based on alleged 'urgency' or 'emergency' are used too frequently, thus eroding the good 'open competition' principle. Furthermore, the evaluation of bids and the selection decision are usually made by a handful of officials in secrecy, allowing manipulation and inviting corruption in the process. Transparency of the decision-making process is thus of the essence for avoiding manipulation and corruption. Indeed, it is the best guarantor that procurement rules are actually applied.

To devise a framework for removing the widespread distortions in public procurement constitutes a classic task and responsibility of the WTO. It can hardly come as a surprise, then, that a plurilateral WTO Government Procurement Agreement (GPA) has been in force since January 1996. And although it contains some basic transparency requirements, it fails to reduce the problem because it has few signatories. Developing countries in particular have refrained from acceding to the Agreement since it also contains market access or no-discrimination rules under which importing countries cannot offer any preferences to infant industries or domestic bidders. Because fair non-discrimination rules in procurement are so central to the multilateral trading system, and because the existing GPA is inadequate both in substance and number of adherents, work on a new procurement agreement has been ongoing since the first Ministerial in Singapore 1996.

The WTO Ministerial Meetings in Seattle (November/December 1999) and Doha (November 2001) had before them draft texts (submitted by the European Commission and by Hungary, Korea and the US) for a new Agreement on Transparency in Government Procurement. The proposed new agreement is no longer burdened by market access clauses and thus in principle more acceptable to developing countries, and constitutes a vast improvement in terms of transparency. It explicitly requires:

- the publication of laws, procedures, judicial decisions and administrative rulings
- timely public notification of bidding opportunities
- information on qualification requirements
- publication of tender documentation, including information on technical specifications and criteria for awards
- transparent qualification and contract award decisions
- information to the unsuccessful bidders as to why they lost and why the winning bid was chosen, and
- independent fora and procedures for review.

Considering the rather opaque processes still in use in many countries, and the unwillingness of many bureaucrats to allow public access to information they regard as the exclusive property of the executive, these proposals will require and hopefully engender significant changes in the actual procurement practices of most countries. By curtailing secrecy and the corruption it breeds, this new agreement could make an important contribution towards reducing a major obstruction to the goal of trade-fostered development.

While all of the WTO's membership stand to profit from transparent procurement rules, there can be little doubt that poor developing and transition countries stand to gain most. With their high levels of indebtedness and their dramatically fallen volume of FDI, they need every penny that can be rescued from misallocation of resources. Yet in Doha, as in previous years, a number of developing countries managed to block the start of negotiations on the proposed Agreement on Transparency in Government Procurement.

And while the resistance of developing countries to the proposed new procurement agreement continues unabated, some northern countries (e.g. Switzerland, the EU, the USA, etc.) have added fuel to the fire by arguing that the scope of a future agreement should cover goods and services.[10] The reasoning is varied. It includes critiques of the artificiality of separating goods and services, as many procurement contracts involve both, and many service contracts have significant goods components. And it maintains that a WTO agreement on goods alone would be a step backward compared with other international agreements. Indeed, there is no intrinsic reason for providing less transparency in service procurement than in goods procurement. In the context of the trade negotiations, bringing services into the discussion raises additional questions, including whether transparency issues relating to services ought not to be handled in the GATS, which in turn opens up a whole new Pandora's box of controversy.

Although all of these questions need clarification, they are not, in TI's view, any reason why an agreement on procurement, whether or not including services, should not be concluded. Most of the outstanding points are of a more or less technical nature and, with goodwill, could have been resolved long ago. According to some procurement experts, the work that has been done to date has addressed virtually all major issues on the subject. It should not, therefore, be difficult to move into an active negotiation, and complete that negotiation in a matter of months.

From the point of view of economic and development costs entailed in the prevailing, at best opaque, at worst massively corrupt, procurement practices, the failure to reach agreement on new rules is even less understandable. The persistence of developing countries in the view that the proposed procurement agreement with its transparency rules is mainly in the interest of industrialized countries, is to deny the reality that those very opponents of the reforms are the main victims of cross-border corruption.

The substantial differences continue to exist, as documented in the July 2003 report by the WTO's Working Group on Transparency in Government Procurement. There is still little consensus on whether multilateral rules on transparency are needed at all, whether procurement should relate only to the federal state and not to local entities, whether to include services into the negotiations, and in how far domestic review procedures and dispute settlement should be part of an agreement on transparency. The report concludes that after six years of consultation the work on clarifying issues, let alone on achieving a consensus, has not yet been completed. Divergence of views continues to exist in relation to most issues, so that not even a pre-negotiation stage is currently achieved. Some members still deny a WTO's mandate to address problems of corruption directly, calling it a moral issue that members must address individually. They continue to interfere with the work on GPA at Cancun in September 2003.

The stalemate over procurement transparency is but one of a series of binds shackling the WTO. The reluctance, in some cases strong opposition, prevailing in many developing countries *vis-à-vis* further trade liberalization in general and WTO rule-making in particular, seems highly unlikely to be overcome by further perfecting proposals suspected of being primarily in the interests of the

North. This suspicion is a relict of the wrong assumption that dominated thinking about corruption for a long time: that corruption is mainly a responsibility of the South. This myth has long been overcome: international corruption is as much the responsibility of northern companies. Hence the control of corruption will be as much addressed to them as to southern decision-makers. Resistance to many useful reforms, some much overdue, seems to emanate from a deep mistrust born of negative experiences with rushed or opaque decision-making processes. In the view of some insiders and many conscientious WTO-watchers, nothing short of institutional reform stands a chance of resolving the political and legislative stalemate crippling the WTO's work.

Conclusions

Notwithstanding the commendable efforts of governments, international organizations and multi-stakeholder coalitions to contain corruption, the empirical evidence sadly shows that cross-border trade corruption continues to be pervasive, its distortive effects on trade and investment considerable, and the resultant destruction of development opportunities deplorable. Corruption is a major impediment to international trade. It renders bureaucratic decisions arbitrary, increases the time managers waste negotiating with public servants and adds to protectionist entry regulation. Corrupt countries therefore suffer from reduced FDI and other capital inflows. Honest international investors lose market shares to the unscrupulous.

With the exception of the WTO, all of the important organizations of global governance have not only recognized that corruption exerts a severe drag on economic and human development but have also initiated programmes to conquer this major obstruction to development. Civil society organizations have demonstrated their ability to support both governments and/or private sector groups in devising strategies and tools to combat corruption, thereby proving that corruption must not be considered an unavoidable disaster. Although a considerable scope of approaches for fighting corruption can be usefully applied, full transparency of government functions represents the best way to deter and combat corruption.

The need for trade-focused corruption prevention policies and mechanisms remains undiminished. The World Trade Organization has both a unique responsibility and opportunity to contribute to a global pro-development solution. As the current trade negotiations have been proclaimed a Development Round, a major WTO initiative to tighten the noose on trade corruption is more imperative than ever.

Acknowledgements

A special acknowledgement is due to Shirley van Buiren and Johann Graf Lambsdorff, senior advisers to Transparency International, for their valuable contributions to this chapter.

Notes

1 In addition to being Chairman of Transparency International, the author is a visiting scholar at the Carnegie Endowment for International Peace and a professorial lecturer at the School of Advanced International Studies. Transparency International is the leading non-profit organization engaged in the fight against corruption worldwide (www.transparency.org).
2 For an empirical review of the various adverse consequences of corruption, see Lambsdorff (1999). Lambsdorff (2000b) proves a negative impact of corruption on productivity in a cross-section of countries.
3 Winston (1979); Mauro (1998) proved an adverse effect of corruption on the share governments allocate to education; Gupta *et al.* (2001) provided evidence for a cross-section of countries that corruption increases arms purchases.
4 As of 1 June 2003, Ireland was the only OECD member not yet to have ratified the OECD Anti-Bribery Convention.
5 Progress reports on the implementation of the convention can be viewed at the OECD Anti-Corruption Unit website: <http://www.oecd.org/daf/nocorruption>.
6 For a more detailed discussion of 'International Actors and Mechanisms', see Transparency International (2000: 153–64).
7 In 2000, Transparency International was instrumental in bringing together 11 leading international banks to announce their agreement on the Wolfsberg Anti-Money Laundering Principles. The new guidelines on business conduct in international private banking state: 'Bank policy will be to prevent the use of its world-wide operations for criminal purposes. The bank will endeavour to accept only those clients whose source of wealth and funds can be reasonably established to be legitimate.' The principles, signed on 30 October 2000, also deal with the identification and follow-up of unusual or suspicious activities. See <http://www.transparency.org/pressreleases_archive/2000/2000.10.30.wolfsberg.html>.
8 Strombom (1998), Frisch (1994).
9 Karachi 'Integrity Pact', press release, Karachi/Berlin, 27 February 2002, <http://www.transparency.org/pressreleases_archive/2002/2002.02.27.karachi.html>.
10 WTO Working Group on Transparency in Government Procurement, WT/WGTGP/M/11, 19 December 2000.

References

Broadman, H.G. and Recanatini, F. (1999) 'Seeds of Corruption – Do Market Institutions Matter?', *World Bank Policy Research Working Paper*, no. 2368, Washington, DC.
Djankov, S., La Porta, R., Lopez-de-Silanes, F. and Shleifer, A. (2000) 'The Regulation of Entry', *National Bureau of Economic Research Working Paper*, no. 7892, Cambridge.
Frisch, D. (1994) 'The Effects of Corruption on Development', Paper presented to the Africa Leadership Forum on 'Corruption, Democracy and Human Rights in Africa', Cotonou, Benin, 19–21 September.
Gatti, R. (1999) 'Corruption and Trade Tariffs, or a Case for Uniform Tariffs', *World Bank Policy Research Working Paper*, no. 2216, Washington, DC.
Gupta, S., de Mello, L. and Sharan, R. (2001) 'Corruption and Military Spending', *European Journal of Political Economy*, vol. 17, no. 4, pp. 749–77.
Kaufmann, D. and Wei, S.-J. (1999) 'Does "Grease Money" Speed up the Wheels of Commerce?', *National Bureau of Economic Research Working Paper*, no. 7093, Cambridge.

Lambsdorff, J. Graf (1999) 'Corruption in Empirical Research – A Review', *Transparency International Working Paper*, November <http://www.transparency.org/iacc/9th_iacc/papers/day2/ws1/d2ws1_jglambsdorff.html>.

Lambsdorff, J. Graf (2001) 'Exporters' Ethics – Some Diverging Evidence', *International Journal of Comparative Criminology*, vol. 1, no. 2.

Lambsdorff, J. Graf (2003a) 'How Corruption Affects Persistent Capital Flows', *Economics of Governance*, vol. 4, no. 3, pp. 229–43.

Lambsdorff, J. Graf (2003b) 'How Corruption Affects Productivity', *Kyklos*, vol. 56, no. 3, pp. 457–74.

Mauro, P. (1998) 'Corruption and the Composition of Government Expenditure', *Journal of Public Economics*, vol. 69, pp. 263–79.

OECD (2002) *The Size of Government Procurement Markets*, OECD Report, March.

Strombom, D. (1998) 'Corruption in Procurement', *USIA Electronic Journal, Economic Perspectives*, November.

Transparency International (2000) *TI Source Book 2000. Confronting Corruption: The Elements of a National Integrity System.*

Transparency International (2002) 'The Bribe Payers Index 2002', <http://www.transparency.org/surveys/index.html#bpi>.

Wei, S.-J. (2000) 'How Taxing is Corruption on International Investors', *Review of Economics and Statistics*, vol. 82, no. 1, pp. 1–11.

Winston, G.C. (1979) 'The Appeal of Inappropriate Technologies: Self-Inflicted Wages, Ethnic Price and Corruption', *World Development*, vol. 7, no. 8/9, pp. 835–45.

13 The case of corruption in Nigeria

Soji Apampa

Introduction: the situation in Nigeria

Through the moral sanctions of collective opinion across the world Nigeria has become something of a pariah state. Nigerians receive 'special treatment' when they apply for visas or arrive at foreign ports of entry, or try to open a bank account or transact any form of business outside their homeland. They are relatively less free to move around the globe than citizens of most other countries; they may not participate as freely in the emerging global economy. Even where the country belongs to international groupings like the Commonwealth or the Economic Community of West African States (ECOWAS), the question must surely cross the minds of other actors as to just how much liberty members should be allowed for fear of having the same liberties extended to Nigeria and Nigerians by induction. Why is the country and her citizens the subject of such nervousness?

Stereotypes of Nigerians abound. Some common derogatory examples describe them as the flamboyant, arrogant, loud, pushy, overconfident Africans whose self-assurance comes from wealth derived from wastage and corruption on a grand scale, or even drug trafficking and elaborate scams. By definition, these stereotypes emanate from exaggerations, distortions and generalizations of some real observations but the effect is very significant – both on the rest of the world and on Nigeria and her citizens. For those who see Africa as a huge untapped market, Nigeria, with approximately one-fifth of the population of the continent, and its oil wealth, is potentially a lucrative entry point. The apprehension towards all things Nigerian, however, serves to keep many out of venturing to unlock this probable gold mine. The recent inability of the government of Nigeria to muster the expected foreign enthusiasm towards the privatization of its national telephone company, NITEL, is a case in point.

If the annual Corruption Perception Index published by Transparency International is anything to go by, Nigeria has consistently been perceived to be the most corrupt country on earth. For the purposes of this discussion I shall define corruption to be:

> *The perversion of, or the attempt to pervert, the legal or right process within an entity; the creation of, or the attempt to create, bottlenecks within a system for private profit or personal gain.*

As may be inferred from that definition, corruption in Nigeria is viewed to be largely systemic.[1] The formal rules of behaviour governing transactions, contracts or cooperation between parties cannot always be upheld due to weaknesses in key institutions.

The role of standards

When a group outlines the standards of behaviour that should

1   guide the definition of its goals and objectives,
2   guide the establishment of all its processes,
3   guide the definition of acceptable outcomes from activities,
4   govern the interaction of its members, and
5   govern the interaction between members and outsiders,

this set of standards or rules of behaviour may be referred to as the norms of that group. These rules are best known in the form of written codes, although in a great number of cases they are not written but passed on through the culture of that group. Within a professional group, a set of standards for such norms may be referred to as the ethics of that profession.

Let us now imagine a group with unlimited knowledge, unlimited resources and a high sense of morality. It is very likely that this group will set for itself very high standards. On the other hand, imagine a group with limited knowledge, limited resources and a weak moral stance.[2] This type of group would tend to set relatively lower standards for themselves than would members of the first group. So, if indeed we agree that standards are generally set bearing in mind limitations and constraints, then perhaps we can conclude that the more limited and constrained you are the lower the standards you are likely to set yourself. We may readily agree that the Nigerian business sector, for example, can be adjudged to be more limited in its access to information (best practice) and resources, and therefore more constrained, than the business sectors of, say, the US, Germany or the UK. Further, if the Nigerian business sector does not have the necessary leadership, capacity (including resources), or institutional arrangements, and is not in the habit of comparing notes and harmonizing standards with those of other economies, then it is not likely that it will exhibit the minimum universally acceptable standards necessary to make behaviours more predictable and thus reduce the potential for mistakes and conflicts that may arise from unpredictable behaviour. For that to happen it needs to interact frequently with others.

In the light of the foregoing, Nigeria being perceived as the most corrupt country in the world is probably a self-fulfilling prophecy. One may expect that it should suffice to frequently interact with other locals so as to make behaviour locally predictable and thus limit corruption in a locally perceived context. However, experience in Nigeria shows that local principals suffer much the same fate as the foreign, and the local context seems to be a microcosm of the larger picture. In search of a possible explanation, permit me to introduce the idea of a 'psychology of scarcity'. A psychology of scarcity prevails where people (who are or perceive themselves to be; were or perceive themselves once to have been deprived for a protracted period) act from very basic instincts borne out of a real or imagined fear of scarcity. Take for example Nigeria's first republic, 1960–1966:

> [It] was wrecked by two related factors: The politics of ethnicity and the theory of winner-takes-all ... most politicians had made a desperate and successful struggle to escape from rural poverty. The *frantic accumulation of wealth* was meant to build a wall between themselves and poverty, between their children and poverty and like their predecessors, the Warrant Chiefs, whom in some ways they resembled, they were expected to be generous, by western standards, absurdly generous, to relations, fellow townsmen and constituents. A successful man had to be seen to be successful – to wield power, to display wealth, to spread it freely – or his constituents would begin to wonder if he was really successful at all.
>
> (Isichei 1983)

The Nigerian value system (which is also an indicator of norms and standards) seemed to have been governed at the time under review by a real or imagined perception of scarcity (limited resources) and settled at a level too low by comparison to international (Western) standards of the time. This argument is an attempt at uncovering and understanding the mechanisms which perpetuate corruption rather than an attempt at justifying the actions of the corrupt.

A little-known fact perhaps is that the corrupt of Nigeria are really not proud of it. It is often the case that people feel that they do not have an alternative to corruption as a means to a livelihood and survival in Nigeria. The idea of a 'psychology of scarcity' as many might well argue, does not and cannot negate the fact that had there been sound governance in place, corruption should not have flourished so. This has been the consistent drone from anti-corruption campaigners over the years. When a particular line of action applied repeatedly over the years yields little or no change it should indicate to us that there is perhaps more to the solution than we have been applying. A good understanding of the effects of the 'psychology of scarcity' on the collective value system of the Nigerian people might well be a new tool to add to the inventory of those seeking to induce lasting positive change.

Domestic barriers to dealing with corruption

A cursory glance at the political and business environment in Nigeria will show ample evidence of poor budgetary outcomes, declining manufacturing output, over-dependence on oil revenues and a difficult atmosphere in which to conduct any type of economic activity. For repair, many would look towards isolating the governing forces in order to design suitable interventions. It is generally assumed that issues such as governance, a focus on development priorities, the establishment of strong oversight institutions, ensuring the accountability of actors, the promotion of the watchdog initiative, guaranteeing competition and the action of market forces, etc. would combine somehow to shape the environment. However, similar to arguments made above, sole reliance on this approach has yielded poor results thus far in Nigeria.[3] To understand the character of the political and economic environment one must also recognize and acknowledge the structure of the society itself, how wealth is held and distributed, the role of public office and the complex relationships, alliances and pacts that hold it all together.

It is expected that society should divide itself neatly into cute little boxes like 'government and politics', 'the military', 'business and civil society', for example, but Nigeria's amorphous society is not that easily resolved. Take the current civilian President of Nigeria, who is an ex-military Head of State. He is currently the owner of a large mechanized farm and owner/founder of an activist NGO. He typifies the blurred boundaries of Nigerian society.[4] Most of the wealth of individuals is held outside the formal economy, as their linkages are not so readily known or established. It is difficult to predict where or how wealth is held in Nigeria just by looking at statistics on the formal economy. The economy, being dominated by sales of crude oil, and the centre (executive and legislative arm of government), being responsible for the allocation of scarce resources, makes public office, mainly at the centre, particularly important to wealth and influence in society. This 'wealth', concentrated in the centre and derived from oil revenue, is referred to in Nigeria as the 'national cake'. In Nigeria, political power is synonymous with great wealth and great wealth is synonymous with political power. You may not have one without the other. Wealth is concentrated at the centre of political power. To have access to the centre you need to be aligned to one of the powerful 'constituencies'[5] made up of a mixture of ex- and serving politicians, civil servants, military leaders, business folk, monarchs, etc. The alliance is sealed with a pact that, 'loosely stated', allows your 'constituency' continued access to the centre whilst keeping other groups out. In return for this they do what it takes to get you into office. This also means that you perpetuate the system of patronage (as you are indebted to your 'constituency'). How well you deliver on this basic understanding determines your survival and longevity in that office. These days, the national cake is a shrinking one, and competition for access is all the more fierce and deadly.

The stereotypical elites (those with access to the centre[6]) therefore see life as a 'zero-sum game' – the progress of others is perceived to be at their expense. Their preoccupation is on how to increase personal wealth and power. They see the establishment of production and industry to be largely futile, except that they can have some sort of monopoly or protection from competition. In a country where transaction costs are high, where banks carry a relatively large portfolio of non-performing loans, where there is a high incidence of fraud, the central bank naturally requires relatively high cash reserves. Add to this all other risks and it is not surprising that lending rates in Nigeria are amongst the highest in Africa. Banks would rather not take long-term positions. Access to capital through financial intermediaries is very expensive, even prohibitive for certain types of economic endeavour. Access to public office (or public office holders) at the centre is a better calculation. The author is certain that were a survey on the background of politicians at the centre to be undertaken, it would return a figure as high as 70 per cent of them being engaged in some economic venture or other whilst in office. The cynic might conclude that public office for most means access to affordable finance. Show them an alternative to corruption as a means to that end and you could begin to catch their attention.[7] The top three deterrents to development, according to roughly one out of every two business enterprises in Nigeria, are absence of affordable finance, inadequate infrastructure and unacceptable levels of inflation (Kwanashie *et al.* 2002). They need a mechanism that can assure them of the wealth, status and prestige that they seek. To enjoy influence, recognition and acknowledgement both at home and internationally they need to be mobile and have access to such affordable finance, international trade flows and markets, innovation, know-how and entrepreneurial assets. This should make the 'national cake' begin to look small in their eyes and not worth the trouble.

The middle class, or should I say 'the middle poor' (as many would rather be called), see themselves as a sort of 'wasted generation': the choices are to stay stunted, emigrate with the hope of a better life or 'shut up and safeguard the future as best as one can'. They look the most for self-definition, and self-actualization through well-rewarded professionalism and industry. If they could find it without emigrating or resorting to dubious means, you would begin to catch their attention. They need a mechanism that can assure them of a level playing field. To deliver a level playing field you need the capacity to establish acceptable standards, offer appropriate rewards to reinforce acceptable behaviour and be in a position to apply effective sanctions to discourage deviant behaviour. One might ask at this point what role the justice system has been able to play in assuring investors of protection of property rights. The inability to find sufficient foreign direct investment flows into the economy is probably an indication of the level of confidence investors are able to place generally on the justice system.

The chambers of commerce and industry (and other trade/professional associations) in the country seem to be largely ineffective. The playing field needs to be level between local and international actors, and amongst local actors in order to promote trust and reduce uncertainty and risk. This could be achieved by having common standards agreed between actors and parties to a transaction, having the means to deploy effective sanctions against deviant behaviour, and being in a position to expect appropriate rewards to follow acceptable behaviour. It is also about the ability to guarantee property rights, and to reduce the chances for opportunism and asymmetric information access in principal–agent relations and thereby reduce transaction costs. The foundation for this requirement is built on many things, including the ability to blow the whistle on corruption, and the functioning rule of law. Some key findings of a recent Governance and Corruption Diagnostic Study of Nigeria (Kwanashie *et al.* 2002) indicate that businesses believe that a major obstacle to using courts is that of a long process (justice delayed is justice denied); the second most important obstacle is that court decisions are influenced by corruption. Of the extra-judicial methods used to settle disputes amongst business enterprises in Nigeria, turning to friends/family, respected members of the business community and using a lawyer without going to court appear to be the most favoured options – in that order. In other words, some form of 'peer review' and, failing that, the ability to exert some form of 'peer pressure' are the alternative methods most frequently used. On the issue of reporting corruption, over 50 per cent of the people (households) do not know what process to follow. Sixty-four per cent indicated that they had witnessed corruption by a public official in the last two years but only 14 per cent had reported this. In other words, blowing the whistle against corruption is not a common occurrence.

The poorest in society see only the phenomenon of 'state capture': 'The elites have high jacked society.' If that were the case, better the elites from my tribe, old school, religious grouping or gender, etc. than others because I at least stand to gain somewhat from their flamboyant acts of benevolence. This probably accounts for the observed phenomenon that public servants, who are benevolent leaders in the eyes of their ethnic group – even when indicted for corruption – may still be recognized for their contribution to the welfare of their clan and blessed with a chieftaincy title. The common folk look for the fruits of good governance, the promise of those things for which the state was created. If they can find sustained development in their lives, you could begin to distract them from looking to receiving a share of corrupt proceeds as the way out. On the quality and availability of public services, more than one in three households believe the services delivered by the water board, public health departments, public education, power authority, national telecommunications company and many other essential services to be poor/very poor, and the worst rating they reserved for the Nigeria Police (Kwanashie *et al.* 2002). Effective, efficient service delivery by the state and the delivery of sustained improvements in their standard of living are the capacities required to make the mechanism of development work for them. At this point one might ask: What is the situation with local governance and service delivery at the grassroots of Nigerian society? In 1998, Integrity published its findings from a survey of the perception of citizens on local government service delivery and corruption. A summary of the findings is listed below:

- 75 per cent did not know how local government (LG) came about its budget
- 75 per cent did not know of avenues for consultation on the budget
- 99 per cent of citizens were unaware of money earmarked for key projects to be undertaken by their LG
- 67 per cent said that 'little or no consideration' is given to community interests in deciding projects

- 90 per cent of LG staff claimed there were avenues for consultation on the budget
- Not one of the 20 local governments in Lagos was willing to give its current budget (2000) to researchers halfway through the financial year!
- Of the 18 broad functions of LG only 30 per cent of citizens could identify five
- About 30 per cent of LG staff could mention five also
- 78 per cent of citizens thought that corruption is 'extremely much/very much/much' of a problem in LG
- 68 per cent of LG staff felt that corruption is 'not much of/not a' problem in LG offices

The following hypothetical questions were posed to respondents to aid further understanding of perceptions of corruption:

1   You have a close relation who is a chairman of local government or a councillor. Would you expect him/her to favour you with contracts? Two in every five expected to be favoured.
2   If you know it's an offence for which he/she (your relation) would be punished, would you still expect him/her to favour you? Of those who expected to be favoured with contracts, the majority – 90 per cent – would not expect their relations to favour them if that would lead to punishment.

The author's opinion, therefore, is that public officials – and indeed the public – do not expect corruption to be detected; if detected they don't expect it to be punished; if prosecuted they expect they can 'share' and get off the hook (in much the same way as Abacha in his initial unilateral goodwill gesture to return US$700 million of his father's loot when faced with the prospect of prosecution). This opinion is supported to some extent by the finding that approximately one in every two households in Nigeria believes that corruption is perpetrated by politicians and bureaucrats. Corruption in the public sector is believed to be one of the major impediments to development by as many as 85 per cent of the people. More than one in every three households believe that there is no sincere desire and will to combat corruption in Nigeria (Kwanashie *et al.* 2002). It is precisely this sort of indifference to very high levels of opportunism and impunity that helps corruption in Nigeria to continue unabated. In fact, in the same study, when asked about the first and second things they would do to curb corruption if they were in a position of responsibility, the people (households) of Nigeria would rather punish offenders first, then provide employment (ensure people have a means of livelihood), and then encourage leaders to lead by example. Paraphrased, they would first demonstrate that corruption is unacceptable and intolerable, then ensure that people have viable alternatives to corruption (a means of livelihood) and then consolidate progress by ensuring leaders lead by example.

For the sake of completeness I will also mention that the world is looking to get Nigeria out of being that 'basket case' by making a good international citizen out of her. Nigerians yearn for the dividends of democracy rather than continue to reap the costs of corruption. Seventy-seven per cent of public officials, 65 per cent of households and 42 per cent of enterprises believe a system of patronage exists with public office holders (threatening the principle of equity). Seventy per cent of public officials, 60 per cent of households and 42 per cent of enterprises believe that bribes paid to public officials to avoid taxes and regulation have a very significant/significant impact on their well-being. In other words, corruption threatens the sustainability of government programmes meant to deliver improvements in the standard of living of the people – and the public officials know it! Sixty-seven per cent of public officials, 50 per cent of households and 34 per cent of enterprises believe that contributions by private interests to political parties and election campaigns have a very significant/significant impact on their well-being. In other words, the element of state capture can rob them of their power to participate meaningfully in and influence those processes that determine and shape their future (Kwanashie *et al.* 2002).

How do we find a mechanism for making Nigeria a good international citizen, given that it is not quite yet a true democracy buoyed by the capacity for ensuring equitable and broad participation of citizens in the processes that determine and shape their future? Another question also comes to mind. How possible is this, given that democracy in Nigeria still has more to do with the influence and manoeuvrings of special 'constituencies'?

In the light of the discussion so far, what role is there for an independent anti-corruption commission whose head is answerable to the President and whose activities get funded through the budget of the executive arm of government? One out of every two households in Nigeria believes corruption is worse now than at the start of the current Obasanjo regime (Kwanashie *et al.* 2002).

The role of leadership

Let us liken the leadership needed to bring lasting positive change in Nigeria to the energy expended by a minority[8] to cause movement from a present state towards a clearly articulated, desirable, future state in the common, greater good of the majority – such energy having been expended to ensure that movement once made is maintained, welcomed and embraced by all.

To produce sustainable change against corruption in Nigeria, we need the following:

1   Strong credible leadership
2   A compelling mission
3   Incentives for stakeholder engagement[9]
4   Institutional arrangements (mechanisms) to support those incentives
5   The capacities required to deliver on the incentives

Who should provide this sort of leadership?

1   Government and legislature?
2   The judiciary?
3   Organized business (through chambers of commerce)?
4   The anti-corruption commission?
5   Civil society organizations?

Ideally it should come from a matrix of institutions including all of the above. However, in the light of the situation in Nigeria, the action of even a small collective could indeed act as the much-needed catalyst for change, with a view to becoming as inclusive as possible as the group becomes productive. The ideal lead should be from government. However, Nigerians (Kwanashie *et al.* 2002) when asked to identify those institutions that in their opinion are useful for combating corruption in Nigeria, pointed to religious organizations (62 per cent), the mass media (56 per cent), NGOs (50 per cent), academics and teachers (49 per cent), and to some extent the anti-corruption commission (38 per cent). Many expect change to start from small, homogeneous, principled groups with acceptable standards of behaviour and an ability to sanction or reward their own. Contrast this to the feeling expressed by 60 per cent of households who believe, for example, that the police have not helped at all.

It is always tempting to assume that change begins with instituting good governance, which will establish an enabling environment for industry and in turn create opportunities for wealth creation and influence development, leading eventually to Nigeria being seen as a good international citizen. This would appear to be a logical sequence. It would also seem to be supported by the direction of aid programmes and the content of various external interventions. Judging however, from the extent to which state capture holds as an observable fact, the reverse of that sequence is probably closer to reality. We need to get Nigeria to be that good international citizen denouncing corruption, whilst giving alternative routes to power and wealth so that the stranglehold on the state can be loosened. Then an enabling environment for enterprise and industry can be established, giving even more room for the state to focus on effective and efficient service delivery and sustained improvements in the standards of living of the people.

What the author is saying in effect is that with reference to Figure 13.1,[10] Nigeria would need first to focus on:

1   building trust and lowering the costs of business transactions,
2   achieving macro-economic stability,
3   looking to improve service delivery, and
4   attaining better standards of governance generally.

The full reintegration of Nigeria into the international community of nations and the gaining of access to trade and investment opportunities by Nigerians is

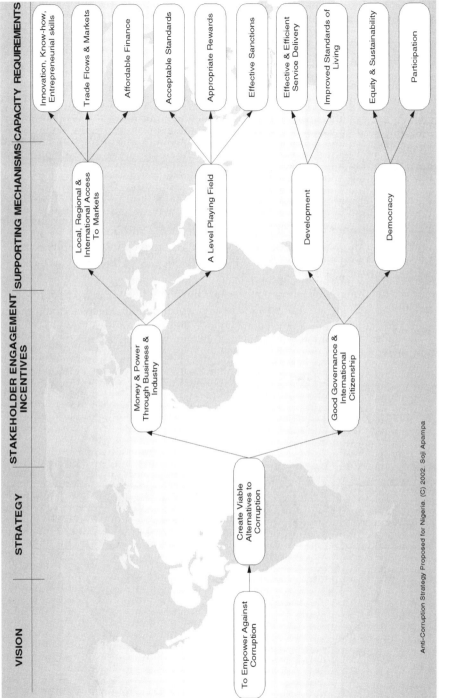

VISION | STRATEGY | STAKEHOLDER ENGAGEMENT | SUPPORTING MECHANISMS | CAPACITY REQUIREMENTS
INCENTIVES

To Empower Against Corruption

Create Viable Alternatives to Corruption

Money & Power Through Business & Industry

Good Governance & International Citizenship

Local, Regional & International Access To Markets

A Level Playing Field

Development

Democracy

Innovation, Know-how, Entrepreneurial skills

Trade Flows & Markets

Affordable Finance

Acceptable Standards

Appropriate Rewards

Effective Sanctions

Effective & Efficient Service Delivery

Improved Standards of Living

Equity & Sustainability

Participation

Anti-Corruption Strategy Proposed for Nigeria. (C) 2002 Soji Apampa

Figure 13.1 Anti-corruption strategy proposed for Nigeria.

a prime requirement for creating a virtuous cycle of change (see Figure 13.2) – but how do we do this without getting burnt?

The initiative

Nigeria needs full integration into the global economy for her to make progress on dealing with corruption. For this reason, business transactions must be empowered against corruption, ineffectiveness and inefficiency by establishing robust rules of engagement capable of encouraging all parties to a transaction to do two things:

1   Assume normal business risk.
2   Assume normal terms of trade.

This should ensure that business-risk considerations and trade terms for those companies with business integrity will not be according to the stereotypes for Nigeria but rather will hinge on the basis of the quality of their corporate governance after normal due diligence checks.

The reader may wonder for a moment if this should be the correct approach to follow in seeking a solution to the issue of corruption in Nigeria. Should the

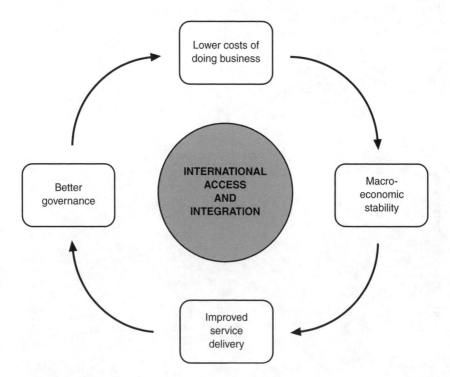

Figure 13.2 Virtuous cycle required to reinforce strategy.

regulation of conflicts of interest not be given the highest authority? The author has described a situation where interests are so intertwined that the borderlines between corruption, favours, reciprocity and gift-giving are blurred and the term 'bribe' loses its meaning. In the opinion of the author there are many ways one could approach the problem. The approach of trying to deal with corruption 'from the top' has been used repeatedly with very little result. Resolving the conflicts of interest decisively would require very high levels of political will. Such will, if present today, is extremely weak. The *Nigeria Governance and Corruption Diagnostic Study, Final Report* (Kwanashie *et al.* 2002), reveals that the executive, political parties, national assembly and local government councils are believed to be corrupt by 60 per cent, 73 per cent, 74 per cent and 59 per cent, respectively, of households in Nigeria.

The strategy adopted (see Figure 13.1) is to reposition corruption by demonstrating viable alternatives to corruption as a necessity for survival in Nigeria. This approach, whilst admittedly indirect, serves the purpose of attempting a fix at the causes rather than to continue with attempts to treat the symptom.

Normal business risk

For normal business risk, a reasonable assumption of the existence of a level playing field must be possible. Acceptable standards must be defined, agreed and adhered to and there must be incentives or rewards for compliance. Sanctions must also be defined, agreed and made enforceable in order for them to be effective. These three elements will form the working rules of a new collective, which will be happy to sideline corruption and prepare for international trade and exchange on a level playing field.

Normal terms of trade

We need to ensure local, regional and international access to:

1 affordable finance and investment (inclusive of supplier credits),
2 trade flows and markets, and
3 innovation, know-how and entrepreneurial skills.

Having discussed mechanisms required for this ambitious mission in generic terms, I would now like to describe an initiative created and first launched in Nigeria on 2 October 1997 and relaunched on 4 July 2002 to establish the capacities needed for turning this concept into an institution.

The convention on business integrity (components)

The Convention on Business Integrity (CBI) is a declaration against corruption and corrupt practices in business. It is a stand for integrity – ethical conduct, competence, transparency, accountability, and a commitment to doing what is right, just and fair.

The primary purpose of the CBI initiative is to encourage the establishment of a minimum standard for business integrity in Nigeria. It is hoped that with time it will reposition the fast-spreading idea that Nigerian business is fraudulent and instead foster domestic and international relationships that can lead to meaningful exchange. The code does not assume moral rectitude on the part of the intending signatory but rather that the intending signatory is willing to participate in a coalition that expects high standards from those who join. Assistance in achieving the standards will be provided through the CBI secretariat. The standards defined in the code are considered to be the endpoint all signatories are striving towards. A simple road map is provided to signatories to lead them towards the endpoint. Having ratified the Code on Business Integrity and signed the convention, periodic compliance checks will also be carried out by the CBI secretariat by means of an integrity rating system. The rating system merely measures how far along the compliance road map an entity has travelled (see Figure 13.3).[11] All stakeholders are empowered by the code to act as whistle-blowers, and so compliance will be largely self-policing.

After a representative of a nation-state has signed a United Nations convention, it must be ratified by the home government and passed into local law for that country to be held to its terms. The mechanism for adopting the Convention on Business Integrity consists of similar steps. First, it is worth noting that the document is not a legal document; rather, it represents a moral contract between consenting parties. It is binding in honour only – as a moral contract

Stage 0	Stage 1	Stage 2	Stage 3	Stage 4	Stage 5
Integrity markets convention to business community	Firms make commitment to Integrity's principles, prepare a policy statement and apply for membership	Firms introduce procedures as required	Firms undertake internal audits	External audit	Formal accreditation and awards ceremony
Integrity prepares model policy statements and procedures		Integrity provides consultancy support and training as required			
	Training of external auditors				Verification of external audit

Figure 13.3 The road map.

between peers. Having said that, with its provisions for applying sanctions, the code has the capacity to cause pressure to be exerted against deviant behaviour. Intending signatories are required to show good faith first by making a public declaration against corruption at a media event. Ratifying the Code on Business Integrity (which involves streamlining standards of corporate business processes with the requirements of the code; that is, 'passing it into their local laws') then follows. When compliance has been satisfactorily achieved, the organization is celebrated with a special seal of accreditation which they can use on their letter-headed paper.

The capacity areas of the Convention on Business Integrity are as follows:

1 *Peer review mechanism*
   The declaration
   The code
   The rating system
2 *Peer pressure mechanism*
   Stakeholders acting as whistle-blowers
   Provisions for sanctions and appeals
   The website
3 *Advocacy focus*
   Primarily a pull strategy (through Nigerian diaspora, trade and diplomatic bodies, chambers of commerce and industry, development agencies, etc.)
   Push strategy (quarterly signing ceremonies, publication of success stories, direct marketing)
4 *Oversight mechanism*
   General assembly of signatories
   The core group
   The secretariat

The rating system

Subscription to the Convention on Business Integrity requires a demonstration of good faith by intending signatories to streamline their business procedures to comply with the Code on Business Integrity. What follows thereafter is a process of application, verification and rating to ensure commitment and adherence to the core values of the Convention. In measuring compliance, the management of the entity under review will be asked to fill out a questionnaire on implementation of the code (which deals largely with standards of business processes). A similar questionnaire will then be administered on a number of employees chosen at random from each level. The same will be done with shareholders, auditors, registrars, customers, suppliers and other stakeholders as deemed necessary. As integrity is not hidden but easily ascertained by the testimony of one's stakeholders, the level of agreement between the stakeholders will be directly related to the true level of compliance of the entity.

The integrity rating system (Table 13.1) takes into account the following factors:

- *One star: bona fides*
  Is the entity what it purports to be?
- *Two stars: ethics and morals*
  We check the value system of the organization to ensure it has articulated acceptable ethical and moral standards for itself by way of credos, codes or policy statements. We pay particular attention to processes that require that such values are published to relevant stakeholders and imbibed throughout the organization.
- *Three stars: transparency and accountability*
  We check processes put in place to ensure timely and accurate disclosure of information to stakeholders (as much as a particular stakeholder has a right to), both at pre-agreed intervals and at unscheduled times. We check processes put in place to ensure that independent verification of such information, as may be required by key stakeholders, is possible and welcome. We check processes put in place to ensure that the board and management cannot act *ultra vires*.
- *Fours stars: will and power to do the right thing*
  We check processes, put in place to ensure audit of organization compliance with stated business processes, as well as continuous enhancement of such processes. We check that the processes include self-audits of compliance with the values of the code by a board-level member of the organization with sufficient powers to define and execute any remedial action identified as necessary.
- *Five stars: commitment*
  We check for anecdotal evidence of a track record of sanctioning deviant behaviour and a history of rewarding and reinforcing acceptable behaviour within the organization, about which the average stakeholder should be able to testify. This gives an idea of commitment to entrenching the stated values into the culture of the organization. A demonstrated time-related will and power to review and enhance integrity continuously would imply the full implementation of the Code on Business Integrity.

The reader might wonder at this stage what might happen to the initiative if a scandal broke out concerning one of the signatories. With it being driven and funded by members would there not be a tendency to try to 'cover up' or limit the damage in order to safeguard the interests of majority?

To avoid such a conflict of interest, Integrity will not be auditing the signatories to the Convention on Business Integrity. This role is reserved for non-member auditors trained in the use of the instrument. Integrity shall use the rating system for information it publishes on its signatories. Having said that, Integrity is called upon from time to time to provide a rating on non-members, and, in that scenario, it will be free to carry out its own audits.

Table 13.1 The five-star rating system

Factor/rating	One star	Two stars	Three stars	Four stars	Five stars
Professional competence assured	✓	?	?	?	?
Acceptable ethical and moral standards	✓	✓	?	?	?
Acceptable level of transparency and accountability	✓	✓	✓	?	?
Demonstrable will and power to protect integrity	✓	✓	✓	✓	?
Proven time-related commitment to integrity	✓	✓	✓	✓	✓

Notes

1 This is the view held of corruption in Nigeria by Integrity (Nigerian CSO), which was set-up in 1995 to empower people, systems and institutions against corruption by providing viable alternatives to corruption and by assisting with the establishment of the capacities and mechanisms required for supporting such alternatives.
2 A weak moral stance may not necessarily be the result of a poor understanding of morality but of a reflex from apathy, plus resignation arising out of incapacity to deal with opportunistic free-riders within the group, for example.
3 These issues are indeed the subject of various reform agendas, but the returns are poor on such projects in Nigeria even where they are donor assisted.
4 The author does not seek to make any value judgements on this and merely states this by way of illustration.
5 Ethnic, religious, gender, old school, business networks, etc. are woven into complex networks of influences that make up a 'constituency'.
6 In Nigeria, the bulk of business is with or on behalf of central government. Nigeria still has a pariah status in international trade. Grand corruption involving large sums of money occurs mostly at the interface of the private and public sectors.
7 By implication, if one were able to provide meaningful alternative sources of afford-able finance and access to bigger 'cakes', such as through international trade flows and markets, a majority of the current political class could be persuaded to stay out of public office. Radical reforms, including political reforms, might then succeed in ush-ering in a new crop of political leaders with a real interest in governance and improv-ing the standard of living of the people.
8 Olson's Logic of Collective Action, according to institutional economists, is most commonly remembered for predictions that small, homogeneous groups would be best able to overcome free-riding and engage in collective action as common interests within a group would not lead to collective action to further those interests if some members had the opportunity to free-ride on the efforts of others to provide the collective goods.
9 The incentives described as important for one stakeholder are by no means the only possible ones. The incentives for one stakeholder group could easily pass as incentives for other groups; however, the most important one has been chosen for each group. There must be strong incentives to attract members and effective intermediation of members' interests to keep them from quitting.
10 Figure 13.1 is divided into five sections reflecting what needs to be accomplished by leadership to create a homogeneous small collective that can spearhead change. The incentives required to attract the interest and possible participation of all sections of

Nigerian society are included. Under supporting mechanisms, the major drivers of change are outlined. They do not rely on the morality of the actors but rather on processes and procedures, systems and standards that could be used to balance the carrot with the stick. The Capacity Requirements section outlines the competencies that must be provided by the collective to keep members interested and participating.

11   The road map (Figure 13.3) is a contribution of Irwin of Irwin Grayson Associates, UK. It is gratefully acknowledged.

References

Isichei, E. (1983) *A History of Nigeria*, London.

Kwanashie *et al.* (2002) *Nigeria Governance and Corruption Diagnostic Study, Final Report*, USAID/World Bank, Washington, DC.

Pound, R. (1922) *An Introduction to the Philosophy of Law*, New Haven.

Shaffer, J.D. (1995) 'Institutions, Behavior and Economic Performance: Comments on Institutional Analysis', Department of Agricultural Economics, Staff Paper no. 95-52, September, Michigan State University, <http://www.msu.edu/user/schmid/shaffer.html>.

Schein, E.H. (1988) *Organizational Psychology* (3rd edn), Prentice-Hall International Editions.

Index

Page numbers in *italics* refer to tables and figures.

Date Due	Date Returned
T 21, 06	DEC 1 1 2006
	JAN 0 4 2015
http://w	er.ca/